The Microelectronics Race

ECONOMIC COMPETITION AMONG NATIONS

Series Editors

Alan Wm. Wolff, R. Michael Gadbaw, Thomas R. Howell, and William A. Noellert

Dewey, Ballantine, Bushby, Palmer & Wood, Washington, D.C.

Paradoxically, in an era of growing economic interdependence, commercial and technological rivalry among nations is intensifying. International competitiveness has moved to the center of the U.S. public policy debate and has become the focus of increasing attention in Europe, Japan, and the developing world. This series examines the public policy issues that affect competition among nations and lead to international economic conflict. Its goals are to contribute to the policy debate by examining underlying sources of economic conflicts, providing policy suggestions for their resolution, and fostering the knowledge that can make a more integrated world economy possible.

FORTHCOMING IN THIS SERIES

Intellectual Property Rights: Global Consensus, Global Conflict, R. Michael Gadbaw and Timothy J. Richards

Steel and the State, Thomas R. Howell, William A. Noellert, and Alan Wm. Wolff

The Microelectronics Race

The Impact of Government Policy on International Competition

Thomas R. Howell, William A. Noellert, Janet H. MacLaughlin, and Alan Wm. Wolff

Westview Press / Boulder and London

Economic Competition Among Nations Series

This Westview softcover edition is printed on acid-free paper and bound in softcovers that carry the highest rating of the National Association of State Textbook Administrators, in consultation with the Association of American Publishers and the Book Manufacturers' Institute.

Copyright © 1988 by Westview Press, Inc.

Published in 1988 in the United States of America by Westview Press, Inc.; Frederick A. Praeger, Publisher; 5500 Central Avenue, Boulder, Colorado 80301

Library of Congress Cataloging-in-Publication Data
The microelectronics race: the impact of government policy on
international competition/by Thomas R. Howell . . . [et al.]
    p. cm.—(Economic competition among nations series)
    Includes index.
    ISBN 0-8133-7551-7
    1. Microelectronics industry—Government policy. 2. Competition,
International. 3. International economic relations. I. Howell,
Thomas R., 1949–   . II. Series: Westview special studies in
science, technology, and public policy/society.
HD9696.A2I588 1988
338.4′76213817—dc19   87-31733
                                                                        CIP

Printed and bound in the United States of America

The paper used in this publication meets the requirements of the American National Standard for Permanence of Paper for Printed Library Materials Z39.48-1984.

6   5   4

This book is dedicated to those individuals in the U.S. Government who have begun to recognize the full implications of the challenge which this country confronts in microelectronics, and who are beginning to take steps to deal with that challenge. In that regard, special recognition and respect is due the late Secretary of Commerce, Malcolm Baldrige.

Contents

List of Tables

List of Figures

Foreword

The invention of the transistor at Bell Telephone Laboratories in 1947 signalled the beginning of the worldwide revolution in microelectronics. That revolution is still in progress, and is transforming all facets of life so profoundly that the period which began forty years ago is increasingly referred to as "the information age." Information age technology has been made possible by microelectronics' capability to detect, measure, record, process and communicate information at real-time speeds or for long-term storage -- information which may be in the form of audio, video, data, text, graphics or images, and which may be transmitted across distances as short as house to house or as distant as from earth to the moon. A revolution of this magnitude inevitably affects the political, social, economic, and defense interests of all nations.

The United States, with its microelectronics technology leadership and its tremendous economic resources, has championed an open exchange of ideas, trade and people between the nations of the free world. Our political beliefs, coupled with our technological and economic strengths, have led us to aid all friendly nations in the various areas of information technology. Our assistance has ranged from providing "know-how" to offering our open market, with U.S. consumers and businesses purchasing a substantial proportion of the world's output of microelectronics-based goods and services.

However, many nations, notably Japan, Korea, and some European countries, have elevated industrial endeavors in microelectronics from the level of actions by individual firms and entrepreneurs to that of governmentally-directed national policy. The microelectronics sector is promoted as a strategic industry, essential to economic growth, the national standard of living, and national security. American firms -- privately-owned and driven by the profit imperative -- are increasingly pitted against foreign, governmentally-directed cooperatives of many firms and institutions. This competition has resulted in the progressive erosion of our manufacturing base, and is now jeopardizing our technological leadership.

Since its inception the Semiconductor Industry Association has sponsored a number of studies on the international competitive environment in microelectronics. This most recent book arose from a concern that the disparity between our own government policies toward the microelectronics sector and those of our principal trading partners is leading to the erosion of U.S. leadership in this industry. Because of the importance of this problem, SIA gave its support to the research leading to the publication of this book, which explains what is happening today and urges the United States to reassert its position in the information technologies.

The future of U.S. competitiveness in all industries in international markets depends on the success of realistic federal, industry, and company policies with regard to microelectronics. A cooperative exchange of views, leading to the formulation of effective national policies, is now essential.

Andrew A. Procassini
President
Semiconductor Industry Association

Acknowledgments

The authors would like to acknowledge the contributions of a number of individuals at Dewey, Ballantine, Bushby, Palmer and Wood to the preparation of this study. Todd Krieg and Cheryl Hesse performed statistical analysis and research. Kathleen Boylan prepared the graphics and oversaw the layout and physical production of the study. Bernice Grandsoult typed the initial drafts of the study and assisted with the preparation of the tables. The library staff, supervised by Daria Proud, tracked down many of the research materials which were needed. Susan Forrester coordinated the conversion of the manuscript to typeset format, which was performed by Pandick Technologies, Inc. in Washington, D.C. The word processing unit at Dewey Ballantine revised many drafts of the study, and we are indebted to Joe James and Martha Myricks, the supervisors, and Joyce Harris, Julie MacGregor, Reginald Spence, Nancy Cernick, Dennis Curtin, Neal Johnson, Reba Lawson, Wini Parker, Gerald Philpott, and Sharon von Bergener for their work on this project.

Introduction

The United States' ability to shape the course of world events has been a standing assumption since the end of the Second World War. At that time both U.S. policymakers and the general public clearly understood that the industrial strength and technological leadership of the United States provided the basis for the successful prosecution of the War. The subsequent ability of the U.S. to drive postwar reconstruction through implementation of the Marshall Plan, the creation of the Bretton Woods institutions, and the extension of regional and bilateral aid was likewise predicated on U.S. industrial and technological superiority.

In recent years, however, U.S. ability to sustain major international economic initiatives has proven more constrained. Global economic events have become less manageable. The current era has been characterized by slower world economic growth, exchange rate instability, the massive buildup of developing country debt, and the emergence of the United States as the world's largest debtor. A substantial portion of the U.S. industrial base has eroded, and public concern is mounting over the loss of American competitiveness. In the formulation of U.S. economic and trade policy, the linkage between America's industrial strength and the world role which the United States is capable of playing -- so obvious in wartime -- has been largely forgotten.

The outcome of current international competition in semiconductors is directly relevant to these larger issues of American power. Few segments of the U.S. industrial base are more vital to national economic well-being and defense than the industry which produces these miniature electronic circuits. The silicon chip is revolutionizing the world economy in much the same way that the harnessing of steam power transformed human economic endeavor in the eighteenth and nineteenth centuries, and oil and the internal combustion engine transformed the twentieth. It is profoundly significant, therefore, that another country, Japan, is overtaking the United States in this key industrial sector.

Japan has established a national goal of achieving preeminence in microelectronics, and has coordinated its government policies and industry efforts in a manner designed to achieve its goal. Japanese firms have surpassed the United States in world sales of semiconductor chips and have become dominant in many areas of the semiconductor device, equipment, and materials industries. They are gaining on U.S. firms in virtually every area of semiconductor device and process technology, and in some areas, hold a technological edge. Other nations, observing Japan's success, have begun to implement their own ambitious promotional programs in microelectronics and related information sectors.

In marked contrast to these foreign efforts, the U.S. Government has no clear policy goal. Government policies which affect the microelectronics industry are dispersed among numerous departments and agencies, many of which pursue priorities which are irrelevant or even detrimental to U.S. commercial competitiveness. Most Government R&D in microelectronics is directed toward military technologies which have limited commercial applicability. Direct Government intervention in the commercial arena, to the extent it has occurred, has consisted of ad hoc, temporary reactions to Japanese initiatives that have escalated into trade disputes. Both inside and outside the Government, there is substantial resistance to the notion that the commercial competitiveness of this (or any other) industrial sector is a relevant consideration in the setting of Government policies. The events of the past five years, however, suggest that a reappraisal is in order.

In the late 1950s a series of spectacular Soviet successes in space jarred the American public and policy establishment, prompting the creation of new U.S. science and space programs and an overhaul of the U.S. system of education in the sciences. As a result, in 1969, a U.S. astronaut became the first man to walk on the moon. There will probably be no equivalent of Sputnik, however, in microelectronics -- the erosion of U.S. leadership is occurring in areas which are generally obscure from public view. It is manifested in the disappearance of small firms which produce semiconductor manufacturing equipment; in the increasing inability of U.S. firms to match Japanese R&D expenditures; and in individual companies' decisions not to invest in the production of certain types of devices which can no longer be made profitably. But while the full magnitude of the present technological challenge confronting the United States in microelectronics is less evident, its implications for this country are no less significant than those posed by the Soviet space effort three decades ago.

This study outlines the nature and dimensions of that challenge. It examines and compares the government policy measures which have been taken in Japan and the United States that are affecting the international competitive balance in microelectronics. It analyzes the role which such policies have played and are now playing in Japan's ascendancy, and describes the intensifying efforts under way in Korea and Europe to benefit from comparable measures.

The parallel promotional efforts in microelectronics which are now under way in many countries are closely linked to national aspirations, driven by a belief that the outcome of the microelectronics race will determine a nation's position in the world economy in the next century. This intensifying competition carries with it a substantial potential for conflict, and some bitter disputes have already begun to erupt in microelectronics. It is the hope of the authors that this study will help inform U.S. policymaking and contribute to the formulation of a set of appropriate responses, based on a clearer understanding of U.S. national interest -- an interest which encompasses both the maintenance of an open international trading system and the preservation of the international competitiveness of the U.S. microelectronics industry.

1

THE INFORMATION REVOLUTION
AND THE UNITED STATES

The world economy is currently undergoing a fundamental transformation as a result of new electronics technologies which process, transmit and store information -- computers, telecommunications systems, and the microelectronic components upon which they are based. The "information revolution" is increasingly being viewed as nothing less than a "new industrial revolution," transforming every aspect of human economic activity from agriculture to manufacturing.[1] The West German Federal Minister for Research and Technology commented in 1984 that

> *The production, processing and dissemination of information in modern industrial societies is increasingly assuming the character of an independent factor of production along with capital and labor.*[2]

During the past decade, awareness of the significance of the information technologies has spread rapidly throughtout the industrialized and developing world. Most major nations have recognized their stake in these industries both from an economic and a military perspective, and are reordering their

---

1   French Minister of Industry Laurent Fabius in *Electroniques Actualites* (October 14, 1983).

2   Dr. Heinz Riesenhuber in *Informationstechnik* (1984).

national priorities to ensure that they will hold a position in them in the next century.[3]   Competition between nations for leadership is intensifying, reflecting the belief that the nation that dominates the electronic information industries "will stand astride the world economy like a 21st century Colossus."[4]

The Office of Technology Assessment concluded in 1983 that "[I]f there is any single industry whose technological progress and competitiveness are critical to the economic growth and national security of the United States, it is electronics."[5]

The United States should seemingly be well positioned to enter this new era. Leadership in the information technologies depends on the ability to master the development, design, and manufacture of new electronics technologies -- areas in which the United States has traditionally been preeminent.   Most of the major technological breakthroughs in the information sector have been achieved in American laboratories and the United States remains unsurpassed in basic science and R&D. U.S. firms have enjoyed a competitive edge not only in information systems -- telecommunications equipment, computers, and office equipment -- but in the microelectronic components which are the key to these systems, as well as in the "upstream" industry sectors which supply the equipment and advanced materials necessary to fabricate these components. Reflecting that edge, and a vigorous entrepreneurial spirit, U.S. firms have enjoyed a position of international market leadership in the information technologies for over twenty years.

However, at present, this situation is deteriorating. A severe recession has shaken major segments of the U.S. information industry and at the same time Japan has launched a major competitive challenge to the United States. Important segments of the U.S. information sector are contracting and in some cases disappearing altogether. In 1986, as shown in Figure 1.1, the U.S. experienced a trade deficit in high technology products. This deficit was a dramatic reversal of the $27 billion surplus which the U.S. enjoyed as

---

3   French Prime Minister Jacques Chirac commented in 1986 that "Beyond its own economic weight, [the information] sector is vital to the development of a nation like ours. It is the source of improvement in the ability of all industries and the services sector to compete. It is strategic to both the military and civilian worlds." *Zero un Informatique* (May 1986).

4   *Fortune* (October 13, 1986), p. 28.

5   Office of Technology Assessment, *International Competitiveness in Electronics* (Washington, D.C.: U.S. Government Printing Office, 1983), p. 463.

FIGURE 1.1

U.S. TRADE BALANCE IN HIGH
TECHNOLOGY PRODUCTS
($ Billion)

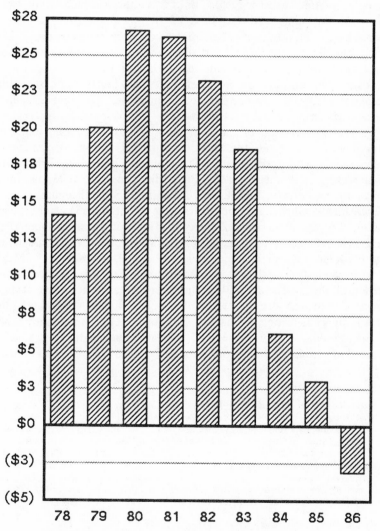

SOURCE: U.S. Department of Commerce Bureau
of the Census, FT-210, FT-610, various issues
(DOC3 definition).

recently as 1980.[6] These trends are now provoking widespread concern within the U.S. Government, the scientific community, and the defense establishment.[7]

The electronic information industries comprise a vast industrial complex resembling an inverted pyramid. At the apex are the "upstream" industries that produce the advanced materials and manufacturing equipment which are needed to produce semiconductor chips. "Midstream," at the middle of the pyramid, is the semiconductor device industry which manufactures semiconductor chips. At the base of the pyramid are the numerous "downstream" industries -- computers, telecommunications, factory automation, defense electronics -- that depend on semiconductor technology to provide the basis for their final products and systems. Because these industries comprise an interdependent, integrated fabric, the destruction or substantial weakening of any significant portion of the complex will have ripple effects throughout the entire system.

The principal erosion of the U.S. industry position in the information sector has occurred at the apex and center of the pyramid -- in semiconductors and in the "upstream" sectors which produce semiconductor manufacturing equipment (SME) and advanced raw materials for the semiconductor industry. In 1985 and 1986, the U.S. semiconductor industry suffered losses which have been estimated at between $1 and $2 billion;[8] between 1983 and 1986 it lost 20 percent of its world market share (Figure 1.2); and in 1985 and 1986 it laid off over 27,000 workers, the first such work force reduction in over a decade (Figure 1.3). The "upstream" SME and materials industries which supply the semiconductor industry have experienced the contraction of their customer base as if they were "at the end of a whip, or the caboose on the end of a train," [9] suffering substantial losses and in some cases exiting the market. Moreover, according to many analysts, the longstanding U.S. technological edge in semiconductors, SME and advanced materials is eroding, with Japan moving toward ascendancy in many

6   U.S. Department of Commerce, International Trade Administration, *An Assessment of U.S. Competitiveness in High Technology Industries* (February 1983) addresses the definition and importance of high technology industries. In electronics products, the U.S. balance of trade shifted from an $8 billion surplus in 1980 to an $8 billion deficit in 1985. Defense Science Board, *Task Force on Semiconductor Dependency* (Office of the Under Secretary of Defense for Acquisition, November 30, 1986).

7   C.H. Ferguson, *American Microelectronics in Decline* (MIT Draft, December 1985). DSB, *Task Force on Semiconductor Dependency*, p. 59.

8   Dan Klesken in the *Washington Post* (May 10, 1987).

9   Brad Wait, Vice President of Siltec Corp., in *San Jose Mercury News* (December 1, 1986), p. 50.

FIGURE 1.2

WORLD SEMICONDUCTOR SHIPMENTS
($ Billion)

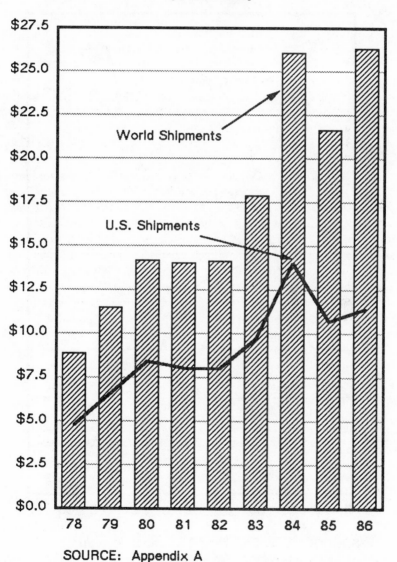

SOURCE: Appendix A

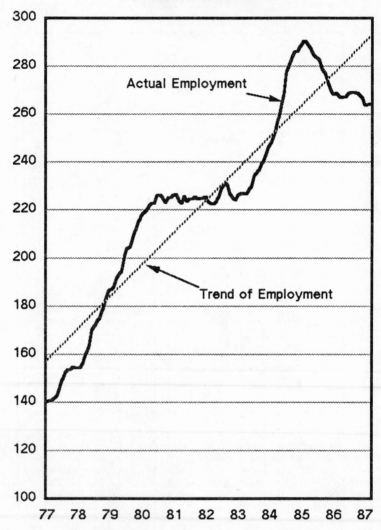

FIGURE 1.3

SEMICONDUCTOR INDUSTRY EMPLOYMENT
(1000 Workers)

Actual Employment

Trend of Employment

SOURCE: U.S. Department of Labor, Bureau
of Labor Statistics, Employment Hours
and Earnings.

areas of microelectronics device, process and materials technology. Table 1.1 shows that the U.S. semiconductor industry continues to spend a higher percentage of its sales revenue on R&D than any other U.S. industry; but as the Defense Science Board concluded, "the problem is that this has simply been insufficient by worldwide standards." [10]

The difficulties of the U.S. semiconductor industry are particularly serious because semiconductors provide the underlying technologies that are a prerequisite to remaining competitive in the information sector as a whole.[11] A Korean analyst commented in 1985 that

> *[T]he nucleus of the information industry is the semiconductor. . . . Nurturing the information industry is limited without the backing of semiconductor technology. . . . The semiconductor has enormously wideranging effects, from various office automation equipment to aircraft and the defense industry.[12]*

Because of its strategic position at the center of the information technologies, many analysts believe that

> *The semiconductor chip means as much to the nation's wellbeing as did natural resources like iron, timber, coal and water in the earlier industrial age.[13]*

The defense implications of the erosion of the semiconductor industry are extremely serious, because the United States has become almost completely reliant on "smart" semiconductor-based weapons systems to offset the numerical superiority of the Warsaw Pact forces. According to two U.S. military experts:

---

10   DSB, *Task Force on Semiconductor Dependency*, p. 59.

11   As the President of the Italian electronics firm SGS commented in 1986, "[A]s soon as the leading role of an enterprise in the development of semiconductors is lost, it becomes dependent upon the supplier of base technology and is degraded to being a dealer in electronic systems produced by others, and when it no longer has command over semiconductor technology, it loses control over its own industrial fate." (*VDI Nachrichten*, July 11, 1986, p. 2.) The West German government observed in 1984 that "In the long run, neither the data processing industry nor the communications industry can be conceived of as being successful without microelectronics." *Informationstechnik* (1984), p. 2.

12   Chung Hung-yol in *Wolgan Chonggyong Munwha* (July, 1985).

13   *Washington Post* (May 10, 1987).

TABLE 1.1

1986 RESEARCH AND DEVELOPMENT EXPENDITURES
AS A PERCENT OF SALES

Industry	R&D as a Percent of Sales
Semiconductors	12.2
Computers	8.3
Drugs	7.8
Software/Services	7.7
Peripherals	7.0
Instruments	6.7
Leisure Industries	5.9
Telecommunications	5.1
Office Equipment	4.8
Aerospace	4.5
Electronics	4.4
Chemicals	4.1
Automotive	3.7
ALL INDUSTRY COMPOSITE	3.5
Electrical	3.3
Machinery (Tools, industry, mining)	3.3
Oil Service/Supply	3.3
Machinery (Farm, Construction)	3.0
Misc. Manufacturing	2.8
Personal & Home Products	2.6
Tire & Rubber	2.6
Conglomerates	2.6
Automotive parts	2.4

Note: The *Business Week* data understates actual semiconductor R&D because included in the denominator are sales of products other than semiconductors for multiproduct firms.

Source: *Business Week* (June 22, 1987)

[I]t is safe to say that there is not a single western military system that is not critically dependent for its operation on semiconductor integrated circuits.[14]

U.S. "downstream" manufacturers of systems based on microelectronics technology -- firms which constitute much of the U.S. defense-industrial base -- are already beginning to feel the effects of the erosion of U.S. semiconductor capability. Some U.S. producers of high performance computers, which are essential to many conventional and nuclear defense systems, are now completely dependent on their direct Japanese competitors for critical components which they need in order to remain competitive.[15]

The speed with which the U.S. industry's competitive position in microelectronics has eroded, coupled with the strategic significance of the industry, has generated a lively debate over underlying causes and possible remedial actions.[16] Some explanations for the relatively sharp decline of the U.S. industry in microelectronics focus solely on macroeconomic factors, such as the relatively high value of the U.S. dollar from 1980-1985[17], or conclude that they are the result of competitive failures by U.S. entrepreneurs, scientists and engineers. However, while factors such as exchange rates and individual managerial decisions have had definite economic effects, a crucial factor underlying relative Japanese market and technological gains has been the implementation of a coordinated promotional strategy in microelectronics by the Japanese Government, working closely with industry and the scientific community -- in contrast to intermittent *ad hoc* reactions by the U.S. Government to Japanese initiatives. The Defense Science Board observed in 1987:

---

14   A.L. Gilbert and B.D. McCombe, "Joint Services Electronics Program: An Historical Perspective," cited in Office of Technology Assessment, *Microelectronics Research and Development* (Washington, D.C.: U.S. Government Printing Office, March 1986).

15   DSB, *Task Force on Semiconductor Dependency*, p. 71.

16   The problems in U.S. microelectronics have been the subject of recent studies by the National Security Council, the National Materials Advisory Board, the Defense Science Board, the National Science Foundation, and a number of leading academic institutions.

17   See Appendix A for an econometric analysis of the impact of exchange rates and other economic factors on U.S. trade in semiconductors. The analysis indicates that variations in the real yen/dollar exchange rate are a relatively minor factor in explaining variations in the volume of trade in integrated circuits between the United States and Japan compared with more fundamental demand and supply factors. Figure 1.4 shows estimated U.S. exports and imports of integrated circuits plotted against simulated imports and exports assuming the exchange rate had held constant from 1981 to 1986. (The estimated values are from the regression results under actual conditions as disucussed in Appendix A.) Under such an assumption, the real volume of cumulative exports would have been 3.4% higher over the period than actual exports while imports would have been 4.0% lower.

FIGURE 1.4

EXCHANGE RATE EFFECTS ON U.S. INTEGRATED CIRCUIT TRADE WITH JAPAN 1981 Q1 TO 1986 Q4 ($Million)

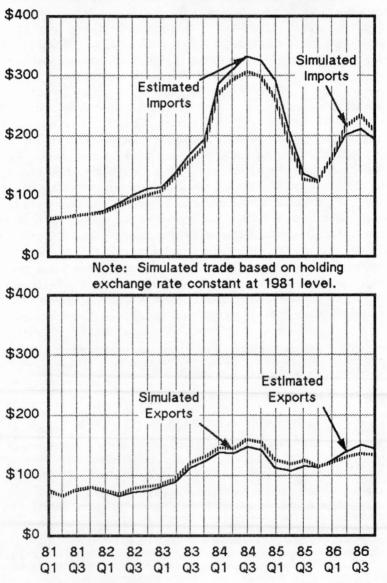

Note: Simulated trade based on holding exchange rate constant at 1981 level.

Source: Appendix A

[T]he principal factor affecting the relative shift in strength of the U.S. and Japanese semiconductor industries is the fact the Japanese established a strategic goal and effectively brought together all the resources, government, industry and academia, needed to pursue that goal. The U.S., at its own discretion, elected not to pursue such an organized focus, and as a result is finding that it is unable to compete in the marketplace as it has been defined by the Japanese.[18]

The competitive situation confronting the United States in microelectronics actually consists of long-term adverse trends in a number of interrelated spheres. None of these trends is solely a reflection of differing government policies, but such policies have played an important, if not decisive role in each sphere:

- *Trade.* Widespread Japanese dumping in commodity memory products between 1984 and 1986 destroyed U.S. semiconductor industry profitability and forced U.S. firms to abandon production in strategically important product areas. At the same time, it has proven impossible for U.S. firms to achieve more than an 8-10 percent share of the Japanese market (which now accounts for almost 40 percent of world consumption of semiconductors).

- *Manufacturing.* The Japanese industry, with government support and direction, has demonstrated a consistent ability to master the process of semiconductor manufacturing, and to produce high quality semiconductors efficiently. This mastery is particularly evident in the high volume product areas which drive the evolution of semiconductor manufacturing technology across the entire product spectrum. The U.S. industry is rapidly abandoning these product lines, and if this trend continues, they are threatened with an across-the-board loss of manufacturing competitiveness.

- *Investment Spending.* The U.S. industry is now being substantially outspent by the Japanese industry in microelectronics investment in plant and equipment and R&D, a disparity which is directly linked to the eroding U.S. technological and market position. U.S. companies must not only pay more for capital, but their continued access to it is jeopardized by their unprofitability. Japanese producers have access to lower cost capital than U.S. firms and the Japanese industrial structure provides Japanese firms with more secure access to capital.

---

18 DSB, *Task Force on Semiconductor Dependency*, p. 79 (original emphasis).

Japanese firms enjoy a lower level of investment risk due to government support and direction, and captive sources of demand within the Japanese semiconductor companies.

● *Industry Structure.* The U.S. semiconductor producers and their equipment and material suppliers are disaggregated and have little tradition of cooperation or mutual support. In the face of encroachment by large Japanese industrial groups, substantial segments of the U.S. information infrastructure are at risk of being acquired by Japanese firms or disappearing altogether.

A series of initiatives is currently being considered in the United States by the industry, by the scientific community, and by the U.S. Government to address these problems:

● The Administration has entered into a bilateral agreement with Japan designed to curb Japanese dumping and improve foreign market access in Japan. The Administration has imposed tariffs on Japanese electronics products to secure adherence to that agreement.

● The U.S. semiconductor producers and their upstream suppliers have formed a consortium, SEMATECH, which is intended to reverse the erosion of the U.S. position in semiconductor manufacturing by developing, proving and demonstrating state-of-the-art semiconductor manufacturing processes, tools, and materials. The industry is seeking Department of Defense investment in SEMATECH.

● Several proposals have been advanced for a national advisory body to coordinate government policies in microelectronics, and workshops have been held to explore ways in which the national laboratories and U.S. companies can work more closely together in the semiconductor field.

● The Department of Defense is exploring the measures which must be taken to reverse a growing U.S. dependency on foreign components.

Most of these initiatives are in their incipient stages and some are controversial -- particularly those which call for changes in existing U.S. government policies and industry-government relationships. However, regardless of how these issues may be resolved in the United States, Japan and other foreign countries will continue to pursue leadership in microelectronics through a concerted industry-government approach because they believe such an approach is most effective and therefore in their national interest. It is important, therefore, that in considering which U.S. policy measures may be appropriate in the current context, that the impact of government policies -- U.S. and foreign -- on international competition in microelectronics is fully appreciated.

2

THE GLOBAL MICROELECTRONICS
INDUSTRY IN TRANSITION

The global microelectronics industry is currently in a state of upheaval. Revolutionary new technologies have altered the dynamics of the industry, destabilizing established patterns of production and trade. Over the last decade the industry has become more R&D and capital intensive and subject to significant economies of scale. These factors favor larger firms, and coupled with overcapacity and extreme swings in demand, are driving smaller U.S. firms out of the market. Surviving firms are rapidly forming systems of alliances, many of them transnational, which will alter the structure of the industry and the nature of international competition in ways that are not yet wholly discernible.

National industrial policies have been an important factor contributing to this industrial transformation. However, in order to assess their impact objectively, it is necessary to review briefly the broad economic and technological forces which are driving international microelectronics competition.[19]

---

19 Appendix B, "The Economics of Semiconductor Production and Competition" contains a more detailed examination of the theoretical and empirical issues addressed in this chapter.

THE SEMICONDUCTOR INDUSTRY

The initial development of semiconductor technology was undertaken by established electronics firms in the United States.[20] Further innovations in device and process technology resulted in the appearance of smaller, independent firms whose primary business was the manufacture of semiconductors -- the "merchants". The competitive dynamics of the industry resulted in the explosive growth of the merchant sector and in rapid technological progress in the semiconductor industry as a whole.[21] By the early 1980s, the merchants accounted for approximately two thirds of U.S. semiconductor production; the remaining third was attributable to "captive" firms, OEMs which manufactured semiconductors for their downstream products.[22]

Many U.S. and foreign industry analysts have concluded that the creative competitive dynamism of the U.S. merchant semiconductor industry has been an important factor underlying U.S. leadership in the information technologies as a whole, and the merchants have accounted for a large proportion of the more recent technological breakthroughs which have occurred in microelectronics.[23] However, because of their size, the merchants lack the financial resources, internal demand base, and work force stability of larger, vertically integrated electronics firms. These characteristics have become important factors for survival since the introduction of VLSI technology. (See Glossary for technical terms.) As a result, merchant firms have proven vulnerable during periods of economic downturn.

---

20   In 1947, AT&T invented the transistor, which would eventually displace vacuum tubes as the essential component in telecommunications and computer equipment. Texas Instruments developed a silicon-based transistor in 1954, and the following year IBM sold the first computer system built with transistors rather than vacuum tubes. See, for example, E. Braun and S. Macdonald, *Revolution in Miniature* (Cambridge: Cambridge University Press, 1978), for a history of the origins of semiconductor technology and the development of the industry.

21   The U.S. merchant sector has historically been characterized by the continual start-up of new firms (often funded by venture capital), rapid commercialization of new technologies, intense competition, and frequent changes in market position among contending firms. Since the early 1980's, there have been no new U.S. firm entries into the commodity memory market.

22   The term original equipment manufacturer ("OEM") refers to a company which manufactures end-products which incorporate semiconductors. "OEM" includes captive producers as well as electronics firms which consume, but do not produce semiconductors.

23   M. Borrus, *Reversing Attrition: A Strategic Response to the Erosion of U.S. Leadership in Microelectronics* (University of California, Berkeley: BRIE Working Paper No. 13, March, 1985), p. 1.

The recent economic and competitive shocks have affected the U.S. merchant sector with such severity that some analysts question its ability to survive over the long run.[24] Over the past decade, numerous merchant firms have been acquired by both foreign and domestic conglomerates.[25] At the same time, Figure 2.1 shows that the U.S. merchants' share of the world semiconductor market has fallen sharply since 1980, while the share of Japanese producers has risen dramatically.[26]

In the upstream sectors which produce raw materials and semiconductor manufacturing equipment ("SME") for the semiconductor industry, the U.S. industry is principally composed of numerous small companies which share many of the strengths and vulnerabilities of the merchant semiconductor producers.[27] These firms also have proven highly innovative[28] and U.S. technological leadership in semiconductor equipment and materials has been

---

24   "Is It Too Late To Save the U.S. Semiconductor Industry?", *Business Week* (August 18, 1986), pp. 62-67; Ferguson, *American Microelectronics in Decline.*

25   Carmela S. Haklisch, *Technical Alliances in the Semiconductor Industry* (New York: New York University Press, 1986) and United Nations Centre on Transnational Corporations, *Transnational Corporations in the International Semiconductor Industry* (New York: United Nations Publication, 1986), Table VI.E.

26   The market share data is based on value of shipments expressed in U.S. dollars, a methodology which is necessary to arrive at world market shares but which, given the large fluctuations in the dollar in the last few years, distorts the absolute percentages for any given year, especially 1986. Nevertheless, the trend in market shares is clear and is not an exchange rate phenomenon. The market share data in this study includes all production that can be traded and that competes in commercial markets. The product must be fungible with devices made by other producers in the industry. The market share data does not include production of nonstandard (captive) devices that are not fungible and do not compete with products of other companies. Thus the production of nonstandard semiconductors by captive producers like IBM are not included in the market share analysis. IBM, for example, has had a policy for 25 years of not selling any semiconductors on the merchant market. See Appendix A, "World Market Share Methodology" for a more detailed discussion of these issues. Unless otherwise indicated, all references to market share in the text will refer to market share measured in U.S. dollars.

27   There are about 1,000 companies in the United States in the semiconductor manufacturing equipment and materials industry. U.S. Department of Commerce, *A Competitive Assessment of the U.S. Semiconductor Manufacturing Equipment Industry,* (Washington, D.C.: U.S. Government Printing Office, March, 1985), p. 41.

28   On February 10, 1982 the French journal *Industries et Techniques* observed that "True independence with respect to integrated circuits presupposes two things: mastering the basic technologies and design capabilities, but also having one's own manufacturing machines. The United States is the only, or almost the only, country in this position."

FIGURE 2.1

SEMICONDUCTOR WORLD MARKET SHARE
(Percent of World Shipments)

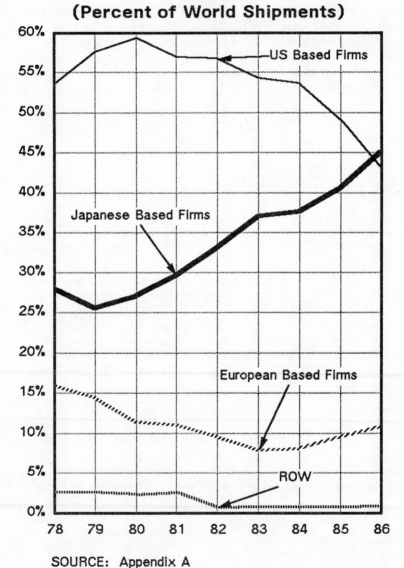

SOURCE: Appendix A

an essential element in overall U.S. leadership in microelectronics.[29] However, the shift in semiconductor production from the United States to Japan which began in the late 1970s also resulted in a transfer of SME and material demand from the United States to Japan. The Japanese Government has pursued a range of policies designed to promote the SME and materials industries and to enable them to satisfy this demand through domestic production. As a result, the Japanese share of these two sectors has increased steadily since the late 1970s. The share gains are shown in Figure 2.2 and discussed in greater detail in chapter 3.

In contrast to the United States, the semiconductor industries in Japan, Europe and Korea have been dominated by a comparatively few, large, diversified manufacturers which use semiconductors in their end products. Typically upstream SME and materials vendors are linked by capital or other ties to these large electronics producers.[30] These conglomerates are frequently affiliated with large financial institutions and usually possess substantial financial resources, which has enabled them to survive periods of reduced demand such as the one which began in 1984.[31]

Japan. The Japanese semiconductor industry is principally comprised of less than ten large, diversified, vertically-integrated firms which produce virtually all of Japan's semiconductors and consume a substantial portion of Japan's total semiconductor demand. These firms own or enjoy direct relationships with most of Japan's upstream SME and material companies.

Europe. Like the Japanese industry, the European semiconductor industry is made up primarily of large, vertically integrated firms, principally Siemens, Phillips, Thomson and SGS, who produce semiconductors for internal use. For a variety of reasons related to market fragmentation, inability to commercialize promising technologies effectively, and cultural resistance to innovations, the European semiconductor industry has never been able to

---

29 *Nihon Keizai* observed on December 6, 1985 that "One factor behind U.S. strength [in SME] is the special ability for creativity and concept making. The United States and Japan are not that different in fundamental technologies; however, in terms of being able to create new ideas, the United States holds the lead."

30 In contrast to U.S. merchant firms, semiconductors generally account for a relatively small percentage of the foreign producers' total sales. Semiconductor sales as a percent of total sales are 6.7% for Fujitsu, 4.1% for Hitachi, 3.8% for Mitsubishi and 17.8% for NEC. *New Scientist* (May 1, 1986).

31 Siemens, for example, the largest semiconductor manufacturer in Europe, possesses such financial resources that it is sometimes characterized as a "big bank with a manufacturing arm attached." *Electronics* (June 2, 1986). The major Japanese semiconductor producers are affiliated with banks which are among the largest private financial institutions on earth.

FIGURE 2.2

SEMICONDUCTOR MANUFACTURING EQUIPMENT WORLD MARKET SHARE
(Percent of World Shipments)

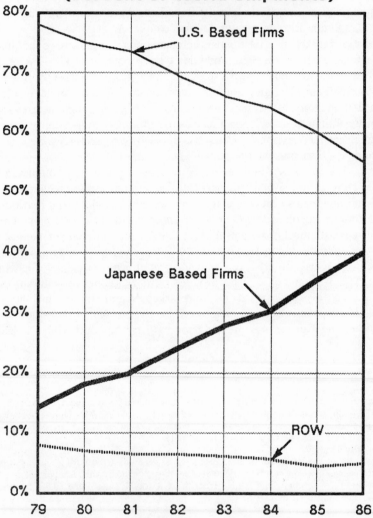

SOURCE: 79-85,VLSI Research, Inc.; 86, authors' estimate.

achieve a significant position in the world market. European micro-electronics has chronically lagged technologically behind producers from the United States and Japan.[32]

Korea. Until the early 1980s Korea was primarily a base for assembly operations by U.S. and Japanese electronics firms. However, in 1982 the Government of South Korea stepped in to promote the development of an indigenous semiconductor industry, principally centered on large, vertically integrated electronics firms (Samsung, Lucky-Goldstar, Hyundai and Daewoo). South Korean semiconductor manufacturers have entered the international market at a time when competitive pressures are intense and have begun to emerge as a significant competitive factor.

The more oligopolistic microelectronics industrial structures which evolved abroad have proven less conducive to innovation than the structurally diverse U.S. industry.[33] National governments in Europe, Korea and Japan have observed the creative dynamics of the U.S. merchant sector and have concluded that their national capacity to innovate would be enhanced by the formation of a larger number of small venture start-up firms along American lines.[34] As a result ambitious efforts are now under way in Japan and Europe to establish "new Silicon Valleys," using subsidies, financial incentives, and regional development measures to overcome some of the obstacles to the establishment and survival of small, innovative firms.[35] Thus, at present, as some U.S. observers are forecasting the imminent demise of the U.S merchant semiconductor industry and its upstream affiliates, foreign countries are systematically seeking to replicate their own versions of those industries in order to ensure the long-run competitiveness of their national information industries.

---

32   See also United Nations Centre on Transnational Corporations, *Transnational Corporations in the International Semiconductor Industry*, pp. 230-257.

33   See generally F. Malerba, *The Semiconductor Business* (Madison: University of Wisconsin Press, 1985); *Der Spiegel* (October 29, 1985).

34   The Rotterdam *NRC Handelsblad* observed on July 29, 1983 that "the essence of a real Silicon Valley lies in a large collection of small, rapidly growing, independent companies which constantly branch off into new ones."

35   For a comprehensive account of Japan's programs to encourage high technology venture businesses and to establish 19 "clones" of Silicon Valley, see Sheridan Tatsuno, *Japan's Technopolis Strategy* (New York: Prentice Hall Press, 1986). On similar efforts in West Germany, see *VDI Nachrichten* (October 5, 1984); *Handelsblatt* (August 12, 1985); in France, *La Tribune De L'Economie* (January 16, 1986), p. 15 and *Bulletin de Liason de la Recherche en Informatique et Automatique* (June-July 1986); in Sweden, *Dagens Nyheter* (November 7, 1983).

RECENT TRENDS IN GLOBAL PRODUCTION, MARKET SHARES AND PERFORMANCE

Over the long run, as Figure 2.3 shows, the growth in demand for semiconductors has been dramatic and is expected to increase rapidly for the foreseeable future.[36] At the same time, however, semiconductor demand has been highly cyclical, reflecting fluctuations in demand from manufacturers of "downstream" products such as video games, telecommunications equipment and personal computers. As a result profitability in semiconductors is much more cyclical than in other industries as shown in Figure 2.4. Fluctuating demand for semiconductors in turn produces a cyclical pattern of demand for "upstream" products such as advanced materials and semiconductor manufacturing equipment.

In 1983-84 a boom in semiconductor consumption occurred, fueled in significant part by the demand for semiconductors to manufacture personal computers.[37] This boom collapsed in late 1984 as personal computer producers experienced a sharp fall in demand and began cancelling many previously-booked orders for semiconductors. During 1985, world semiconductor consumption declined by approximately 20 percent from its height in 1984, just as many producers both in the United States and Japan were bringing new capacity on stream.[38] Japanese producers maintained a high level of output in commodity memory products, sending prices downward and selling large volumes of devices substantially below the cost of production.[39] As a result, as shown in Figure 2.5, the U.S. semiconductor industry capacity utilization rate sank to less than 50 percent in 1985, and

---

36   U.S. shipments of semiconductor devices have grown dramatically over the last three decades, from $151 million in 1957 to $11.4 billion in 1986. World semiconductor shipments have tripled in the past nine years, from $8.91 billion in 1978 to $26.35 billion in 1986. There are estimates that world semiconductor sales will rise to $160 billion annually by the year 2000. *Electronics* (May 14, 1987), p. 8.

37   Downstream companies, fearful of a "chip shortage," engaged in multiple booking of orders with semiconductor vendors to ensure an adequate supply of components.

38   In one product line, dynamic random access memories (DRAMs), U.S. consumption plunged by 51 percent from $630.6 million in 1984 to $311.1 million in 1985. U.S. International Trade Commission, *64K Dynamic Random Access Memory Components from Japan* (U.S.I.T.C. Publication No. 1862, final, June 1986), p. A-30.

39   This is discussed in greater detail in chapter 3.

FIGURE 2.3

U.S. MERCHANT SHIPMENTS OF SEMICONDUCTORS 1958 TO 1986 ($ Billion)

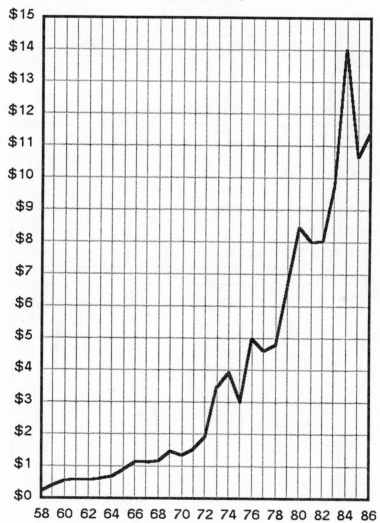

SOURCE: 1958-77 data from Richard C. Levin, "The Semiconductor Industry", (1982), Table 2.16, p.60; 1978-86 data from Appendix A.

FIGURE 2.4

PROFITABILITY OF SEMICONDUCTOR INDUSTRY COMPARED TO ELECTRONICS AND ALL MANUFACTURING

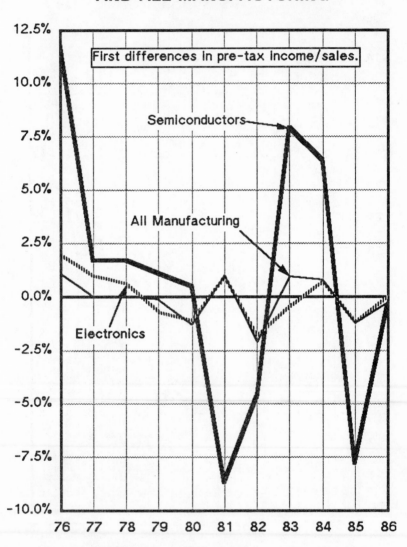

SOURCE: Semiconductor Industry Association,
U.S. Department of Commerce.

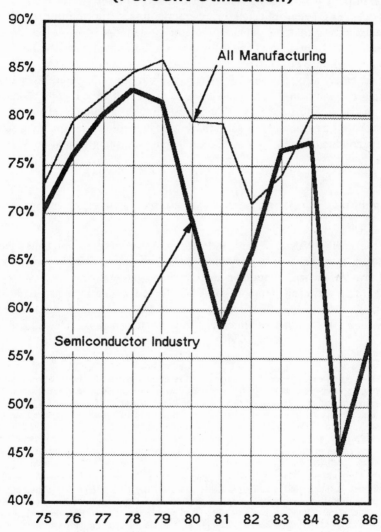

FIGURE 2.5

SEMICONDUCTOR INDUSTRY CAPACITY UTILIZATION COMPARED TO ALL MANUFACTURING
(Percent Utilization)

SOURCE: Semiconductor Industry Association, FRB

many U.S. and foreign producers suffered major losses.[40] U.S. manufacturers sharply curtailed their orders for new production equipment and raw materials -- sending the U.S. SME and materials industries into a major recession. World consumption improved in 1986, but in real terms (correcting for exchange rate effects) demand was still significantly below the 1984 level.

As indicated above, the U.S. merchants have been battling a steady erosion in their world market share since 1980. The recent decline in sales and prices has been reflected in operating losses for these companies. Figure 2.6 shows that the merchant sector posted operating losses in the seven quarters from 1985 Q1 to 1986 Q4. On an annual basis the losses in 1985 and 1986 were equal to 6.5 percent and 6.1 percent of total sales. These losses adversely affected the U.S. industry's ability to raise capital. In 1986, spending on plant and equipment by U.S. firms fell by an unprecedented 45%. In absolute terms, this was the lowest annual spending level since 1979 and measured as a percent of sales the lowest level of capital spending since the Semiconductor Industry Association began publishing capital investment data in 1976.

STRUCTURAL CHANGES IN THE INDUSTRY: THE ADVENT OF VLSI

In the early 1980s the semiconductor industry reached a technological watershed, the transition to very large scale integration (VLSI) technology, which involves devices containing 1000 or more gate equivalents on a single chip.[41] The technical demands of VLSI forced major changes in device design, manufacturing techniques, and device technology, and placed unprecedented pressure on microelectronics enterprises. The course of

---

40   The recession which began in 1984 was global in scope and placed substantial pressure on foreign producers as well as U.S. firms. However, these firms were generally vertically integrated and able to assure their semiconductor divisions at least some continued internal demand. In addition, some foreign semiconductor producers received subsidy injections from their governments to cover their operating losses. The French Government Microelectronics Plan for the 1983-86 period, for example, provided 900 million francs in subsidies to French semiconductor firms to cover their operating losses. *Electroniques Actualites* (June 10, 1983).

41   Progress in integrated circuit production has primarily been directed at increasing the density of circuit elements per chip. In the mid-1960s, Medium Scale Integration (MSI) was the norm, defined as involving 10 to 100 digital logic gates (for logic devices). By the mid-1970s, the industry was producing Large Scale Integration (LSI) devices, which contained 100 to 1000 gate equivalents. In terms of the largest volume memory devices, DRAMs, the LSI period began with production of the 16K DRAM, while VLSI began with production of the 256K DRAM.

FIGURE 2.6

U.S. SEMICONDUCTOR MANUFACTURERS' PRE-TAX INCOME TO SALES
(Percent of Sales)

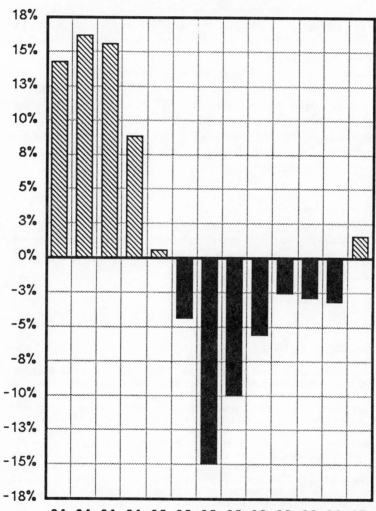

SOURCE: Semiconductor Industry Association

technical change in the industry, especially with the advent of VLSI, has dramatically increased the minimum efficient scale of operation, reflecting increased capital and R&D costs.[42]

VLSI devices themselves have become so complex that they must increasingly be designed by computers. The cost of device design also has escalated substantially -- the cost of designing a 32-bit microprocessor is estimated at $50 million. The cost of production equipment for VLSI devices has undergone a quantum jump, reflecting the complex process technologies required to produce devices of the requisite density, as well as the need to automate virtually all aspects of manufacturing to improve yields.[43] According to some estimates a world class wafer fabrication facility today costs $200 million for the factory alone; by 1995, the cost of a fabrication facility is forecast to reach $1 billion.[44] Even more significantly, the capital/output ratio has dramatically increased from approximately 1:9 in the mid-1970s to 1:2 in the mid-1980s with a ratio of 1:1.8 projected for the early 1990s.[45] These changes have resulted in tremendous capital requirements for volume manufacturing in an industry that at one time had few entry barriers. As a result, high volume integrated circuit production is increasingly becoming possible only for large corporations.[46]

---

42 While scale economies associated with minimum outlay contraints were not considered significant in the early years of the semiconductor industry, learning economies have always been important in integrated circuit fabrication. Richard C. Levin, "The Semiconductor Industry," in *Government and Technical Progress*, ed. Richard R. Nelson (New York: Pergamon Press, 1982), pp. 20-22.

43 The Defense Science Board estimated in 1987 that "to tool a modern one megabit production line costs well in excess of $100 million." DSB, *Task Force on Semiconductor Dependency*, p. 16.

44 *Forbes* (February 9, 1987).

45 Integrated Circuit Engineering Corporation. *Status 1987: A Report on the Integrated Circuit Industry* (Scotsdale, Arizona: ICE, 1987), p. 6-15.

46 The significance of learning economies has imparted a tremendous strategic importance to certain types of semiconductors for which significant unit demand exists -- and which can thus be produced in high volumes -- but which are also highly complex. The mass production of such extremely complex devices generates "learning" about complex production processes which can be applied to a much wider range of other device types which are produced by a company in lower volume. Such high-complexity, high volume "technology drivers" are widely viewed as a prerequisite to remaining competitive in semiconductors over the long run. Consequently, these product areas have been the principal areas of international competition in microelectronics since the early 1970s. At present, the most common "technology drivers" are advanced computer memory devices for which high volume demand exists -- dynamic and static random access memories (DRAMs and SRAMs) and erasable programmable read only memories (EPROMs). This is discussed further in Appendix B.

The increasing scale of R&D investments has made it impossible for even the largest firms to remain entirely self-sufficient technologically. In order to acquire necessary additional technology, semiconductor firms are entering into an increasing number of interfirm alliances, many of them transnational.[47] In this environment, the value of developing a new technology is thus twofold -- a company can commercialize the technology itself, but can also utilize it in exchange for needed technologies from other companies.[48] While some observers of the transnational alliance phenomenon comment that it reflects a trend toward global cooperation, others comment that "patterns of technical cooperation that are evolving are part of the growing intensity of competition."[49] Firms which possess the most advanced technology are able to further enhance their position through a well-managed system of technical alliances and exchanges.[50]

The quest for progressively greater device density and performance continues to push existing production processes and device and materials technologies to their physical limits, requiring a series of quantum leaps to entirely new technologies:

- *Process Technology.* Photolithography, the process by which circuits are projected on a wafer by transmitting light through a mask onto a photosensitive emulsion, confronts limitations as circuit widths go below 1 micron. The need for further reduction in circuit size is forcing the introduction of entirely new lithographic techniques -- the "direct writing" of circuits on a wafer through computer-controlled beams of electrons, ions, or x-rays.

---

47 Transnational technology exchanges virtually never involve joint research; the dominant pattern is exchange of one developed technology for another. One noteworthy exception to this general pattern is the Siemens-Philips Mega-Projekt, involving joint R&D on DRAM and SRAM technology by a German and a Dutch firm.

48 The Tokyo *Computer Digest* reported in March, 1980, when MITI announced that patents from its VLSI project would be opened for licensing to foreign firms, that the measure would "facilitate beneficial dealings when importing foreign technologies and negotiating with foreign industries. . . . The VLSI patents are expected to be used as 'chessmen' captured and available for use in acquiring superb foreign technologies."

49 Haklisch, *Technical Alliances*, p. 1. The technologies themselves "are increasingly being used as bargaining chips in a high stakes game of industrial technology." Tatsuno, *Technopolis Strategy*, p. 43.

50 The *Financial Times* observed on October 17, 1986 that "In the computer industry, both Fujitsu and NEC have gained immeasurable competitive advantage from a welter of partnerships in complementary technologies and geographic markets. Fujitsu's partners, for example, include Texas Instruments, GTE, ICL, Amdahl, Siemens, and Telefonica of Spain."

- *Three Dimensional Devices.* The desire to increase function density has led to efforts to move from the traditional two-dimensional character of semiconductor devices to three dimensional or "stacked" devices.

- *Non-silicon Materials.* Increasing function density is revealing the limits of silicon as a medium and compelling the development of alternatives to silicon, notably gallium arsenide (GaAs).

- *Optical Semiconductors.* The desire for enhanced device speed is leading to development of an entirely new class of devices -- optoelectronic and optical semiconductors -- which conduct light instead of electricity, and can deliver speeds hundreds of times faster than conventional electronic-based devices.

The cost of research and development into these and other advanced technologies is proving beyond the resources of very large individual firms in the United States and foreign countries, and even national governments.[51] An executive for the Dutch electronics firm, Philips, complained in 1986 that

The tragedy of Philips is that it is a really big company in a really small country with a small budget.[52]

The semiconductor industry has always been characterized by competition to achieve progressively greater device capability and quality at increasingly reduced cost:[53]

---

51   France concluded in the mid-1980s that the cost of remaining abreast in microelectronics R&D was beyond the resource capability of the nation as a whole. As a result, despite a strong tradition of economic nationalism, the French government decided that it needed to merge its efforts with those of its European neighbors to attain the necessary scale. *Eletroniques Actualites* (March 29, 1985).

52   *NRC Handelsblad* (December 6, 1986).

53   In DRAMs, the standard technological advance between product generations involves the doubling of the density of circuits which can be etched on a two-dimensional surface, which quadruples the number of components. The number of electronic functions that can be packed onto a single DRAM chip has been doubling every year since the early 1970s; at the same time, the cost per function has fallen several thousand-fold during the past two decades. Thus, successive generations of DRAMs have been the 1K (kilobit, or 1000 bits of memory) DRAM, and the 4K, 16K, 64K, 256K DRAM and currently, the 1M (megabit or 1,000,000 bits of memory) DRAM.

- *Enhanced device capabilities* are achieved by intensive commitments of human and financial resources to research and development of new device designs and production technologies.

- *Reductions in production cost* are achieved primarily through "learning economies" or "learning-by-doing" -- that is, the cumulative experience gained through the actual manufacturing of large numbers of semiconductors.

- *Enhanced quality* of finished devices is likewise made possible through the experience gained by producing large numbers of devices and by "designing in" device quality at critical points in the production process.

These competitive imperatives foster a race to enter commercial production of a new device type quickly, and to achieve volume production in advance of competitors, with concomitant advantages in cost reduction and device quality achieved through learning-by-doing.

Finally, product life cycles are extraordinarily short, often only 3 or 4 years, so that these large investments must be recovered very quickly -- making investment an extraordinarily risky proposition. A Korean analyst commented in 1985 that

> *It would take at least several hundred million won to set up one [DRAM] factory, but the facility would become outdated in 3 years at the longest. Since such a facility could not even be converted to produce other products, it would become a heap of scrap metal. . . . [A] great loss is inevitable unless the huge capital investment is completely recovered within 3 years.*[54]

The U.S. merchants have traditionally raised most of their funds through a combination of reinvested retained earnings and equity investment, with commercial success in a given product generation making funds available for investment in the next product generation. This reliance on retained earnings and equity has forced U.S. firms to place a substantial emphasis on remaining profitable.[55] The large Japanese, European and Korean firms -- more closely affiliated with large financial institutions -- generally enjoy a

---

54 Chong Hung-yol in *Wolgan Chonggyong Munwha* (July, 1985).

55 Losses not only reduce retained earnings, but depress stock prices and limit a firm's ability to raise debt.

more stable access to capital and are able to rely more heavily on debt financing. Thus, they are less driven by short-run profit concerns.

Historically, the existence of a large venture capital market in the United States has generally ensured that promising new innovations received the funding necessary for initial commercialization, whereas the conservative character of the large banks has retarded venture startups in Japan and Europe.[56] However, U.S. capital markets are ultimately subject to the desire for a return on investments. The losses incurred by U.S. information sector firms are slowing the flow of venture capital to semiconductor companies[57] at the same time that governments in Japan, Korea and Europe are taking steps to make venture capital more readily available to their own small, innovative firms.[58]

The nature of VLSI devices is also forcing the development of new relationships between upstream, midstream and downstream firms. VLSI devices are so complex that they are themselves often complete subsystems or systems, and their performance characteristics have major implications for the end users who incorporate them into their own larger systems.[59] The increasing systems orientation of VLSI virtually compels the development of much closer relationships between upstream, midstream and downstream companies than has traditionally characterized the information sector,[60] and, therefore, has resulted in a shift in competitive advantage in manufacturing to vertically integrated firms.

Such changes in design, process and device technology are affecting the structure of the industry substantially. The economics of VLSI increasingly

---

56 *Frankfurter Zeitung/Blick durch die Wirtschaft* (September 30, 1985). "During the 1970s and early 1980s there was in effect no city bank capital available for new ventures in Japan." M. Therese Flaherty and Hiroyuki Itami, "Finance" in *Competitive Edge: The Semiconductor Industry in the U.S. and Japan* eds. Daniel I. Okimoto, Takuo Sugano, and Franklin B. Weinstein (Stanford: Stanford University Press, 1984), p. 148.

57 U.S. venture capital investment is reportedly shifting from high technology investment toward leveraged buyouts of established companies, pizza shops, athletic apparel concerns and other businesses unrelated to the commercialization of new technology. *New York Times* (February 6, 1987).

58 *Frankfurter Rundschau* (March 23, 1984); *Hanguk Kjongje Sinmun* (February 5, 1984).

59 One manifestation of this phenomenon is the dramatic growth in the market for semistandard and application specific integrated circuits (ASICs), which are VLSI devices specifically tailored for the needs of a particular user.

60 For example, a semiconductor vendor designing a "system-on-a-chip" for an end user must become privy to many of the technological secrets of that end user in order to design and produce a satisfactory component. Similarly, the semiconductor producer needs to divulge certain aspects of its own technology to its equipment and materials vendors to ensure that it secures the tools and materials necessary to produce the devices.

favor larger firms with extensive financial resources. New firms, funded by venture capital, are still entering the industry, but the rate of entry has slowed -- the costs of entry are higher, and the risks correspondingly greater.[61] A number of firms are exiting segments of the semiconductor market, concluding that they no longer possess the resources necessary to sustain competition in those product areas or products' areas.

The severity of the semiconductor recession which began in 1984, coupled with the various structural and financial stresses associated with the transition to VLSI, would have forced major adjustments on the U.S. semiconductor industry even in the complete absence of foreign competition. However, these developments occurred simultaneously with the dramatic emergence of Japan as an aggressive challenger in the international competitive arena.

---

61   In the United States, the new venture start-up firms now tend to be concentrated in the "niche" product areas rather than in the high-volume, technology driver product lines.

3

THE JAPANESE CHALLENGE

The most fundamental competitive fact of life which the U.S. microelectronics industry confronts in the 1980s is Japan's extraordinary move toward global leadership in microelectronics. Figure 3.1 shows that Japanese semiconductor producers have gained 20 percentage points in world market share since 1978, primarily at the expense of U.S. firms. Japanese firms now hold the largest share of the world semiconductor market.[62] The three largest semiconductor vendors in the world are now Japanese firms (NEC, Hitachi, and Toshiba), although their emergence as leaders partially reflects the high value of the yen. Japanese producers dominate all major technology-driver product areas -- DRAMs, SRAMs and EPROMs -- and are steadily eroding U.S. firms' share in design-intensive product areas such as ASICs and microprocessors.

Japanese semiconductor investment spending levels have been substantially greater than those of the U.S. industry as a percent of sales since the mid-1970s. As shown in Figure 3.2, this higher rate of investment spending resulted in the Japanese industry overtaking the U.S. industry in absolute spending levels in 1983. While U.S. semiconductor producers lead all other U.S. industries in terms of reinvestment of sales revenues in R&D. the volume of investment has nevertheless been insufficient.[63] Japanese

---

62 Sales for Japanese semiconductor producers more than doubled between 1982 to 1984, rising from $4.6 billion to $9.8 billion. Total semiconductor sales for Japanese producers declined to $8.8 billion in 1985 but rose to $11.9 billion in 1986.

63 DSB, *Task Force on Semiconductor Dependency,* p. 64.

FIGURE 3.1

CUMULATIVE CHANGE IN WORLD SEMICONDUCTOR MARKET SHARE SINCE 1978
(Percentage Points)

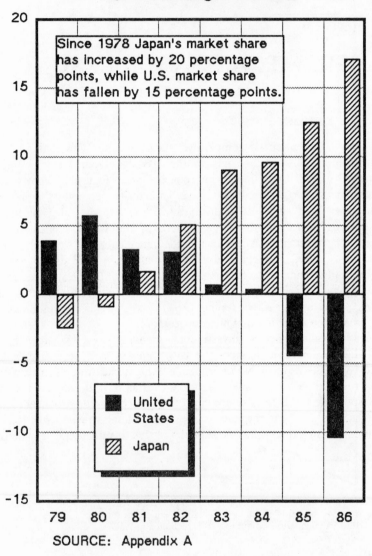

Since 1978 Japan's market share has increased by 20 percentage points, while U.S. market share has fallen by 15 percentage points.

United States

Japan

SOURCE: Appendix A

FIGURE 3.2

SEMICONDUCTOR INVESTMENT
EXPENDITURES

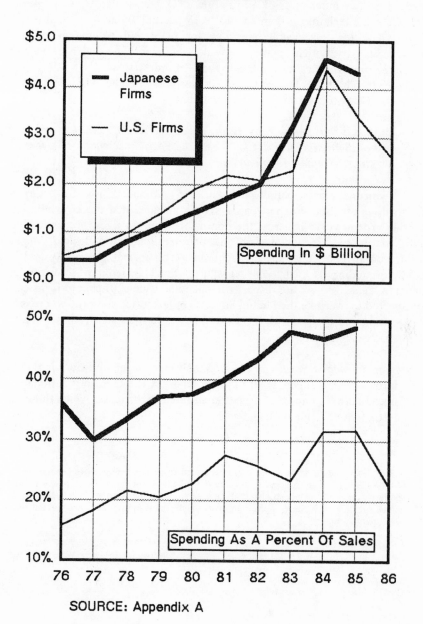

SOURCE: Appendix A

semiconductor R&D expenditures have exceeded U.S. levels as a percent of sales for over a decade and, as illustrated in Figure 3.3, are approaching aggregate U.S. spending levels.[64] This is particularly significant in light of the fact that Japanese R&D spending is more efficient and less duplicative because of the large number of cooperative R&D projects in Japan. Furthermore, a much greater proportion of Japanese R&D is spent on manufacturing technology than the 10 to 15 percent spent by U.S. firms.[65] Figure 3.4 shows that overall spending for plant and equipment by the Japanese industry, both as a percent of sales and in absolute dollar terms, has been increasing significantly relative to the U.S. industry.

These trends have led to grim forecasts about the U.S. industry's prospects. One observer predicted in 1986 that

My forecast is that by the early 1990s, the Japanese will dominate every segment of the market worldwide -- with the possible exception of a few custom chips. Nothing American industry can do will stop them.[66]

In semiconductor technology itself, the ultimate basis for market leadership, a number of expert panels have concluded that the U.S. industry is losing ground virtually across the board to Japan. In a few areas, notably nonsilicon products, new materials, and high density memory devices, Japan, in the view of many analysts, has achieved technological superiority and is rapidly expanding its edge. The erosion of the U.S. industry's position is shown in Table 3.1. As the disparity in spending widens, Japanese firms can be expected to overtake the United States in other device and process areas.

The Japanese challenge to the United States in microelectronics consists of two basic elements:

● *Gains in Market Position.* The first, and most visible, element is the inroads which Japanese firms have made in the U.S. international market position and the structural and financial stresses which those inroads are placing on U.S. firms.

---

64 U.S. R&D spending, through 1985, has continued to exceed Japanese R&D spending in absolute dollar terms. Appendix A, Table A.3. However, because of differences in how the Japanese and U.S. industries classify investment spending as either R&D spending or capital spending, it is more appropriate to examine trends in what has been termed total investment spending.

65 Congressional Budget Office, *The Benefits and Risks of Federal Funding for Sematech* (September, 1987), p. 32; Edward C. White, Jr., "Electronics Industry Weekly Notes" (E.F. Hutton Industry Review, September 22, 1987).

66 Clyde Prestowitz in *Business Week* (August 18, 1986), p. 63.

FIGURE 3.3

SEMICONDUCTOR R&D EXPENDITURES

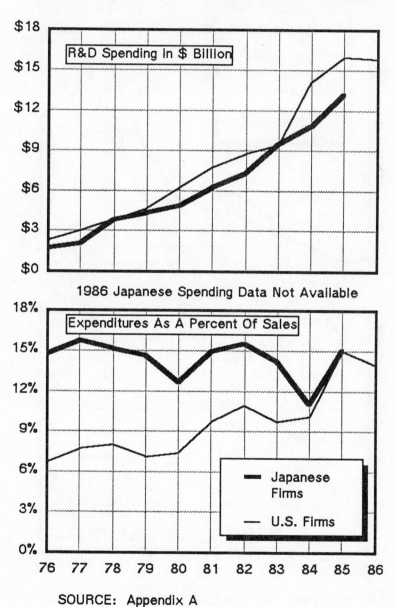

SOURCE: Appendix A

FIGURE 3.4

SEMICONDUCTOR CAPITAL EXPENDITURES

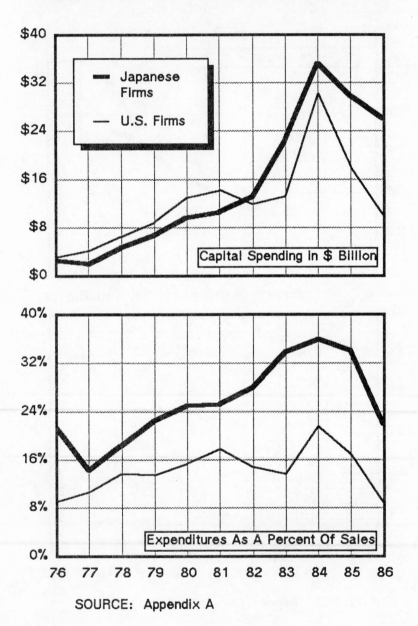

SOURCE: Appendix A

TABLE 3.1

STATUS AND TRENDS OF U.S. SEMICONDUCTOR TECHNOLOGY RELATIVE TO JAPAN

	U.S. LAG			Parity With Japan	U.S. LEAD		
	Substantial	Clear	Slight		Slight	Clear	Substantial
Silicon Products							
DRAMs		<	•				
SRAMs		<	•				
EPROMs				<		•	
Microprocessors					< •		
Custom, Semicustom Logic				•	<	•	
Bipolar		<					
Nonsilicon Products							
Memory			<		•		
Logic			<				•
Linear					• <		
Optoelectronics	<		•				
Heterostructures		<	•				
Materials							
Silicon			<	•			
Gallium Arsenide		<			•		
Processing Equipment							
Lithography							
Optical				<			
E-Beam					<	•	
X-Ray				<		•	
Ion Implantation Technology					< •		
Chemical Vapor Deposition				• <			
Deposition, Diffusion, Other				<	•		
Energy-Assisted Processing*			<				
Assembly				• <			
Packaging		< •					
Test			<		•		
CAD				<			•
CAM		<			•		

*N/A in 1979 - 1980   • U.S. Position 1979 - 80 (IQ)   < U.S. Position 1986 - 87 (IQ)

Source: U.S. Government InterAgency Working Group on Semiconductor Technology

● *Technological Gains.* A second, and less widely recognized, element consists of the rapid Japanese gains in the semiconductor device, manufacturing and materials technologies that will be critical to competitive success in the 1990s and beyond.

Japanese achievements both in the market and in technology are partially attributable to competitive factors such as the strong technological, manufacturing, and marketing capabilities of Japanese firms. However, Japanese gains have been predicated, above all, upon the close and highly effective working relationship forged between the Japanese Government and the Japanese industry.

Both the Japanese and U.S. Governments have implemented numerous measures which have benefited their respective microelectronics and related information sectors.[67] However, U.S. policies have been implemented piecemeal and have usually been subordinated to other objectives, such as national defense, the enhancement of consumer benefits, and the desire to restrict the flow of U.S. technology to the Soviet Union. In Japan, by contrast, the "elevation" of the microelectronics industries to a position of international preeminence has been an overriding national priority and government policies have been applied in a systematic and coordinated fashion for over 15 years to achieve this objective -- where necessary, at the expense of other objectives. The full impact of this Japanese national effort is now being felt in the market and is being reflected in the market and technological gains Japanese firms are making relative to U.S. firms.

INDUSTRY-GOVERNMENT RELATIONSHIPS: THE UNITED STATES AND JAPAN

The U.S. Government has never established an overall policy goal of promoting U.S. competitiveness in microelectronics. U.S. policies affecting microelectronics are fragmented among many agencies, some of which pursue priorities which are irrelevant or even detrimental to U.S. competitiveness.[68] Japanese policies in the information sector are closely

---

67 Since 1980, for example, the U.S. Government, has provided tax credits for research and development; relaxed antitrust inhibitions on joint research; committed substantial defense-related resources to microelectronics R&D; and extended intellectual property protection to semiconductor mask designs.

68 "It has become a commonplace note that, while numerous public policies exert direct or indirect effects on firms and industries, the American approach is *ad hoc* ... The United

coordinated toward the attainment of a narrow objective; the promotion of the national industry.[69]   While the Japanese Government is far from monolithic, two entities, the Ministry of International Trade and Industry ("MITI") and the Ministry of Posts and Telecommunications ("MPT"), between them play a role in virtually every policy area affecting the information industry and have proven capable of ensuring that promotion of the information sector is accorded priority within the Japanese Government.[70] Competition between MITI and MPT, rather than paralyzing Japanese information policy, has developed into a contest to woo the information industry through the extension of progressively greater promotional benefits.[71]

The Japanese information industry is not subordinated to the state as is the case in centrally-planned economies. The relationship between the government and the industry has been more accurately characterized as a "partnership between central bureaucrats and entrepreneurs:"

> *The bureaucrats never attempt to gain absolute power over the nongovernmental corporations. They guide the economy while using the entrepreneurs as antennae. The central planners . . . know what is happening at the periphery through constant monitoring of the experiences of capitalists trying to find new ways of making money. The mistakes planners undoubtedly make are more than compensated by the unified forces they bring to bear on industrial development. . . . [I]t is a partnership that has an industrial policy and a trade strategy. Freedom of the market is not considered a desirable goal in itself, but only one of several instruments for achieving predetermined effects that are totally subordinated to the ultimate goal of industrial expansion.*[72]

States has avoided promotion, planning, targeting -- the common tools in other countries." Office of Technology Assessment, *International Competitiveness in Electronics*, p. 389.

69   "The main strength of Japanese industrial policies has lain not in any particular instrument or set of instruments, but rather in the way in which these various instruments have been used together to directly or indirectly complement one another." M.E. Janow, "Whither the Future of Japanese Industrial Development Policies," *Michigan Yearbook of International Legal Studies* 11 (1984): 111.

70   For example, MITI has waged a long, at least partially successful struggle with the Ministry of Finance to secure the subsidies and tax benefits needed to promote high technology industries. Similarly, MITI has largely forestalled the exercise of antitrust jurisdiction over the information sector by the Japan Fair Trade Commission.

71   See generally C. Johnson, *MITI, MPT and the Telecom Wars: How Japan Makes Policy for High Technology* (University of California, Berkeley: BRIE Working Paper No. 21, September 11, 1986).

72   K.G. van Wolferen, "The Japan Problem," *Foreign Affairs* (January 1987): 292-93.

The basic relationship between the Japanese Government and the information industry is depicted schematically in Figure 3.5. MITI provides strategic guidance and financial assistance to the industry and jointly participates with Japanese companies in R&D for commercial applications in industry-government joint laboratories. Nippon Telephone and Telegraph (NTT), under the jurisdiction of MPT, jointly designs telecommunications equipment with Japanese companies who then produce the equipment for sale to NTT. The Ministry of Education and Culture funds university research and supports several large national research facilities which are used in electronics R&D.[73]

MITI was the government agency principally responsible for directing Japan's extraordinary postwar economic growth. MITI "has taken the view that Japan's future lies in control of electronics technology." [74] Accordingly, during the 1960s and early 1970s MITI fostered the rapid development of indigenous computer and semiconductor industries through a combination of subsidies for research and development, home market protection, and promotion of an industrial structure suited for international competition.[75] In the late 1970s, after formal import and investment restrictions were lifted, MITI's VLSI Project (1975-79), a government-funded industry- government joint R&D project, enabled Japanese companies to make major strides in

---

73 The Ministry of Education and Culture operates the Photon Factory in Tsukuba Science City, a $60-$100 million synchotron facility where much of Japan's synchotron expertise is concentrated. The Photon Factory's synchotron facilities are used by NTT and by the joint laboratories organized by MITI to perform microelectronics R&D. The Photon Factory also trains company scientists and engineers. *Far Eastern Economic Review* (August 20, 1987); H. Wieder, et. al., *JTECH Panel Report on Opto-& Microelectronics*, (La Jolla, California: Science Applications International Corporation, 1985), p. 2-9, reprinted by National Technical Information Service, Document No. PB85-242402.

74 *Zaikai Tembo* (February 1983).

75 MITI's policies have played a significant role in shaping the current structure of the Japanese microelectronics industry, which is dominated by several large firms. In the industry's incipient phase, MITI restricted entry into the integrated circuit field to established electronics firms through its control over the licensing of technology from Texas Instruments. *Japan Economic Journal* (November 19, 1968). Its subsidized 1973-74 microelectronics R&D projects and the 1975-79 VLSI project were limited to large, established producers, which had the effect of concentrating semiconductor production in these firms. An executive from a small Japanese firm excluded from the VLSI Project complained that "Not having been able to join the VLSI Project was a severe blow .... We are doing our utmost, but we have not caught up with those who were selected to participate in the joint program." *Chuo Koron* (Fall 1981), p. 20, cited in K. Yamamura, "Joint Research and Antitrust: Japanese vs. American Strategies", in *Japan's High Technology Industries* eds. H. Patrick and L. Meissner (Seattle: University of Washington Press, 1986), p. 193.

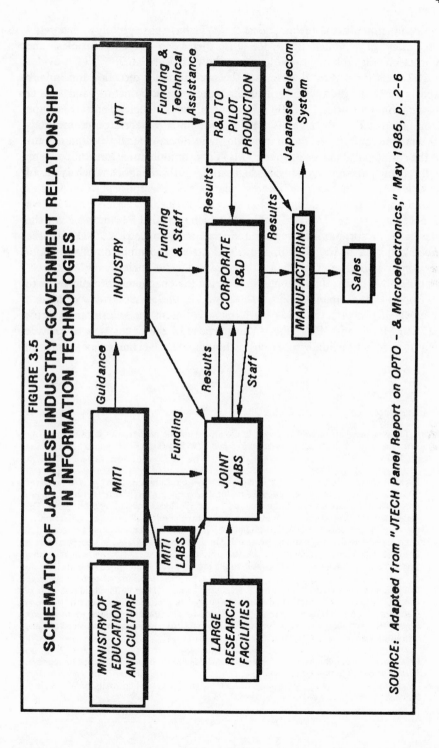

FIGURE 3.5

SCHEMATIC OF JAPANESE INDUSTRY-GOVERNMENT RELATIONSHIP
IN INFORMATION TECHNOLOGIES

SOURCE: Adapted from "JTECH Panel Report on OPTO – & Microelectronics," May 1985, p. 2-6

semiconductor process technologies.[76] MITI has subsequently sponsored a succession of similar joint R&D projects in microelectronics and microelectronics-related technologies as shown in Table 3.2.

MITI has for several decades set the overall policy direction for Japan's export-oriented industries, including the semiconductor and other information industries.[77] MITI influences the strategic direction of the information sector through its participation in a wide range of industry-government committees and associations, and direct contact with the leaders of the principal Japanese firms. MITI's promotional efforts have been undertaken pursuant to special legislation authorizing the provision of subsidies, tax benefits, low interest loans, and exemptions from Japan's Antimonopoly Law for designated priority industries.[78] The most well known of these laws was the "*Kijoho*" (1978-85) which provided a framework for the "elevation" of specific information and machinery industries.[79] During the effective period of the *Kijoho*, Japan's electronics producers moved into a position of world leadership in a number of key technologies.

In 1985 MITI was instrumental in securing the enactment of a successor to the *Kijoho* by the Japanese Diet,[80] the *Basic Technology Research Facilitation Law*, which provides the basis for joint activities in the information sector between MITI and MPT. The stated purpose of the new law is to provide measures which facilitate research in "fundamental" technologies by private

---

76   A Japanese account of MITI's promotional efforts in microelectronics is given in Kyoko Sato, *Japanese Semiconductor Industry Yearbook 1985* (Tokyo: Press Journal, Inc., 1985), pp. 17-26.

77   Each fiscal year MITI's Machinery and Information Industries Bureau draws up an "Outline" of information related policies for the coming year, setting forth the major programs it will sponsor and the funding to be allocated from MITI's budgets. The figures for FY 1986 are set forth in Table 3.3. These "Outlines," however, reflect only a fraction of the assistance MITI mobilizes on behalf of the information sector; it recommends additional funding by the Japan Development Bank and Export-Import Bank of Japan, and regularly presses for the enactment of tax legislation and other government funding initiatives favorable to the industry.

78   In 1957, the Diet enacted the *Law Concerning Special Measures for the Promotion of Specific Electronic Industries*. This was replaced by Law No. 17 of 1971, the *Extraordinary Measures Law for the Promotion of Specific Electronic and Machinery Industries (Kidenho)*. These laws provided the basis for MITI's promotional aid to the semiconductor and computer industries.

79   Law No. 84 of 1978, the *Law for Provisional Measures for the Promotion of Specific Machinery and Information Industries*.

80   *Nihon Keizai* (July 31, 1984) and (August 3, 1984).

TABLE 3.2

MITI-SPONSORED JOINT RESEARCH AND DEVELOPMENT PROJECTS IN MICROELECTRONICS

Project	MITI VLSI	Opto Electronics	Super Computer	New Function Elements	SORTEC**	Optoelectronic Devices**	Fifth Generation Computer
Time Frame	1975-79	1979-86	1981-89	1981-90	1986-96	1986-96	1981-91
Technological Focus	VLSI Manufacturing	Optical Semi-conductors	High Speed Devices	VLSI Device & Process	Synchotron Lithography	Optical Semi-conductors	VLSI logic
Govt. Funding* ($Million)	112	80	135	140	62	42	NA
Participants	NEC Hitachi Fujitsu Toshiba Mitsubishi	NEC Hitachi Fujitsu Toshiba Mitsubishi Oki Sumitomo	NEC Hitachi Fujitsu Toshiba Mitsubishi Oki Sharp	NEC Hitachi Fujitsu Toshiba Mitsubishi Oki Sharp Sanyo Sumitomo Matsushita	NEC Hitachi Fujitsu Toshiba Mitsubishi Oki Sharp Sanyo Sumitomo Nippon Sh. Gls. Matsushita Nippon Kogaku	NEC Hitachi Fujitsu Toshiba Mitsubishi Oki Sharp Sanyo Sumitomo Nippon Sh. Glass Fujikura	NEC Hitachi Fujitsu Toshiba Mitsubishi Oki Sharp

* Yen:dollar conversion average for the period
** Funded through Japan Key Technology Center

Source: Nihon Keizai (May 6 and May 26, 1986);
U. S. Embassy, Tokyo

TABLE 3.3

MITI BUDGET FOR INFORMATION-RELATED FUNDING
Capitalization Denotes Projects Applicable To Microelectronics (Millions of Yen)

		Japanese Fiscal Year	
	1984	1985	1986
Construct software industrialized generator and maintenance aids system	NA	2,500	NA
Inf. Processing Promotion Association	2,682	2,459	2,350
Subsidy for Software Business Operation	1,711	1,383	NA
Subsidy to accelerate information systems in small-medium enterprises	772	965	NA
FIFTH GENERATION COMPUTER PROJECT	5,120	4,776	4,800
R&D on Interoperable Data Base Systems	-	20	20
SUPERCOMPUTER PROJECT	2,248	2,753	2,750
R&D On Optical Instrumentation Control Systems	2,327	3,439	-
NEW FUNCTION ELEMENTS PROJECT	1,478	1,585	1,560
Support Systems for Diagnosis and Treatment	119	110	110
JAPAN DEVELOPMENT BANK LOANS TO JAPAN ELECTRONIC COMPUTER COMPANY (JECC)	65,000	65,000	65,000
Bank loans to finance investment in information processing	3,500	3,000	3,000
Safety measures for information processing service industry	13	12	NA
R&D into unification trends, interoperability of equipment	13	14	"
Arrange data base and information supply service	12	12	"
Investigate trends related to systematization of information	22	16	"
Formation of New Media Communities	96	74	74
Promote New Media Communities concept	-	2	NA
Software Production Industrialization Project	-	-	2,350
Basic technology on information processing for education	-	-	220
Construction of data bases	-	-	1,952
FUNDING FOR THE JAPAN KEY TECHNOLOGY CENTER	-	-	10,000

Source: MITI Machine and Information Industry Bureau, cited in *Denshi Kogyo Geppo*, February and October 1985

firms.[81] The law provides for the use of national research facilities by private firms,[82] licensing of technology by the government,[83] establishment of an industry-government "Key Technology Center," [84] and "any other necessary measures" for the facilitation of research in fundamental technologies to be conducted by private firms and institutions.[85]

MPT, MITI's bureaucratic rival, exercises jurisdiction over NTT, which until 1985 had a monopoly on most telecommunications services in Japan. MPT's administration of the Japanese telecommunications system has been characterized as "conservative, monopolistic . . . bureaucratic, labor-intensive, inefficient and politically driven;" [86] at the same time, NTT's joint development of telecommunications equipment with a "family" of favored Japanese firms (notably NEC, Hitachi, Fujitsu and Oki) has played a major role in the international successes these firms have achieved in microelectronics.[87] NTT develops semiconductor device technology in its laboratories which is transferred to Japanese companies, in some cases reportedly free of charge.[88] NTT was ostensibly "privatized" in 1985, but the government still holds the majority of its stock and will retain a 50 percent ownership. Through the sale of NTT stock and collection of dividends on the remaining shares, the government has generated a huge sum of off-budget

---

81   Chapter I, Article 2. "Fundamental" technologies are defined as technologies used in mining and manufacturing industries, telecommunications and broadcasting services, and radio telecommunications technologies which are under either the jurisdiction of MITI or MPT. As a practical matter this definition embraces the entire information industry.

82   Chapter II, Article 3.

83   Chapter II, Article 4.

84   Chapter III.

85   Chapter II, Article 5.

86   G. Turin, et. al., *JTECH Panel Report on Telecommunications Technology in Japan -- Final Report* (La Jolla, California: Science Applications International Corporation, 1986), pp. 2-5, 2-6, reprinted by National Technical Information Service, Document No. PB86-202330.

87   For example, NTT's first VLSI project (1975-77), undertaken jointly with NEC, Hitachi and Fujitsu, resulted in the development of a prototype 64K DRAM in 1977. *Japan Telecommunications Review* (January 1979). NTT engineers helped Japanese firms overcome technical obstacles to the commercialization of the 64K DRAM, and in 1981, Japanese firms captured a dominant share of the world market for this product. NTT subsequently developed and transferred technology for the 256K DRAM to four Japanese companies, reportedly free of charge, and Japanese firms hold over 90 percent of the world market for this product. *Japan Economic Journal* (May 30, 1978); *Electronic News,* (October 1, 1982).

88   *Electronic News* (October 11, 1982).

funds, a portion of which is now being channeled to support commercial R&D in Japan's high technology industries.[89]

Companies which jointly develop equipment with NTT have found the business to be highly lucrative. NTT pays premium prices for equipment which it procures, leading a former NTT President to characterize NTT procurement orders as "gold mines,"[90] and some observers have characterized NTT procurement as a form of subsidization.[91] NTT procurement gives Japanese producers a secure source of initial demand for the new technologies which they commercialize, diminishing investment risk and enabling them to reduce their production costs through their initial sales.[92]

The Japanese semiconductor industry consists virtually entirely of an oligopoly of vertically integrated firms that both produce and consume semiconductors. In addition to internal vertical integration, each major Japanese semiconductor producer has a large group of closely affiliated "family" companies in electronics and related fields.[93] The Japanese producers have also substantially integrated into upstream sectors such as semiconductor manufacturing and testing equipment. Many of the most important semiconductor equipment manufacturers are subsidiaries or financial affiliates of the leading semiconductor producers as shown in Table 3.4.

---

89   Johnson, *Telecom Wars*, pp. 57-60. Dividends from government-held shares of NTT stock are being channeled into the Japan Key Technology Center, which funds high-risk commercial R&D.

90   Former President Yonezawa in *Nikkan Kogyo* (April 27, 1979). In addition to premium prices, NTT sometimes prepaid 60 percent of the contract procurement sum in order to provide developmental capital for the producer. In addition -- further reducing the risk to producers -- the price to be paid for the product was fixed after production, when actual costs were known so that the price would cover all costs plus allowance for profit. Hitoshi Hiromatsu, *Denwa no Muko wa Konna Kao: Denden Kosha KDD no Uchimaku* (Tokyo, 1980).

91   Flaherty and Itami, *Finance*, pp. 156-157. The Japanese telecommunications equipment industry earns the highest returns of any major Japanese industry, and is the only Japanese industry in which Japanese firms consistently earn higher returns than the equivalent U.S. industry. Turin, *JTECH Panel Report on Telecommunications*, p. 2-9.

92   Former NTT President Akikusa commented in *Asahi* (February 29, 1979) that "manufacturers are brought up on a bed of roses, with orders guaranteed." *Nikkan Kogyo* observed on April 25, 1979 that "participation in [NTT] joint development is a passport for negotiated contracts, and means they have received a promise for the future."

93   Table 3.5 shows that NEC, for example, has over two dozen subsidiaries and affiliate firms which produce communications equipment, electronic parts, consumer electronics products, and other electronic and information industry products.

TABLE 3.4

VERTICAL INTEGRATION OF JAPANESE SEMICONDUCTOR PRODUCERS -- UPSTREAM SECTORS

Equipment Sector	Hitachi	Fujitsu	NEC	Toshiba	Mitsubishi	Matsushita
Lithography	Hitachi			Toshiba	Nikon Machine JOEL	JOEL
Diffusion	Kokusai				JOEL	ULVAC
Ion Implant	Kokusai					ULVAC
Deposition	Kokusai		Anelva	Tokuda-Seisakusho	JOEL	ULVAC
Etch	Kokusai		Anelva; Kaijo Denki	Tokuda-Seisakusho		
Test		Takeda-Riken	Ando-Electric		Nippon Kogaku	
Assembly	Shinkawa		Kaijo Denki	Toshiba-Seiki		

Source: U.S. Department of Commerce, *A Competitive Assessment of the U.S. Semiconductor Manufacturing Equipment Industry,* (March 1985).

TABLE 3.5

DIRECT SUBSIDIARIES OF THE NIPPON ELECTRIC COMPANY
(NEC)

Company	Business	Percent Owned NEC
Shin Nippon Electric KK	Home Electronic products	100
Tohoku NEC KK	Communications equipment & parts	100
Yamagata NEC KK	Semiconductors	100
Akika NEC KK	Semiconductors	100
Miyagi NEC KK	Communications equipment & parts	100
Fukushima NEC KK	Communications equipment & parts	100
Ibaraki NEC KK	Information processing equipment	100
Niigata NEC KK	Data processing terminals	100
Nagano NEC KK	Consumer electronics products	100
Toyama NEC KK	Electronic parts	100
Fukui NEC KK	Semiconductors	100
Shizuoka NEC KK	Communications equipment & parts	100
Hyogo NEC KK	Communications equipment & parts	100
Kyushu NEC KK	Semiconductors	100
Fukuoka NEC KK	Semiconductors	100
Kumanoto NEC KK	Semiconductors	100
Kagoshima NEC KK	Electronic parts	100
Nichiden Inf. Termo Systems	Lease of IP equipment	100
NEC System Constr. KK	Electrical communications construction	100
NEC Field Service KK	Contracting for maintenance products	100
NEC Engineering KK	Design & inspect products of parent	100
Nippon Avionics KK	Electronics equipment for aviation	51
Fujiya Audio KK	Miniature motors and players	100
NEC Lease KK	Equipment leasing	75
NEC Vacuum Glass KK	Glass parts and processing electronics parts	100
Nippon Aviation Elecns. KK	Connectors and electrical equipment for aviation	50
Nichiden Anelba KK	Vacuum and analysis equipment	81
Ando Electric KK	Electronic measuring equipment	50.5
Niko Electronic KK	Automatic vending machines	100
Yonezawa Mfg. KK	Communications equipment & parts	100
Sanei Measuring Equip. KK	Medical electronics & measuring equipment	55
NEC America, Inc.	Communications equipment	100
NEC Telephones, Inc.	Sales of communications equipment	100
NEC Home Electronics, Inc.	Consumer electronics products	100
NEC Electronics USA, Inc.	Semiconductors	100
NEC Australia Prop. Ltd.	Communications equipment	100

Source: *Yukashoken Hokokushu Soran* (March, 1983)

Each major Japanese semiconductor producer is also affiliated with one or more *keiretsu*, larger and more diverse industrial groups bound together by a web of financial, personal and traditional ties, each headed by a major city bank or trust bank.[94] The NEC group of affiliates and subsidiaries, for example, is part of the much larger Sumitomo *keiretsu*, and NEC receives much of its financing from the Sumitomo Bank.[95] Fujitsu belongs to the Furukawa group, one of two groups which comprise the Dai-Ichi Kangyo Bank (DKB) *keiretsu*.[96]

The Japanese industrial system is not one characterized by perfect harmony. Infighting between rival ministries is sometimes intense and the electronics firms and their *keiretsu* compete fiercely among themselves for preeminence. Nevertheless, the Japanese system has functioned with a comparatively high degree of cohesion and effectiveness, both in enabling the Japanese industry to achieve ascendancy in the market in the 1980s and in supporting the industry's bid for technological leadership in the 1990s.

The relationship between the U.S. microelectronics sector and the U.S. Government is substantially different. As a matter of fundamental philosophy, the U.S. Government has traditionally rejected the notion of promoting the interests of any particular industrial sector. The appropriate government role has been viewed as that of a neutral referee, ensuring only that basic conditions of fairness exist as various private interests vie in the marketplace.[97] In pursuit of this role, the U.S. Government has occasionally

---

94   The *keiretsu* are the successors to the prewar *zaibatsu*, industrial groups that were broken up by the American occupation authorities. Some *keiretsu* (Hitachi, Mitsui, Mitsubishi and Sumitomo) are direct descendants of prewar *zaibatsu*. Others, such as the Dai-ichi Kangyo group (formed in 1971 by the merger of the Kawasaki and Furukawa *keiretsu*) are comparatively new organizations.

95   A Goldman Sachs *Investment Research* newsletter noted on August 7, 1986 that NEC was a member of the Sumitomo *keiretsu*, "one of Japan's largest horizontally connected groupings. Among other things, this allows for greater financial support from the *keiretsu*'s financial institutions than in a strictly arms-length relationship. Sumitomo bank owns 5% of the [NEC] equity and Sumitomo Life Insurance another 7%."

96   Hitachi heads its own *keiretsu*, consisting of approximately 40 consolidated and 430 unconsolidated subsidiaries. The Hitachi group is in turn loosely affiliated with several other *keiretsu*, including the Sanwa and Dai-Ichi Kangyo groups. Mitsubishi Electric belongs to the Mitsubishi *keiretsu* and receives much of its financing from the group; Oki belongs to the Fuji Bank (*Fuyo*) *keiretsu*; Toshiba's group (consisting of over 30 consolidated subsidiaries and several hundred affiliated subsidiaries and contractors) is part of the Mitsui *keiretsu*. House Ways and Means Committee Subcommittee on Trade, *High Technology and Japanese Industrial Policy: A Strategy for U.S. Policymakers* (October 1, 1980), p. 2.

97   Herbert Hoover articulated this view of the appropriate role of the Government in the Presidential campaign of 1928: "It is as if we set a race. We, through free and universal education provide the training for the runners; we give them an equal start; we provide in

intervened in reaction to specific crises in microelectronics, but has sought to avoid a larger or more sustained role.[98]

While the U.S. Government has implemented broad policies which have benefited U.S. semiconductor firms (along with other U.S. industries),[99] the panoply of Japanese financial assistance, trade protection and antitrust programs specifically designed to "elevate" microelectronics and related information sectors has no U.S. counterpart.[100] The U.S. Government has pursued the development of microelectronics technologies in the context of the defense and space programs, but both the objectives and end results of such programs have been substantially different than in Japan, and at no time has any U.S. program been undertaken in this industry with the primary goal of enhancing U.S. competitiveness.[101] Moreover, the U.S. Government has implemented a number of policies that have been detrimental to U.S. commercial interests and competitiveness in microelectronics.[102]

The U.S. Government's stance on such issues has been based primarily on strongly held political and economic views about the appropriate role of the government, and only secondarily upon the events that are rapidly unfolding in the marketplace in the 1980s. An intensive competitive struggle has been joined between the U.S. and Japanese industrial systems in microelectronics, and in the related upstream and downstream sectors and Japan is making spectacular headway. These trends, if not checked, will result in Japanese domination of virtually all of the microelectronics technologies required for industrial leadership and national defense in the next century. While the

---

the government the umpire of the fairness of the race. The winner is he who shows the most conscientious training, the greatest ability, and the greatest character." R. Hofstadter, *The American Political Tradition* (New York: Vintage Books, 1974), p. 38.

98   For example, in 1982-83, the U.S. Department of Commerce and the Office of the U.S. Trade Representative committed substantial personnel to a series of bilateral discussions with Japan as a result of U.S. industry allegations of Japanese dumping and market barriers. This effort led to the conclusion of a bilateral accord, the so-called High Tech Working Group Agreement, at which point virtually all of the staff working on the semiconductor issue were reassigned to other projects. The Agreement itself collapsed within a year.

99   Such policies include tax credits for research and development and relaxation of antitrust inhibitions on joint research. These benefits are available to all U.S. industries.

100   "The very notion of objectives or "goals" for [electronics] policy, in any but the most immediate sense, has been anathema for policymakers here." Office of Technology Assessment, *International Competitiveness in Electronics*, p. 393.

101   For a recent summary of defense-related federal funding of microelectronics R&D, see Office of Technology Assessment, *Microelectronics Research and Development*.

102   *National Academy of Sciences, Balancing the National Interest* (Washington, D.C.: National Academy Press, 1987), pp.254-77; *Aviation Week & Space Technology* (December 15, 1986), pp. 88-89.

Japanese Government's role in this process might be regarded in many respects as wholly inappropriate for emulation by this country, it has undeniably been effective.

JAPAN'S MARKET ASCENDANCY

The most dramatic and visible gains made by the Japanese semiconductor industry in the mid-1980s have been in the marketplace itself. In 1986, Japanese firms for the first time captured a larger share of the world semiconductor market than the U.S. industry, the culmination of several years of rapid Japanese inroads into U.S. market share.[103] Japanese gains are more significant than market share numbers alone would suggest, since the initial Japanese share gains have occurred in strategic "technology driver" product lines.

Although the Japanese industry overtook the U.S. industry in world semiconductor market share in 1986, Figure 3.6 shows that the Japanese industry surpassed the U.S. industry in MOS memory products in 1984. MOS memory products consist principally of DRAMs, SRAMs and EPROMs, the key technology process drivers which were the initial targets of intensive Japanese investments. However, U.S. market share losses have not been confined to the MOS memory segment, but have occurred over a broad range of product categories as shown in Figure 3.7. The Japanese industry overtook the U.S. industry in MOS logic products (microprocessors, microcontrollers, etc.) in 1986. Even in bipolar digital ICs, a low-growth market segment upon which the Japanese industry has not placed a major emphasis, U.S. firms have experienced substantial market share losses to Japanese (and European) firms since 1980.

These market share losses have been accompanied by the contraction of important segments of the U.S. semiconductor device, SME and materials industries -- the Japanese industry's principal international competitors. Recent Japanese successes in the marketplace will be reflected in enhanced Japanese competitiveness in microelectronics and ultimately, throughout the information sector.

---

103 The fact that the crossover occurred in 1986 reflects the strengthening of the yen against the dollar, which increases the dollar value of Japanese sales. However, the general trend of Japanese market gains transcends fluctuations in the exchange rate. Appendix A contains a detailed discussion of this issue.

FIGURE 3.6

MOS MEMORY WORLD MARKET SHARE
(Percent of World Shipments)

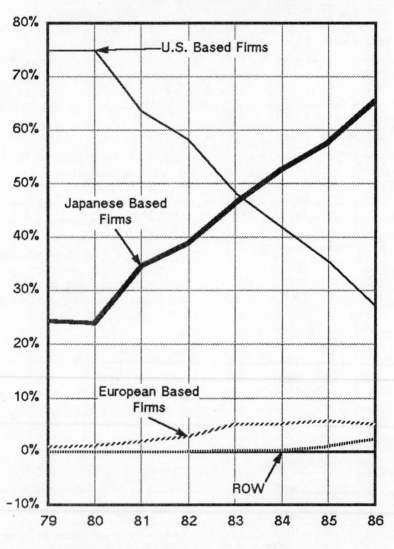

SOURCE: Dataquest

FIGURE 3.7

INTEGRATED CIRCUIT WORLD MARKET SHARES
MOS LOGIC AND BIPOLAR DIGITAL

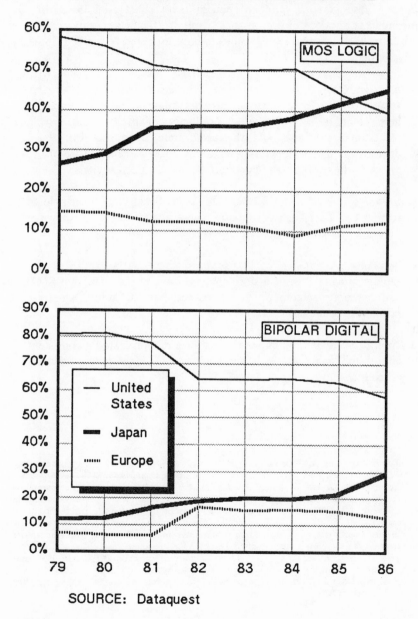

SOURCE: Dataquest

The Elements of Japanese Market Success

In the semiconductor market, the Japanese industry has pursued a strategy based on expanding market share rather than maximizing profitability. It has achieved dramatic gains in market share since 1980, and from available evidence, these gains have been "bought" with substantial losses by the semiconductor divisions of the Japanese firms.[104] The competitive challenge which Japanese semiconductor producers have mounted to the U.S. industry has five basic aspects:

- *Intensive Capital Investment and Sustained Below Cost Pricing.* Japanese firms have pursued an extraordinarily aggressive capital investment policy, expanding production capacity even during recessionary periods. At the same time, Japanese firms have demonstrated a willingness and ability to sell semiconductors at prices far below the cost of production for sustained periods.

- *Control of the Japanese Market.* Japanese firms have been able to restrict U.S. firms' access to the Japanese market, which, as shown in Figure 3.8, is now the world's largest semiconductor market.

- *Increasing Dominance of the Infrastructure.* Japanese firms are rapidly moving toward a dominant position in the upstream SME and materials sectors which are essential to sustaining a market position in semiconductors.

- *Manufacturing Skill.* Japanese firms have demonstrated a consistent ability to manufacture large numbers of high quality devices efficiently.

---

104 The semiconductor divisions of the major Japanese producers do not report separate operating results, and "all concerns in the business treat their profits as top-secret information." *Japan Economic Journal* (July 30, 1985). However, statements by executives from these firms indicate massive operating losses have occurred in semiconductors. "If I said we were making a profit, I'd be lying." *Japan Economic Journal* (July 30, 1985); "The semiconductor recession is the biggest cause of the business deterioration ... In addition to a sales slowdown, declining prices had more effect on the company's profitability." Hitachi Vice President Yasuo Miyauchi in *Toshi Keizai* (December 1985), pp. 56-57. *Tokyo Shimbun* reported on October 30, 1985, that the interim accounts of the five largest electronics firms showed major declines in profit, and that this was a reflection of the losses suffered by their semiconductor divisions. See also *Electronics News* (April 29, 1986).

FIGURE 3.8

WORLD SEMICONDUCTOR CONSUMPTION BY MARKET
(Percent of World Shipments)

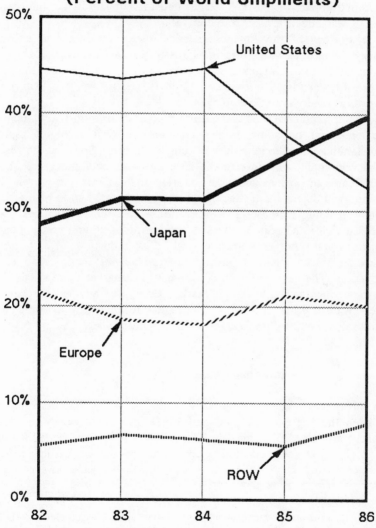

SOURCE: WSTS, SIA

● *Dominance of the Consumer Electronics Market.* Japanese firms dominate the world consumer electronics industry, an OEM market which accounts for about 30 percent of world semiconductor consumption.

The Japanese industrial structure, coupled with past and present government policies, has contributed to this combination of elements, which has had a devastating impact on the U.S. semiconductor industry in the international arena. These effects are illustrated in Table 3.6.

The strategy of the Japanese semiconductor producers in expanding capacity ahead of demand, pricing aggressively to achieve market share, and limiting access to the Japanese market cannot be rationally understood in the context of conventional microeconomic and trade theory. New concepts of competitive rivalry must be employed.[105]

Technological innovation is the driving force of this industry. Standards of behavior based on static models of atomistic firms are not useful in understanding commercial rivalry in semiconductors. Spending on research and development, and investment in plants and equipment are the key determinants of present and future market share. Past and current R&D spending will determine technological progress and the pace of innovation. Capital spending increases for fabrication and assembly facilities lead to increased yields and scale economies, further reducing unit costs. Learning economies and other economies of scale drive reductions in costs, making worldwide market share a crucial determinant of the average cost of production. The positive feedback loop between market share increases and cost reductions make losses in market share, for any given technology, extremely difficult to recapture.[106] The same technological dynamic confers significant competitive advantages to firms with privileged access to specific markets.

Japanese Capital Investment and Pricing

A major factor in Japan's growing market advantage in microelectronics has been the aggressive capital and R&D investment policy pursued by Japanese producers since the late 1970s. Japanese firms repeatedly invested heavily in R&D designed to accelerate the introduction of new products.

---

105 See Appendix B.

106 See Kenneth Flamm, "Internationalization in the Semiconductor Industry" in Joseph Greenwald and Kenneth Flamm, *The Global Factory* (Washington, D.C.: The Brookings Institution, 1985), pp. 68-94, for a discussion of U.S. losses to Japan in transistors. "The lesson learned was that a competitive advantage, once lost, is exceedingly difficult to regain."

TABLE 3.6

COMPETITION IN MICROELECTRONICS
JAPANESE GOVERNMENT POLICIES AND THE ELEMENTS OF JAPANESE MARKET SUCCESS

Competitive Element	Relevant Government Policies	Relevant Industrial Structure Factors
Intensive Capital Investment and Sustained Below Cost Pricing	- Designation of microelectronics as a national priority - Short depreciation schedules (3-4 years) - Direct government loans and support of Japan Electronic Computer Co. (JECC) - Implicit guarantee that government will not allow a major producer to fail	- *Keiretsu* banks support - Vertical integration permits cross-subsidization of semiconductor divisions - Low cost of capital - Implicit guarantee that *keiretsu* banks will not allow a major producer to fail
Control of the Japanese Market	- Long history of protectionism - Weak antitrust enforcement - Continuing protection of "infant" sectors	- Microelectronics end-markets dominated by Japanese OEMs - Japanese OEMs control much of the distribution system in Japan - Japanese industry is oligopolistic and has a history of excluding foreign firms
Growing Dominance of the Infrastructure	- Promotion of investment in SME and materials through subsidies and other incentives - NTT procurement of SME prototypes - MITI encouragement of industry rationalization	- SME and materials suppliers vertically linked to large electronics firms - Keiretsu banks support
Manufacturing Skill	- Government Funding of R&D in commercial manufacturing techniques - NTT development and proving of manufacturing techniques	- Low employee turnover - Close relationships between tool-makers and device makers.

They have consistently invested in capacity expansion at a rate permitting them to grow substantially faster than the rate of world demand growth and they have sustained high investment levels even through recessionary periods.[107] Such intensive investments, coupled with sustained below cost pricing, led one analyst to conclude that the Japanese firms were seeking to "spend their way into a leadership position".[108]

Intensive Japanese investments have had a pronounced impact on international semiconductor competition. The combination of heavy R&D and capital investment has enabled them to commercialize new products on a mass-production basis ahead of their competitors -- Japanese firms were the first to introduce 64K and 256K DRAMs. During recessions (1974-75, 1981-82, and 1985-86) U.S. firms, confronted by a combination of slack demand and Japanese pricing pressure, were forced to curtail capital investment to minimize their losses. Their Japanese counterparts, on the other hand, continued to invest. At the end of each recession Japanese firms have emerged with a larger market share.[109]

Aggressive Japanese product development and capacity expansion has been combined with equally aggressive pricing tactics. The same financial resources that enable Japanese firms to undertake intensive investments have made it possible to sell large quantities of semiconductors at prices far below the cost of production for protracted periods. Japanese firms are willing and able to endure sustained losses because of the strategic nature of the product. An executive from Mitsubishi commented in 1986 that

> *You can't imagine the big loss [we had] in semiconductor operations. . . . We use DRAMs as the technology driver for developing new generation integrated circuits. All six major Japanese semiconductor companies are pushing hard to come out with 1-megabit and 4-megabit DRAMs, which will take a major advance in technology to sub-micron line geometries on devices. None of them will drop DRAMs, no matter how unprofitable*

---

107 A West German observer commented in 1983 that "With the policy of creating production capacities that are larger than the medium-term expected world market volume, the Japanese constrained themselves to forced export, which excludes normal competition." Dieter Rath in Essen *Elektro-Anzeiger* (February 1983), pp. 14-15.

108 M. Borrus, *Reversing Attrition*, p. 7.

109 The Defense Science Board observed in 1987 that "as the semiconductor economy emerged from each succeeding downturn, more and more U.S. competitors were found to drop out of the market altogether, whereas their Japanese counterparts tended to emerge with ever larger market shares upon which to base the next round of growth." DSB, *Task Force on Semiconductor Dependency*, p. 85.

they may be, because we need that base to develop 1M-bit and 4M-bit DRAMs.[110]

While aggressive Japanese pricing is sometimes attributed to Japanese cost efficiency, Japanese prices during the 1984-86 period were substantially below the costs of even the most efficient Japanese producers.[111] While their motives may have varied, one important motive was clearly the expansion of market share.[112]

The U.S. industrial system is not organized in a manner which permits individual firms to respond effectively, over the long run, to a combination of intensive capital investments and massive, sustained below cost sales. The U.S. Government does not seek to channel capital into the semiconductor industry by direct or indirect means -- capital must flow to the industry as a result of individual decisions by private investors. Such investment is attracted by the prospect of a return, not to finance a "bloodbath" designed to expand market share; in the 1980s even large conglomerates have proven unwilling to finance sustained losses by their U.S. semiconductor subsidiaries. Japanese investment and pricing strategies, therefore, have had the effect of reducing the volume of capital available to U.S. firms.[113]

The predictable consequence of such differences between the U.S. and Japanese systems has been U.S. disinvestment in the product areas which Japanese firms have elected to dominate through aggressive investment and

---

110 *Electronics News* (April 29, 1986).

111 In 1986, the U.S. Commerce Department investigated allegations of Japanese dumping of EPROMs and DRAMs and found, after a detailed review of Japanese production costs, that Japanese firms were indeed selling below cost (dumping), frequently by enormous margins. The dumping "margin" is the percentage by which the export price of the product must increase in order to cover the cost of production and a reasonable return on investment.

112 An NEC executive commented on the competitive "bloodbath" which occurred in 64K DRAMs in 1981-82 that "The Japanese perspective is that when you are still making inroads into a market you can't afford the luxury of making money." *Business Week* (May 23, 1983).

113 One U.S. industry analyst, observing the Japanese capacity buildup in 1985, warned potential investors that "Currently there is excess capacity in Japan. Capital spending increased an estimated 100% in 1984 over 1983 and is expected to increase another 25% or more in 1985, further aggravating the overcapacity situation. The severe imbalance between supply and demand should result in further sharp price declines in 1985. . . . The price declines, which could average 20% in Japan, will be the most severe in modern semiconductor history and will obviously have a deleterious impact on the worldwide industry. Profitability, which was exceptionally high in 1984, is expected to plummet in 1985." J. J. Lazlo, *The Japanese Semiconductor Industry: Aggressive Capital Spending Could Deleteriously Impact Industry Profitability in 1985* (Hambrecht & Quist, January 31, 1985); pp. 2-3.

below cost pricing.[114]   The U.S. International Trade Commission found in 1986, after investigation, that a "massive price collapse" had occurred in 64K DRAMs in 1985, and that dumped Japanese DRAMs "contributed to the downward price spiral" which resulted in "staggering losses during 1985, and the subsequent withdrawal of a number of major [U.S.] companies from DRAM production." [115]   In effect, competition in these product areas has become a contest to determine which firms can sustain the largest losses -- a contest which U.S. firms cannot win because of the very nature of the U.S. industrial system.   As a former Commerce Department official observed in 1986,

> *Japanese policies result in chronic dumping in U.S. market, as well as sales below cost in all other markets. With everyone losing money, the winner is not the most efficient producer, but the one with the deepest pockets. Since the Japanese semiconductor companies are all part of large conglomerates owned by major banks and ultimately backed by the Japanese government, theirs are deeper.*[116]

Sources of Capital

Japanese firms' ability to sustain such intensive capital and R&D investments is attributable to several factors. The cost of capital is lower for Japanese producers than for U.S. producers.[117]   The *keiretsu* banks, which are now the largest private financial organizations on earth,[118] provide a

---

114 A recent Japanese perspective was that "Excessive investment will lead to excess production, which may lead to excess exports. Although it is unfair to call Japan a 'looter' of the memory market, as a key figure with a major U.S. semiconductor firm has, the Japanese side has to understand the pain of the side that lost the market." *Denshi Kogyo Geppo*, No. 4, 1986.

115 U.S. International Trade Commission, *64K Dynamic Random Access Memory Components from Japan*, pp. 19-20. The U.S.I.T.C. made similar findings in its investigations of the impact of Japanese dumping on U.S. producers of EPROMs and 256K DRAMs.

116 Clyde Prestowitz in *Wall Street Journal* (September 26, 1986).

117 While this has been challenged by some analysts, the weight of opinion supports the view that Japan's cost of capital is lower, even when adjusted for inflation differentials. See generally the Report of the President's Commission on Industrial Competitiveness, *Global Competition: The New Reality* (Washington, D.C.: U.S. Government Printing Office, January 1985), Vol. II, p. 113.

118 The Dai-Ichi Kangyo Bank (which heads the *keiretsu* to which Fujitsu belongs) is the largest private banking institution in the world. Dai-Ichi Kangyo's assets reached $207 billion in the first quarter of 1986, compared with second-ranked Citicorp's $176 billion. Four of the top five banking companies in the world are Japanese *keiretsu* banks (Dai-Ichi Kangyo, Fuji Bank, Sumitomo Bank, and Mitsubishi Bank). *Time* (August 11, 1986).

principal source of capital for their affiliated semiconductor producers, a relationship which has no U.S. counterpart.[119]

The Japanese semiconductor firms also enjoy massive internal resources. All of the major producers are large, diversified companies with the ability to support semiconductor investments with retained earnings from their other divisions.[120] Japanese dominance in televisions and VCRs thus helps to support large-scale investments in the microelectronics technologies which are necessary to sustain the competitiveness of their other products.

Government Policies. The Japanese Government has played a significant role in ensuring that adequate financial resources were available for microelectronics and its related upstream and downstream sectors.[121] Most importantly, its designation of the microelectronics sector as a priority industry has served to increase its attractiveness to lenders.[122] In addition, the lending policies of the Japan Development Bank (JDB), which makes loans to designated priority sectors at MITI's recommendation, have served to signal commercial banks that the government favors the activity in question and served to mobilize capital for the semiconductor and related information sectors.[123] Procurement of OEM products by several government entities also indirectly contributes to Japanese firms' earnings,

---

119 During the 1970s the Japanese semiconductor producers' relationships with the *keiretsu* banks enabled them to finance aggressive capital expansion through heavy borrowing. While in the 1980s the leading Japanese producers have reduced their reliance on debt as a source of capital, their special relationship with the banks remains a critically important asset.

120 "A...potent source of advantage for large, diversified Japanese electronics firms, particularly in periods when markets are expanding rapidly, stems from their ability to allocate funds internally, using monies generated in other lines of business to finance high rates of spending on R&D and new production capacity." Office of Technology Assessment, *International Competitiveness in Electronics*, p. 33.

121 In recent years this effort has required MITI to engage in a running battle with the Ministry of Finance (MOF) for tax concessions and allocations from the state budget to support MITI's ambitious high technology agenda. *Nihon Keizai* (August 10 and September 15, 1984). The MOF position on such issues is that "the private sector has enough power to develop techniques and to raise funds by itself." *Nihon Keizai* (July 6, 1984).

122 MITI "gather[ed] information and help[ed] form a consensus among the semiconductor firms and financial community in Japan. The very articulation of a rational industrial policy to foster a certain industry undoubtedly increased the attractiveness of that industry as a lending target, even though there was no general government loan guarantee." Flaherty and Itami, *Finance*, p. 155.

123 MITI stated in 1979 that it decides "whether or not [companies'] proposed plans are necessary to achieve appropriate production scales, work collaboration, specialization, and other items for rationalization, selects qualified corporations and makes recommendations for loans to the Japan Development Bank." MITI Machinery and Information Industries Bureau, *Commentary on the Law for Provisional Measures for the Promotion of Specific Machinery and Information Industries* (1979) Section 3(I)(4).

notably NTT's procurement of telecommunications equipment at premium prices[124] and the purchase of computers by JECC, a government-subsidized computer leasing consortium.[125] Finally, as illustrated in Table 3.7, Japanese tax law permits the complete depreciation of most types of semiconductor equipment in three or four years (in contrast to five years in the U.S.).[126]

Accelerated development. While Japanese companies' heavy R&D spending has enabled them to accelerate the introduction of new products, government R&D assistance has also played an important role. The MITI/NTT VLSI projects of the late 1970s were credited with enabling Japanese firms to commercialize the 64K DRAM six to twelve months ahead of schedule -- a tremendous competitive advantage in an industry characterized by short product life cycles.[127] NTT developed the device prototype for the 64K DRAM in 1977 and helped Japanese firms overcome several technical obstacles to commercializing the device, such as excessive gate oxide thickness and excessive power requirements.[128] NTT developed device technology for the 256K DRAM and transferred it to Japanese firms who went on to dominate the world market for this key product.[129]

---

124 "The Japanese government also seems to have subsidized semiconductor development ... through Nippon Telephone and Telegraph (NTT) procurement." Flaherty and Itami, *Finance*, p. 157.

125 The Japan Electronic Computer Company (JECC) was financed by a combination of government subsidies and contributions from Japanese computer producers. It purchases computers from Japanese firms and leases them on highly favorable terms to Japanese consumers, in effect creating a larger demand for Japanese computers. "The subsidy that actually got passed on to the semiconductor operations probably coincided with the procurement of semiconductors by Japanese computer manufacturers -- that is, by having a larger domestic computer market than would otherwise have existed." Flaherty and Itami, *Finance*, pp. 156-157. For an analysis of the financial benefits to Japanese firms resulting from JECC financing by the government, see M. Anchordoguy, *The State and the Market: Industrial Policy Towards Japan's Computer Industry* (Harvard Business School, January 27, 1987.)

126 See generally J.P. Stern, "Japan's R&D Tax Credit System," *Journal of the American Chamber of Commerce of Japan* (April 1987). The disparity in depreciable equipment lives places U.S. semiconductor firms "at a significant competitive disadvantage!" Laszlo, *Japanese Semiconductor Industry*, p. 18.

127 NEC's Tomihiro Matsumura in *New York Times* (May 18, 1983).

128 *Japan Telecommunications Review* (January 1979); *Japan Economic Journal* (May 30, 1978).

129 NTT reportedly provided free prototype design specifications and manufacturing technology for a 150 nanosecond 256K DRAM to Hitachi, NEC and Fujitsu. *Electronics News* (October 11, 1982).

TABLE 3.7
JAPANESE TAX DEPRECIATION SCHEDULES FOR
SEMICONDUCTOR MANUFACTURING EQUIPMENT

Item	Depreciable Life (Years)
Wire Bonders	3
Burn-in Equipment	4
Mounters	4
CVD Devices	4
Mask aligners and steppers	4
Sputtering equipment	4
Epitaxial crystal growth chambers	4
Probes	4
Furnaces	3
Comparators	4
Oxidation Equipment	4
Photomask cleaners	5
Molding devices	4
Grinders	4

Source: *Genka Shokyaku Shisan to Taiyonensu-to ni Kansuru Shorei* (Ministerial Order Concerning the Depreciable Life of Assets, Schedule 5) Ministry of Finance cited in J.P. Stern, "Japan's R&D Tax Credit System," in *Journal of the American Chamber of Commerce in Japan*, April 1987.

Reduced Risk. The Japanese firms' *keiretsu* affiliations, coupled with government backing, not only serve to make available the capital needed for an intensive investment program, but also to reduce the risks inherent in such a program.[130] The view is widely held that the banks and the government will not allow a major electronics producer to fail.[131] Oki, for example, one of Japan's leading semiconductor producers, was the subject of an NTT "rescue" operation in the mid-1970s when it was suffering from operating losses and a lagging technological position.[132] In addition, Japanese OEMs are in a position to help their components divisions and "upstream" SME and materials vendors better withstand the fluctuations of the demand cycle.[133] Such factors in turn foster an aggressive attitude toward investment and a willingness to accept substantial risks. As one recent analysis notes,

> *It is in the high-growth sectors like semiconductors, and indeed in the whole range of microelectronically driven new technologies, that the differences in financial policies become critical. It is precisely in these critical competitive sectors that the growth-driven financial policies of the* kaisha *[Japanese companies] differ most greatly from those of their Western competitors. Japanese companies in these high growth businesses often employ financial policies considered reckless and unmatchable by Western executives. . . . The combination of aggressive*

---

130 "*Keiretsu* groupings serve to diffuse and reduce risks through intercorporate stockholdings, financial ties of interdependence, and mutual assistance during difficult times. This safety net eases the pressures that buildup rather quickly for highly leveraged companies during business downturns, thereby relieving MITI of the headaches of having to step in directly to rescue firms from the brink of bankruptcy." D.I. Okimoto, "Regime Characteristics of Japanese Industrial Policy," in *Japan's High Technology Industries*, p. 47.

131 When a large Japanese company encounters serious trouble, its affiliated banks intervene to reconstruct the corporation, inserting their executives into management positions in the companies. James C. Abegglen and George Stalk, *Kaisha, the Japanese Corporation* (New York: Basic Books, 1985), pp. 166-67.

132 NTT dispatched the director of its Materials Bureau to take over the leadership of Oki, and furnished the company with semiconductor device technology which NTT had developed with three other Japanese companies. Following an extensive internal shakeup, Oki returned to profitabilty in 1978, and has subsequently become a major international competitor. Hiromatsu, *Denwa no Muko wa Konna Kao*.

133 When demand for semiconductors is high, producers need to expand production capacity quickly, but equipment-makers cannot respond instantaneously to a sharp rise in demand for tools. Equipment delivery times lengthen, and an equipment maker can confer an advantage on an affiliated semiconductor producer by giving it priority for equipment delivery. Conversely, in a depressed semiconductor market, demand for equipment falls off sharply, and the semiconductor producer can aid its tool-making affiliate by ordering what little it needs from that affiliate. U.S. Department of Commerce, *Semiconductor Manufacturing Equipment Industry*, pp. 67-69.

financial policies and fundamentally sound product and marketing strategies can be devastating to competitors.[134]

Dominance in the Home Market

Japanese inroads into foreign semiconductor markets have not been offset by increased foreign penetration of the Japanese market, which is now the world's largest market for semiconductors.[135] During the past 15 years, foreign firms have never been able to hold more than about 10 percent of the Japanese market for any sustained period, a share which had diminished to about 8 percent in 1986. In an industry in which production volume translates directly into gains in cost and quality competitiveness, the inability of foreign firms to participate significantly in this market -- coupled with dramatic Japanese gains abroad -- has made it progressively more difficult for non-Japanese firms to sustain competitiveness on a global scale.[136]

Industrial Structure. While formal Japanese government protection of semiconductor and most OEM markets has been eliminated, foreign penetration of these markets has shown little or no increase since the period when the market was formally protected. This phenomenon appears primarily to be a reflection of the structure of the Japanese industry. Virtually all semiconductor consumption in Japan is attributable to Japanese-capitalized OEMs, reflecting the limited success of U.S. OEMs in penetrating Japanese end-markets.[137] The *keiretsu* member companies tend to favor the products of their affiliated OEMs,[138] and have exercised a substantial degree

---

134 Abegglen and Stalk, *Kaisha*, pp. 154, 157.

135 The strengthening of the yen relative to the dollar has accelerated the growth in the dollar value of the Japanese market, but the trend of that market toward becoming the world's largest -- regardless of exchange fluctuations -- has been apparent for some time. See Appendix A for further discussion of these points.

136 "The advantages of the [Japanese microelectronics] enterprises primarily lie in the fact that they are supported by a domestic market which de facto is reserved completely for themselves" . . . Dieter Rath in Essen *Elektro-Anzeiger* (February 1983).

137 The only major OEM market in which U.S. firms hold a substantial share of Japanese sales is large computers. By contrast, in Europe, U.S. OEMs have established a major presence, which in turn provides market opportunities in Europe for U.S. semiconductor producers.

138 *Nihon Keizai* reported on August 9, 1978 with respect to the sale of computers that "Each big city bank is trying to sell the products of the computer manufacturers under its control to its principal customers, acting like a sales agent for this manufacturer. . . . " Similarly, the 1980 Ways and Means Committee *High Technology* study observed that "In many cases the *keiretsu* creates business opportunities for its members. . . . Hitachi introduced its HITAC system at the Sanwa Bank and the Industrial Bank of Japan. The Sumitomo group favors NEC customers and Oki sells huge quantities of terminals to the Fuji Bank." Ways and Means Committee, *High Technology*, p. 3.

of control over the distribution outlets in Japan for consumer electronics products and office automation equipment.[139] Procurement of telecommunications equipment and office automation equipment by NTT and other Japanese government agencies has always overwhelmingly favored Japanese suppliers.[140]

Thus, in semiconductors, foreign firms' potential sales in Japan are virtually limited completely to Japanese OEMs, who, in many cases, are also Japan's leading semiconductor producers and the direct competitors of foreign semiconductor vendors. Vertically-integrated Japanese firms have generally preferred to procure semiconductors from their own components divisions or from each other rather than from foreign sources. U.S. and other foreign firms' semiconductor sales have generally been limited to products which Japanese firms do not make or cannot supply in sufficient volume. Moreover, when a Japanese product becomes available foreign sales disappear, often with dramatic speed.[141]

Government Policies. While in recent years the Japanese Government has taken steps to encourage larger foreign sales of advanced electronics products in Japan, its policies have played a role in creating and sustaining an industrial structure which resists foreign penetration. In the information sector, MITI engaged in a program of "liberalization countermeasures" in the 1973-75 period designed to offset the effects of formal liberalization by restructuring the computer and semiconductor industries in a manner which enabled them to resist import penetration.[142] MITI also appears to be encouraging similar restructuring of some of the upstream sectors at present.[143] MITI has given "administrative guidance" to domestic industries

---

139 Kozo Yamamura and Jan Vandenberg, "Japan's Rapid-Growth Policy on Trial: The Television Case," in *Law and Trade Issues of the Japanese Economy* eds. Gary R. Saxonhouse and Kozo Yamamura (Seattle: University of Washington Press, 1986), pp. 243-47, 270.

140 NTT's procurement was formally opened to foreign firms in 1981, but NTT has never procured more than a few percent of its products from foreign sources.

141 A Siemens executive commented in 1985 that "Japan is just not buying from outside if firms have their own supplier. So what you can do there is mainly to fill a temporary gap with a product which is not readily available there. As soon as the product is available from local Japanese sources, your chances go down to very close to zero." *Far Eastern Economic Review* (August 22, 1985). *Nihon Keizai* commented on March 20, 1985 that "the most advanced electronic products are developed in the U.S., first, and U.S enterprises also sell them to Japan in an active way. However, when Japanese firms put similar products into use within two or three years, sales by U.S. firms suddenly stop."

142 These measures are documented in Semiconductor Industry Association, *Japanese Market Barriers in Microelectronics*, pp. 49-58.

143 In silicon wafers, for example, a *Chosa Hokokusho* (research report) was prepared in March 1985 by the "High Purity Silicon Issues Study Group," a group of Japanese high purity silicon producers, chaired by MITI's Terue Kataoka, Manager, Electronic Devices

to favor national products after "liberalization."[144]   Protection -- formal or
informal -- has been maintained in OEM markets where the United States
still holds a competitive edge.[145]   Most significantly, Japan's enforcement of
the Antimonopoly Law has been extremely lax, if not nonexistent, in the
advanced electronics sectors, enabling the *keiretsu* firms to exert a substantial
degree of control over the market.[146]

In contrast to Japan, the U.S. market for semiconductors, as well as many
OEM and upstream products, have proven relatively easy for Japanese firms
to penetrate.[147]   The web of structural barriers which confront U.S. firms in
Japan has no U.S. equivalent.   Japanese penetration of OEM and
semiconductor markets in the United States has been rapid, and has in some

---

Department, Electrotechnical Laboratory. This group concluded that "It is expected that
the establishment of production facilities in Japan by foreign makers will enable them to
make a full-scale inroad into the Japanese market.... [A] mechanism for industrywide
interaction by the silicon makers and the device makers must be established so that
standards can be established, specifications can be made uniform, and user needs can be
made more clearly understood . . . [the industry must] strengthen the corporate ground
to meet the entry of foreign manufacturers into the Japanese market."   *Forbes*
commented on August 25, 1985, with respect to MITI's high purity silicon project that "It
is very clear that for all their protestations about wanting to open their markets, the
Japanese continue to pursue national goals that conflict with the idea of free trade."

144   *Denki* (March 11, 1976); *Monthly Report of the Electronics Industry* (January 1976),
reproduced in Ways and Means, *High Technology*.

145   NTT indicated in 1984 that it would not procure communications satellites from foreign
sources. *Kyodo*, 3:17 GMT (Foreign Broadcast Information Service, January 14, 1984).
The Office of U.S. Trade Representative reported in its 1986 *Report on Foreign Trade
Barriers* that "Japanese policy requires that satellite procurement by public organizations
including NTT must be consistent with national development policy'. NTT is effectively
precluded from buying foreign satellites, probably through 1992....Thus far Japan has
refused to let government entities buy U.S.-built satellites." (p. 154).   U.S.
supercomputer manufacturers have complained that Japanese government agencies will
not procure U.S. supercomputers, despite the fact that U.S. machines are superior to
Japanese models.

146   In 1984, the Japan Fair Trade Commission found that in the office equipment market a
number of arrangements with distributors contain "restrictions regarding retail prices,
sales area, retailers to whom the products could be sold, and other matters, which
conflict with the interest of the Antimonopoly Law," p. 278.   Japan Fair Trade
Commission, *Office Computer No Ryutsu Jittai chosa Ni Tsuite*, p. 270, cited in Yamamura
and Vandenburg, "Japan's Rapid Growth Policy on Trial," p. 278.   The electronics
producers have also been found by the JFTC to have engaged in collusive activity with
the effect of restricting market entry in the consumer electronics market. Ibid. Despite
such findings, no sanctions have been imposed against these firms under the
Antimonopoly Law.

147   One exception to this general pattern was the attempt by Fujitsu to acquire Fairchild in
1987. The acquisition would have given Fujitsu access to Fairchild's U.S. distribution
networks and substantially enhanced its ability to sell its products in the United States.
In the wake of criticism of the acquisition by U.S. officials, Fujitsu abandoned the
transaction.

cases has led to Japanese dominance of the U.S. market within several years of their initial entry.[148]

Growing Dominance of the Infrastructure

A fourth aspect of Japan's market success in microelectronics has been the growing Japanese dominance of many of the upstream SME and advanced materials sectors which are essential to the competitiveness of the industry as a whole. U.S. semiconductor producers are rapidly discovering that their only sources for some key materials and tools are Japanese firms which in many cases are affiliated with their direct competitors.[149] Here too the rapid gains achieved by the Japanese industry are attributable, in substantial degree, to the policies of the Japanese government.

Materials. Since the oil shocks of the 1970s, MITI has been pressing Japan's heavy industries to shift their resources into the development and production of "new basic materials," many of which were intended for microelectronics applications.[150] A Japanese official commented in 1985 that

[T]he creation of new materials has grown to be a matter of extreme national importance. The government is pushing forward a variety of policies with the Science and Technology Agency, MITI, and the Ministry of Education taking the lead . . .. MITI, for example, is implementing R&D for measurement technology in connection with research on fine ceramics, materials of film for high-efficiency separation of polymers,

---

148 Foreign observers have been struck by the relative openness of the U.S. market to Japanese penetration; a Dutch journal interviewing C. van der Klugt, the President of the Dutch electronics giant, Philips, reported in 1986 that "[van der Klugt] accuses the American producers of consumer electronics of having given away their marketing position in their home market to the Japanese for a mess of pottage .... [P]eople in the United States have helped the Japanese get the upper hand." According to van der Klugt they have "brought the Trojan Horse into the city." The new President of Philips says that history threatens to repeat itself with the American chip industry. This industry too could disappear in the United States if the government does not stop it ...." [m]any Americans still do not "understand the strategic importance of a number of basic industries." *NRC Handelsblad* (April 23, 1986).

149 Employees of two U.S. semiconductor firms have indicated difficulty in obtaining wafer steppers from Nikon, the dominant firm in this segment, because of Japanese pressure to prevent export. Ferguson, *American Microelectronics in Decline*, p. 83.

150 Kazuo Iwasaki, Director General of MITI's Basic Industries Bureau, commented in 1986 that "Eight years ago when I was director of steel operations, there was an assembly of the Keidanren called the Consultation on the Problem of Basic Industries ... This assembly is now being reorganized into the new Basic Materials Research Society. This can be thought of as a symbolic change." *Jihyo* (April 1986). *Toshi Keizai* observed in October 1985 that "It is not too much to say there are no enterprises of the traditional heavy type which are not tackling any of these fields of advanced technology" (new materials, microelectronics, biotechnology).

materials of polymers with high electricity conduction, materials of polymers with high facility for crystallization ... and composite materials .... This research is based on a law subsidizing costs for the development of technologies that serve to activate the industry.[151]

Japanese industries have responded vigorously to MITI's lead:

• Dowa Mining Company, traditionally a refiner of nonferrous metals, entered the field of new materials to manufacture gallium arsenide wafers and indium phosphorous. These materials are expected to be used extensively in laser diodes and other forms of optical communications.

• Mitsubishi Metal Industries has diversified into IC packaging, silicon wafers, lead frame materials, bonding wire, and compound semiconductor materials.

• Asahi Glass, traditionally a producer of flat glass and furnace materials, has diversified into materials for semiconductors and optoelectronic devices.[152]

Table 3.8 provides greater detail on new materials development for microelectronics. MITI, NTT, and the government Science and Technology Agency have augmented these private efforts through extensive materials R&D conducted in their own laboratories.[153]

---

151 *Purometeusu* (September-October, 1985). MITI began to place a heightened emphasis on new materials in 1984: "The year 1984 then saw discussion on new materials emerge particularly in copious quantities because the policy for FY 1985 of MITI placed weight on new materials as the major target of developmental research, and in connection with this move, various relevant reports and research data were made public in succession by many advisory committees set up for the relevant purpose." *Jidosha Gijutsu* (August 1985).

152 *Toshi Keizai* (October 1985); *Nikko Materials* (March 1986).

153 *Purometeusu* (September-October, 1985). In 1984 MITI's Electrotechnical Laboratory created a gallium arsenide crystal through a technique controlling the formation of each atomic layer. It developed a single crystal of silicon through the same technique in 1985. This technology is expected to be instrumental in developing optoelectronic semiconductors and superlattice devices. *Japan Economic Journal* (June 15, 1985). NTT operates a Materials Laboratory at its Ibaraki Electronic Communications Laboratory. Wieder, *JTECH Panel Report on Opto-& Microelectronics*, p. 11-3.

TABLE 3.8

JAPANESE COMPANIES & GOVERNMENT ENTITIES DEVELOPING NEW
MATERIALS WITH MICROELECTRONICS APPLICATIONS

Materials Technology	Manufacturer	Materials Technology	Manufacturer
IC substrates & package (ceramics)	Kyocera Narumi Pottery Japan Special Pottery	Josephson device	NTT (Musashino) Hitachi
		Three dimensional circuits	AIST (MITI)
GaAs semiconductor	Sumitomo Electric Showa Denko Sumitomo Metal Mitsubishi Metal	Semiconductors of organic compounds	Hitachi Nippon Paint Sharp Matsushita Electric Nippon Kogaku Daini Seikosha
Gadolinium-gallium garnet substrate	Shin-Etsu Chemical Hitachi Metal Sumitomo Metal Tohoku Metal TDK Mitsubishi Chemical	Light transmitting ceramics	NGK Insulator
Single Crystal silicon	Komatsu Electronic Metal Nippon Silicon Osaka Titanium Shin-Etsu Semi- conductor	Optical bistable units Bisimuth silicon oxide Yttrium aluminum garnet (YAG) Multiple quantum well (MQW) semi- conductor laser	Hitachi Ricoh NEC NTT (Mussashino)
Amorphous silicon for solar cells	Sanyo Electric Sharp Fuji Electric Matsushita Electric Sumitomo Electric Taiyo Yuden Asahi Chemical	Lithium nobate Surface acoustic- wave device	Sanyo Toshiba Sanyu Ceramics
Light transmitting ceramics	NGK Insulator		

Source: *Jidosha Gijutsu*, August 1985 (Table 1)

The "High Purity Silicon Issues Study Group," consisting of MITI and representatives of the high purity silicon industry, developed a series of strategic recommendations for the Japanese silicon industry in the spring of 1985. The group called for expansion of domestic production, entry of new companies into the polysilicon field, "capital investment in foreign makers," establishment of a series of joint R&D efforts, standardization of wafer production, and the strengthening of ties with downstream users.[154] Three months later, two of Japan's largest steelmaking companies, Nippon Steel and Kawasaki, announced their entry into silicon wafer manufacturing,[155] and Nippon Kokan, Japan's second largest steel producer, entered the polycrystalline silicon field.[156] This new market entry occurred in an industry already characterized by massive surplus capacity.[157] *Forbes* commented on August 26, 1985 that

Is the world so short of silicon wafer capacity that all this MITI-induced investment is necessary? Hardly .... It is clear, then, that the new Japanese push is inspired not by visions of an untapped market, but by a national decision that Japan ought to try dominating this already well-established market.

Semiconductor Manufacturing Equipment. In 1975, U.S. SME producers accounted for 80 percent of Japan's SME market. Ten years later, nearly 71 percent of SME sales in Japan were attributable to Japanese firms and Japanese SME firms were achieving dominant shares of the world market in a number of key product areas.[158] As indigenous Japanese SME capability has developed, Japanese semiconductor firms -- in many cases affiliated with the upstream suppliers -- have switched from U.S. to Japanese vendors. Two Japanese firms, Ando and Takeda Riken, now hold between them 80 percent of the Japanese market for testing equipment, which is characterized by a "tight buyer-seller union forged by Japanese tester suppliers and memory manufacturers."[159] As the Japanese semiconductor industry has expanded

---

154 Ko-Jundo Shirikon Mondai Kenkyukai, *Chosa Hokukusho* (March 1985).

155 *Japan Economic Journal* (July 22, 1985). Nippon Steel planned to cooperate closely with Hitachi in the new field. *Japan Economic Journal* (July 16, 1985).

156 In July, Toyo Soda, a petrochemical firm, announced a joint venture with a U.S. company to manufacture silicon wafers in Japan.

157 *Japan Economic Journal* (August 30, 1986).

158 *Electronics* (July 22, 1985).

159 *Electronics* (March 31, 1986). Similarly, in lithography, a Japanese SME market valued at $500 million, Canon now controls 90 percent of contact aligner sales and has taken a 60 percent share of the projection-aligner market, which was until recently dominated by

relative to that of the United States, the global market position of the Japanese SME producers has improved relative to that of their U.S. competitors.[160]

The Japanese Government has given a substantial impetus to the development of the Japanese SME industry. As in materials, MITI asked established Japanese companies to enter the SME business.[161] Table 3.9 shows the many periodic grants provided by MITI to one SME manufacturer, Takeda Riken, for research and development. The 1975-79 MITI VLSI project concentrated on process technology and a MITI official commented in 1982 that the project "results could be focused ... in the development of various types of semiconductor device manufacturing equipment."[162] The U.S. Department of Commerce commented in 1985 that

Research cooperation between the SME industry, Japanese chip-makers, NTT, and MITI electrical laboratories was instrumental in the development of the present highly competitive generation of Japanese wafer processing and testing equipment, as well as direct write E-beam and X-ray systems....[163]

In addition to MITI's efforts, NTT buys prototypes of SME equipment from Japanese producers at premium prices which "helps ensure the continued operations of companies at the lower end of the production process."[164]

In contrast to Japan, outside the defense field, the United States Government has pursued virtually no direct policies to foster the

---

Perkin-Elmer. In ion etching, NEC Anelva now dominates the Japanese market with a 65 percent share, and in plasma etching, three Japanese firms hold among them 60 percent of the market.

160 *Nihon Keizai* observed on December 6, 1985 that "in a sense, Japan's strength in the field of semiconductor manufacturing equipment is in the enhanced position of the parent [semiconductor] industry."

161 For example, MITI asked Nippon Kogaku, a camera producer, to enter the wafer stepper business in the 1970s, and the company did so. *Forbes* (April 7, 1986), p. 88.

162 Akie Kataoka, Chief of the Electronic Device Section, MITI Electrotechnical Laboratory, in *Tsusan Janaru* (February 1982).

163 U.S. Department of Commerce, *Semiconductor Manufacturing Equipment Industry*, p. 62.

164 Ibid. p. 92. In the 1980s, the Japanese government has given increasing recognition to the importance of the SME industry to the competitiveness of Japanese semiconductor producers. The New Function Elements Project, originally restricted to semiconductor producers, has expanded to include two major SME firms, Canon and Nippon Kogaku, and these firms are also participating in the newly-organized synchotron orbital radiation project, SORTEC.

TABLE 3.9

MITI R&D ASSISTANCE TO TAKEDA RIKEN, 1961-79
(Japanese Manufacturer Of Automated Testing Equipment)

YEAR	ITEM
1961	Awarded 1961 Research Subsidy by MITI
1963	Awarded 1963 Research Subsidy by MITI
1964	Awarded 1964 Research Subsidy by MITI
1966	Awarded 1966 Research Subsidy by MITI
1968	Atwarded 1968 Research Subsidy by MITI
1969	Awarded 1969 Research Subsidy by MITI
1971	Awarded 1971 Research Subsidy by MITI
1972	Awarded 1972 Research Subsidy by MITI
1973	Awarded 1973 Research Subsidy by MITI
1974	Joined MITI's First Important Technology Development Program With 6 Other Measuring Equipment Producers
1976	Awarded Second Important Technology Development Subsidy By MITI
1978	Ordered By Research Development Corporation Of Japan To Jointly Develop Manufacturing Technology For Magnetic Resonator Element Using Yttrium Iron Garnet (YIG)
1979	Awarded 1979 Subsidy By MITI (For 2 Years)

SOURCE: Takeda Riken, *Takeda Riken Is Up To The Challenge*, attachment to testimony of Allen B. Rosenstein, Chairman of the Board, Pioneer Magnetics, before the House Subcommittee on Science, Research and Technology, Committee on Science and Technology, April 29, 1987

development of U.S. SME and materials technologies, and U.S. defense programs' commercial spillover has been extremely limited.[165] Moreover, the U.S. Government has maintained extensive national security restrictions on the export of U.S. SME which have seriously hurt the international competitive efforts of the U.S. industry. While these restrictions are imposed to prevent the acquisition of U.S. technology by the Soviet bloc, Japan does not impose comparably stringent controls on its own producers.[166]

Japanese Manufacturing Skill

Japanese semiconductors have proven highly competitive in the 1980s, not only because of their low price, but because of their consistently high quality and reliability, reflecting a thorough Japanese mastery of the details of semiconductor manufacturing. The Japanese success in manufacturing is attributable, to a substantial degree, to the sustained emphasis which Japanese firms have placed on the manufacturing process since the mid-1970s. However, structural factors and Japanese government policies have also played an important role.

Structural Factors. Japanese success in semiconductor manufacturing is partially attributable to the stability of the Japanese management and work force, in which skilled scientist and engineer turnover rates are low by U.S. standards. In a typical Japanese production line, for example, there are

> *experts at each station -- epitaxy, masking, and so on -- individuals with long experience on the job, who [can] spot flaws immediately and remove defective parts from the process.*[167]

Similarly, the fact that a number of vertically integrated Japanese firms, such as Hitachi and Toshiba, develop a substantial proportion of their SME in-

---

165   "[U.S.] programs targeted specifically at the SME industry are almost nonexistent," although programs affecting the semiconductor industry itself naturally influence the SME sector. U.S. Department of Commerce, *Semiconductor Manufacturing Equipment Industry*, p. 86.

166   The U.S. Department of Commerce observed in 1985 that "in contrast to the situations in Japan and Europe, the U.S. [export] licensing process appears to hinder SME export sales .... Reports from industry suggest that licensing delays of up to 120 days have resulted in lost sales when competing, for example, with the (reported) 5 day turnaround time in Japanese export license approvals .... [C]ontinued delays in export licensing will have an increasingly negative effect on [U.S.] sales." Ibid., p. 103.

167   Franklin B. Weinstein, Michiyuki Uenohara and John G. Linvill, "Technological Resources" in *Competitive Edge*, pp. 59-60.

house "makes an important contribution to productivity and quality."[168] Even in cases where SME is supplied by an outside vendor, the close relationship which Japanese semiconductor producers frequently enjoy with such vendors has proven important in developing and implementing the manufacturing techniques needed to sustain competitiveness.[169] Finally, the ability to sustain a consistently high level of capital investment has also enhanced Japanese firms' manufacturing competitiveness by enabling them to employ state-of-the-art equipment.

Government Policies. Government policies have also played a role in enhancing Japanese semiconductor firms' manufacturing capabilities and the government has devoted substantial resources to developing and refining semiconductor manufacturing techniques. Most of MITI's 1975-79 VLSI project was devoted to the improvement of commercial semiconductor manufacturing processes. A substantially greater role has been played by NTT, which annually procures billions of dollars worth of telecommunications equipment containing semiconductors and has been a driving force behind Japanese firms' adoption of automated mass production facilities, which manufacture high quality semiconductors efficiently. NTT places such a high priority on improving semiconductor manufacturing techniques that its Atsugi laboratory (where R&D is conducted jointly with Japanese companies) contains

a complete experimental [production] line, from silicon vacuum diffusion furnaces to super LSI production, for materials, designs, fabrication and inspection . . . . [and] a clean room wing where even minute dust particles, the most formidable foe in manufacturing of super LSI, of micron size (one-thousandth of a millimeter) is removed.[170]

---

168 The use of machines made in-house "has the advantage of providing immediate feedback, which facilitates modification." Toshiba makes about 50 percent of its SME, and Hitachi makes over 50 percent. Ibid., p. 63.

169 The U.S. Commerce Department commented in a 1985 study that "Industry experts speak of the "black magic" that is needed to convert a laboratory procedure into one that can be used in the factory. This consists mainly of experience acquired under actual operating conditions, known as beta-site testing, thereby allowing alterations and fine-tuning of the machinery before final marketing. Close equipmentmaker/chipmaker ties, whether formal or informal, are critical in this respect. The Japanese manufacturer can permit scientists and technicians of its tool-making affiliate to have access to the production process for extended periods of time without fear of losing proprietary secrets. This situation is in contrast to the arms-length relationship between U.S. equipmentmakers and chip-makers." U.S. Department of Commerce, *Semiconductor Manufacturing Equipment Industry*, p. 69.

170 *Toki No Keizai* (January 1982). Dr. W.E. Spicer of Stanford visited this facility in September 1983. He reported that "Particular pride was taken in 50,000 square feet of continuously connected Class 10 clean room space. I was shown a pilot production line for ICs such as the 256K RAM. Each processing step was being automated. The wafers

One analyst commented in 1986 that

> *Japan's capacity to compete with U.S. manufacturers in mass memory chip markets is due in no small measure to joint research and the transfer of advanced NTT technology. NTT's groundwork in the development of the 64K DRAM, the 256K DRAM, and the 1M ROM, encompassing device design and production technology, has helped Japanese companies carve out large chunks of world markets. Certainly Japanese producers would not have become competitive so quickly without NTT.*[171]

To be sure, NTT's role as a large procurer of semiconductors is paralleled, to some extent, by U.S. Defense Department procurement of semiconductors, but important distinctions exist between the impact of NTT and DOD procurement programs on manufacturing competitiveness.[172] NTT procures large quantities of devices which can be mass-produced for sale in the commercial market, whereas DOD primarily procures small batches of custom devices for military uses.   Production of the latter generally does not significantly facilitate improvements in commercial manufacturing techniques.[173] While NTT generally procures state-of-the-art equipment, DOD procurement for defense systems with much longer life

---

were transported via an enclosed system by an overhead trolley between the approximately twenty-three processing stations. The wafers were never exposed to the Class 10 atmosphere. By using computers and remote control, the ultimate objective was to remove all personnel from the processing room thus achieving, with the cassette transport, better than Class 1 processing environment. I also noticed in the same clean space as the pilot line, two MBE machines for GaAs-based research -- the latest model Riber plus a Japanese made unit. I estimate that I saw only one-third to one-fourth of the clean room space." Wieder, *JTECH Panel Report on OPTO-& Microelectronics*, p. 2-11.

171 D.I. Okimoto, "Regime Characteristics of Japanese Industrial Policy," p. 56.

172 Both DOD and NTT procurements have provided a stable demand base for vendors. Former NTT President Akikusa, commenting on NTT's procurement system, stated that "manufacturers are brought up on a bed of roses, with orders guaranteed." *Asahi* (February 25, 1979). In the U.S., while military procurement business tends to be less profitable than commercial sales, many companies have remained in the market, citing the stability of military sales as an offset to the volatile commercial market.

173 Most DOD semiconductor procurement orders are characterized by minor differences in specifications for otherwise standard products that makes high volume production impossible.   In 1985, 4-5 thousand unique integrated circuit designs and about 10 thousand separate part numbers were available to designers of military electronics systems. Automated production lines do not adapt well to nonstandard production flows, and the small sizes of most procurement orders makes automated assembly and testing of such devices uneconomical. *Electronics* (October 14, 1985); S. Benz and T. Richards, *Government Procurement of Semiconductors* (Semiconductor Industry Association, 1986).

spans frequently requires continuing the production of obsolete devices with older equipment, which does little to enhance U.S. manufacturing competitiveness.[174] Finally, the quality of devices produced by Japanese firms for sale to NTT and the commercial market can be assured through "designed in" quality techniques which are feasible with automated mass production. DOD attempts to ensure quality through extensive testing and retesting of each device, a method which actually results in reduced quality.[175]

Dominance in Consumer Electronics

A final factor underlying Japanese market success in microelectronics is the Japanese industry's dominance of the consumer electronics industry, which represents one of the largest OEM markets for semiconductors. Japanese firms hold an overwhelmingly strong position in many consumer electronics markets -- notably in the more advanced product lines such as VCRs.[176] In 1984 consumer electronics products accounted for approximately 30 percent of total world consumption of integrated circuits, and Japanese firms accounted for an estimated 59 percent of the ICs sold to this OEM sector.[177] The strong Japanese position in this downstream sector has provided a natural demand base for Japanese semiconductor production which is less volatile than some other OEM sectors, such as computers.[178] In

---

174 A Matsushita executive commented in 1986 that "some [U.S.] military chip manufacturers' equipment is so old that they would be of more use displayed in a museum." Hajima Karatsu, *A Friendly Talk on a Serious Topic* (June 13, 1986). A U.S. semiconductor executive commented in 1986 that "the military uses yesterday's technology today while the commercial industry uses tomorrow's technology today." *Defense Electronics* (February 1986), p. 46. A small industry has sprung up in the U.S. devoted specifically to producing obsolete semiconductors for the military. *Electronics*. (October 14, 1985), p. 43.

175 Device quality and reliability is established by monitoring the defects that occur over time in the production process, and identifying and correcting the cause of the defects. This requires a large volume production flow to generate sufficient statistical data; such flows are usually not possible in military production. Karatsu, *A Friendly Talk on a Serious Topic*.

176 Office of Technology Assessment, *International Competitiveness in Electronics*, p. 122. Japanese electronics firms' emphasis on consumer electronics products is currently diminishing in proportion to products such as computers and communications equipment. However, in 1986 consumer electronic sales were still estimated to account for 39 percent of the Japanese electronics industry's total sales. Integrated Circuit Engineering, *Status 1987*, p. 2-39.

177 Integrated Circuit Engineering, *Status 1985*, p. 5. U.S. firms accounted for 36 percent of this market. Ibid.

178 A Japanese electronics executive commented in 1986 that in the 1984-85 recession, while "the U.S. market fell into a destructive situation suffering from 'computer slumps', the

addition, the profits from Japanese electronics firms' consumer electronics divisions have enabled them to sustain protracted loss operations in their semiconductor divisions.

The factors underlying Japan's move toward dominance in consumer electronics are not without relevance in the present context. Through the late 1960s the Japanese Government sponsored a variety of programs to enhance the competitiveness of the consumer electronics industry.[179] Japanese electronics firms enjoyed the advantage of a protected home market in the 1960s and 1970s as they moved toward international competitive leadership.[180] The Japanese industry rapidly automated its production process and demonstrated a consistent ability to manufacture high quality products at a competitive cost. Finally, in the late 1960s and early 1970s the Japanese industry exported massive quantities of televisions which were priced aggressively (and in some cases dumped), destroying substantial segments of the U.S. television industry.[181] Most U.S. television producers exited the market, were acquired by Japanese firms, or moved their manufacturing operations out of the United States.[182] The Japanese industry ultimately went on to develop new generations of consumer

---

Japanese market was supported by the two markets of industrial and consumer use that play the role of 'two wheels of a vehicle'", the injury the Japanese market suffered from the recession was comparatively slight." Yukio Shimura in *Denshi Kogyo Geppo*, No. 4 (1986).

179   For example, in 1966 MITI financed an R&D program to develop an all solid-state technology for use in monochrome and color televisions. J.E. Millstein, "Decline in an Expanding Industry; Japanese Competition in Color Television" in *American Industry in International Competition* eds. Laura Tyson and John Zysman (Ithaca, New York: Cornell University Press, 1983), p. 106.

180   U.S. electronics firms confronted formal protective barriers through the early 1970s, and U.S. penetration of the domestic market was limited thereafter by the fact that the control exercised by Japanese electronics firms over the domestic distribution system resulted in "virtually closing the Japanese appliance and electronics market to new entrants, both foreign and domestic." Yamamura and Vandenberg, "Japan's Rapid Growth Policy on Trial," p. 253. The various formal and informal protective measures, and U.S. companies' attempts to surmount them, are described in U.S. Government Accounting Office, *United States-Japan Trade: Issues and Problems* (September 21, 1979), pp. 85-91.

181   The U.S. Tariff Commission found in 1971, after investigation, that Japanese firms had been dumping televisions, reflecting the fact that the Japanese electronics firms fixed high domestic prices for various types of televisions and exported televisions at much lower prices. The system by which the Japanese producers collaborated to organize domestic and export pricing -- through a "welter of clandestine groups" -- was revealed after an investigation by the JFTC and is described in Yamamura and Vandenberg," Japan's Rapid Growth Policy on Trial," pp. 253-63.

182   Ibid. Also see Millstein, "Japanese Competition in Color Television."

electronics products associated with television technology, notably the VCR, while the U.S. industry entered a period of decline.[183]

The relationship forged between the Japanese government and industry has thus enabled Japan to mount a major challenge to the United States in the international semiconductor market. Japanese firms have expanded production capacity far more rapidly than the long-run rate of growth in world demand, and have engaged in massive, sustained sales of semiconductors at prices far below the cost of production. At the same time, they have demonstrated a consistently strong capability in the semiconductor manufacturing process. They have maintained virtually complete domination of their own market and they have moved rapidly toward domination of the upstream SME and materials industries. This combination of factors has had a shattering impact on the U.S. market position in the 1980s.

U.S. Competitive Reversals

Japan's market gains in the mid-1980s have largely been achieved at the expense of U.S. firms, and the rapid expansion of Japanese microelectronics capability has been paralleled by the contraction of the U.S. microelectronics industry. Japan has succeeded in establishing an integrated fabric of upstream, midstream and downstream industries in the information technologies. At the same time major segments of the U.S. information industry structure, as shown in Table 3.10, have substantially eroded or collapsed altogether with adverse ripple effects on the elements which remain. This process may be summarized as follows:

- U.S. semiconductor device manufacturers have been driven out of most commodity memory product areas, jeopardizing their ability to remain competitive in semiconductor manufacturing. They are coming under increasing Japanese pressure in other product areas, such as ASICs and microprocessors.

---

183 The Office of Technology Assessment noted in 1983 that in many consumer electronics markets, the U.S. industry was not competitive or was competitive "in only narrow segments of the market." Office of Technology Assessment, *International Competitiveness in Electronics*, p. 112.

TABLE 3.10

IMPACT OF JAPANESE MARKET GAINS ON THE U.S. INFORMATION INDUSTRY

Market Development	Effect On		
	Device Manufacturers	"Upstream" Sectors (Tools and Materials)	"Downstream" Sectors (Computers, Telecommunications, Machine Tools, Consumer)
Japanese dominance of "technology drivers" (commodity memory products)	- Erosion of manufacturing competitiveness across most product lines - Increasing avoidance of manufacturing, growing emphasis on design-only strategies - Loss of revenue base needed to sustain necessary levels of capital and R&D investment	- Contraction of demand base as device makers exit the market, loss of sales volume and revenue - Loss of revenue base needed to sustain necessary levels of capital and R&D investment	- Growing dependency on Japanese competitors for critical components - Eventual loss of competitiveness
Japanese dominance of "upstream" sectors (tools and materials)	- Erosion of manufacturing competitiveness across all product lines - Growing dependency on Japanese sources for state-of-the-art tools and materials - Contraction of demand base, reduction in revenues and sales volume	- Erosion of revenue base needed to sustain necessary levels of capital and R&D investment	- Growing dependency on Japanese competitors for critical tools and materials - Eventual loss of competitiveness
Japanese inroads in "downstream" sectors (consumer electronics, telecommunications)		- Erosion of domestic demand base	- Loss of revenue base needed to sustain necessary levels of capital and R&D investment

- U.S. SME and materials manufacturers have lost much of their Japanese customer base as indigenous producers have displaced them in Japan, and the contraction of their U.S. customer base has thrown them into a crisis. Their difficulties have been exacerbated by the aggressive entry of Japanese SME and materials producers into markets outside Japan.

- U.S. OEMs and captive producers are jeopardized by growing Japanese dominance of the device, SME and materials technologies upon which they depend to remain competitive.

The Commodity Memory Debacle

Between 1981 and 1986, Japanese semiconductor producers achieved a dominant position in three major "technology driver" commodity memory markets, DRAMS, SRAMS, and EPROMs. They expanded production capacity far more rapidly than the growth of actual or forecast market demand,[184] and in a number of cases sold massive quantities of semiconductors at prices substantially below the cost of production.[185] U.S. firms suffered major operating losses and many of them abandoned technology driver markets or ceased operations altogether. The commodity memory debacle has reverberated through the U.S. upstream and downstream industries and has serious long-run implications for the U.S. competitiveness in microelectronics, and ultimately, in the information industry as a whole.

The most dramatic and significant U.S. setbacks occurred in DRAMs, the most important technology driver product line. U.S. firms dominated the world market for the first three DRAM generations -- 1K, 4K and 16K. In 1981-82, however, Japanese firms, commercializing process and device technology developed in the MITI-NTT VLSI projects, captured 70 percent

---

184 Between 1965 and 1984 the world market grew at an average rate of 16.5 percent. In 1984-85, Japanese firms were investing at a rate which would permit a long run growth rate ranging from 33 to 44 percent (Semiconductor Industry Association).

185 In the EPROM investigation, for example, the U.S. Department of Commerce found margins of dumping ranging from 60.1 percent (Toshiba) to 188.0 percent (NEC). In other words, Japanese EPROM prices would need to increase by that percentage in order to cover costs and provide a return on investment. *EPROMs from Japan*, 51 F.R. 29708 (October 30, 1986).

of the world market for the fourth generation device, the 64K DRAM.[186] In 1985, in the wake of massive Japanese dumping of 64K and 256K DRAMs, most U.S. companies ceased production of DRAMs altogether.[187] Figure 3.9 shows the rapid price declines; the imported price of Japanese 64K DRAMs fell from $3.53 in September, 1984, to $0.82 by September, 1985. The imported price of Japanese 256K DRAMs fell from an index of 100 in September, 1984, to 7 by September, 1985. At the end of 1986, Japanese firms held 90 percent of the market for the current generation 256K DRAM and were forecast to dominate future generations of this product, the 1 and 4 megabit DRAM. During the same period, Japanese firms captured 90 percent of the market for SRAMs, another high volume technology driver.

The virtual complete loss of the DRAM and SRAM markets was an ominous development for the U.S. semiconductor industry because surrender of the technology driver product lines threatened an across-the-board loss of competitiveness. U.S. firms responded by seeking to sustain a market position in the remaining potential technology driver, EPROMs.[188] However, by 1984, Japanese firms had captured a dominant share of the world EPROM market and in the 1984-86 period, U.S. EPROM producers were staggered by a wave of dumped Japanese EPROMs which were often sold at a fraction of the cost of production.[189] U.S. firms elected to "stand and fight in EPROMs" rather than surrender market share to Japanese firms,

---

186 This episode is described in Semiconductor Industry Association, *The Effect of Government Targeting on World Semiconductor Competition* (Washington, D.C.: SIA, 1983).

187 AMD ceased production of DRAMs in May 1985. Intel announced its total withdrawal from the DRAM business and the closure of its DRAM fabrication facility in October 1985. Motorola suspended production of DRAMS at the end of 1985. Mostek, a major producer of DRAMs, ceased operations at the end of 1985. U.S. International Trade Commission, *64K Dynamic Access Random Memory Components from Japan*, pp. A-7 and A-8; *Electronics News* (October 14, 1985).

188 *Electronics* (September 30, 1985). The viability of this strategy over the long run has been questioned. One analyst commented that "It seems unlikely that abandoning the DRAM market will contribute to maintaining a semiconductor industry in the United States that is technologically competitive with its Japanese counterpart." Turin, *JTECH Panel Report on Telecommunications*, p. 6-8.

189 Hitachi instructed its distributors to follow the so-called "ten percent rule," repeatedly cutting the price for Hitachi EPROMs by 10 percent until a sale was gained, with Hitachi guaranteeing the distributor a 25 percent profit regardless of the final price. *New York Times* (June 5, 1985); *Wall Street Journal* (June 5, 1985).

FIGURE 3.9

JAPANESE-IMPORTED DRAM
U.S. SELLING PRICES

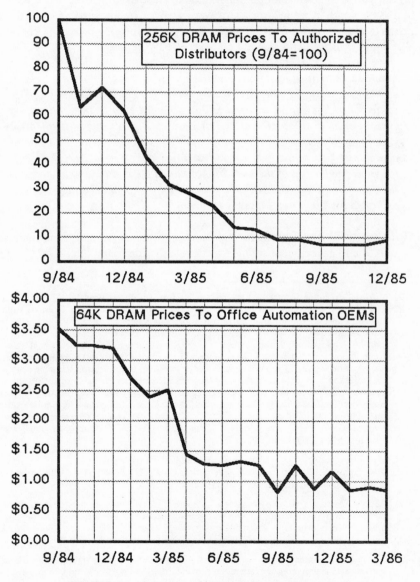

SOURCE: U.S. International Trade Commission

but this decision resulted in massive operating losses.[190] In 1985, the U.S. industry's ratio of operating income to net sales for EPROMs showed a loss of 45 percent; in the first six months of 1986, the ratio was a loss of 50 percent.[191]

The impact of Japanese dumping of commodity memory devices was not limited to U.S. companies. In the European Community, semiconductor producers brought an antidumping action against the Japanese in EPROMs in 1987. South Korean producers were shaken by Japanese 64K DRAM prices that were only a fraction of the Korean producers' production costs.[192] The Seoul *Hanguk Ilbo* observed on March 1, 1985 (p. 4)

> *Japanese manufacturers [have] come out with a dumping offensive to dominate the world semiconductor market from the beginning. They come out with a dumping offensive that does not even recover production costs in order to overturn their competitors . . . Japan's dumping offensive is striking a major blow at our country's semiconductor industry in particular. Our semiconductor industry has only now acquired systems for mass production of the 64K DRAM and is going on the final stages in development of the 256K DRAM and cannot escape bitter struggle as it is disrupted by Japan's bud-nipping tactics.*

However, while the European and Korean firms enjoy sufficient financial resources and government support to survive the "dumping offensive,"[193] U.S.

---

190 An Intel executive commented in 1985, as his firm withdrew from the DRAM market, that "We will stand and fight in EPROMs . . . we could not recoup the necessary capital to justify keeping the dynamic RAM lines open any longer .... EPROMs are really the last commodity battlefield left in memories." *Electronic News* (October 14, 1985). In the 1985-86 antidumping investigation of EPROMs, the U.S. International Trade Commission stated that the U.S. producers "argue that they chose to meet a Japanese-led rapid decline in EPROM prices, in order to maintain production levels and market presence and to benefit from learning economies, as well as to enable them to continue to develop and bring into production new generations of EPROMs. Meeting Japanese price levels resulted in significant financial losses . . . . [T]hey chose to fight Japanese dumping on the basis of price . . ." U.S. International Trade Commission, *Eraseable Programmable Read Only Memories from Japan* (U.S.I.T.C. Pub. No. 1927, final, December 1986), pp. 17-18.

191 U.S. International Trade Commission, *Eraseable Programmable Read Only Memories from Japan*, p. 16. U.S. firms' net pretax loss on EPROMs was $161.6 million in 1985 and $75.1 million in the first six months of 1986.

192 Lucky-Goldstar, a Korean producer, estimated in 1985 that it needed to sell 64K DRAMS at $1.30 or $1.40 per unit to cover materials and production costs. Japanese prices, however, were only about 60 cents per unit. *Maeil Kjongje Sinmun* (November 28, 1985).

193 *Le Monde* commented on September 23, 1983 that "conditions [for the French semiconductor industry] are favorable, provided there be no lack of public money . . ..

firms have been forced to choose between enduring protracted losses or exiting the commodity memory market. The fact that most U.S. firms have embraced the latter option has serious long-run implications for the United States.

The Impact on U.S. Competitiveness

The reversals suffered by U.S. semiconductor producers in the commodity memory product lines in the 1980s represent the loss of markets with multi-billion dollar present and future potential. However, erosion of the U.S. position in several of these technology driver product areas has a larger strategic significance than revenue and operating losses alone. Abandonment of these product areas threatens to undermine U.S. competitiveness in the semiconductor industry and ultimately, in the information sector as a whole:

- Withdrawal from the technology driver product lines will result in an increasing inability to master the manufacturing techniques necessary to remain competitive in the semiconductor industry as a whole.

- The losses suffered by U.S. firms in the 1980s in the technology driver product lines have severely hampered their ability to make the level of R&D and capital investments necessary to remain competitive in microelectronics.

- The erosion of the U.S. market position in technology driver products is adversely affecting the U.S. upstream and downstream sectors.

U.S. merchant firms retain a strong market position in a number of design-intensive product areas where devices tend to be produced in lower volumes and dedicated to specific applications.[194] Some observers believe that the U.S. merchant industry can survive through a strategy based on these "niche" products, avoiding competition with the Japanese in the high volume

---

To succeed, one must manufacture memories. The race being run is, in fact, based on this particular type of ubiquitous circuit. Memories are the "driving force" of the technology which is then applied everywhere else to more specific and highly profitable products. Memories must therefore be manufactured in France under license, even if it means "losing our shirts on it," is the unanimous affirmation of all the specialists. In plain language, this means we cannot avoid stepping, with both feet, into the costly worldwide free-for-all between the Japanese and the Americans. Half measures are out of the question."

194 These include microprocessors, microcontrollers, application-specific integrated circuits (ASICs), and semistandard logic devices (SSL).

commodity memory markets.[195]   Other observers, however, believe that
surrender of the "technology driver" markets will lead inevitably to loss of
market position in the niche markets as well.[196]

There is some evidence that this loss is occurring already.[197] Japanese
inroads into the U.S. market position began in the commodity memory
product areas, but are now spreading to other product lines. Japanese firms
overtook the U.S. industry in MOS memory (which includes DRAMs,
SRAMs, and EPROMs) in 1984. Japanese firms overtook the U.S. industry
in MOS logic products (microprocessors, microcontrollers, etc.) in 1986. The
United States still holds a lead in bipolar digital ICs -- a low growth market
which has been comparatively neglected by Japanese firms -- but even here
there have been substantial losses in market share to Japanese and European
producers since 1980.

Erosion of Manufacturing Competitiveness. Probably the most significant
long-run effect of U.S. industry withdrawal from the commodity memory
product areas is the negative across-the-board impact such a withdrawal has
on U.S. manufacturing competitiveness. The manufacturing of technology
drivers enables producers to learn process improvements that can then be
applied to the manufacturing of their other products, with corresponding
improvements in cost and quality.[198]   As U.S. firms withdraw from these
markets, this ability is being lost.

The strategic significance of technology drivers is rooted in the
semiconductor manufacturing process itself, which is "probably the most
complex mass production process ever attempted." A producers' relative

---

195 *Electronics* (October 21, 1985).

196 Pasquale Pistorio, the President of the Italian semiconductor company SGS, observed in
1986 that "survival in niche markets is possible only until large-scale enterprises
themselves begin to fill these gaps . . . A niche firm . . . can survive and be profitable as
long as the market niche is relatively small and is immediately abandoned as soon as it
becomes attractive for a large-scale enterprise." *VDI Nachrichten* (July 11, 1986), p. 2.

197 Japanese firms already hold 40 percent of the world market in MOS ASICs, and "[They]
have recently entered the American market in CMOS gate arrays with extraordinary
aggressiveness. Japanese firms may capture 33 percent of the CMOS ASIC market [in
1986]." National Science Foundation, Division of Electrical, Communications, and
Systems Engineering, and Consultants, *Effects of a Substantial Loss in Capability of the
U.S. Semiconductor Industry on "Upstream" and "Downstream" Industries* (September 5,
1986, draft), p. 21. *Electronics* commented on November 18, 1985 (p. 82) that "Japanese
companies . . . have their eye on U.S. positions in application-specific integrated circuits
and microprocessors." A Toshiba executive reported in mid-1986 that his firm was
moving rapidly into ASICs to offset the slump in commodity memory demand. *Toshi
Keizai* (July, 1986).

198 For example, one of Texas Instruments' technology drivers, the 256K EPROM, was
expected to yield major benefits transferable to CMOS 8-bit microcontrollers, CMOS
field-programmable logic devices, EPROMs, low power linear devices, and "smart"
power ICs. *Electronics* (September 30, 1985).

success in manufacturing a device is measured by its yield, the percentage of devices which enter the production process which ultimately proves useable.[199] Because of the complexity of the manufacturing process, when new semiconductor products are first manufactured yields are extraordinarily low. As cumulative output increases more devices are produced and the causes of defects can be progressively identified and eliminated increasing yields dramatically.[200] This process requires a constant flow of production to generate the volume of data necessary to analyze the production process; the higher the production volume, the more that is learned about those points in the production process where improvements are necessary. The "technology driver" products are ideal in this respect because they not only can be produced in the necessary volumes, but also are extremely complex so that mastering their manufacture generates learning which is can be systematically applied to most other product lines.[201] An executive from Siemens, which has remained in the DRAM market, commented in 1987 that

the production of memory components is not the real strategic goal. Rather for the firm it is a matter of mastering the submicron structures to such a degree that Siemens will be able to manufacture more and more logic components for the market and for its own products and systems in the next decade.[202]

The increasing difficulty of sustaining manufacturing operations in the commodity memory lines has led a number of U.S. firms to abandon

---

199   William F. Finan and Annette M. LaMond, "Sustaining U.S. Competitiveness in Microelectronics: The Challenge to U.S. Policy," in *U.S. Competitiveness and the World Economy* eds. Bruce R. Scott and George C. Lodge (Boston: Harvard Business School Press, 1985), p. 149.

200   The "learning" process in semiconductor manufacturing has become quite sophisticated. For example, semiconductor producers have adopted a technique known as statistical process control (SPC) or statistical quality control (SQC) to determine whether a particular machine or process is functioning with 100 percent effectiveness. On the basis of a study of the machines and processes in the production line, problem points are identified; failures and causes arranged in a chart of rapidly descending magnitude, and corrective measures rapidly taken. Control charts are drawn up to monitor production flows to identify parameters that could result in a defective product, permitting corrective steps to be taken before a defective device is produced.

201   U.S. firms, for example, sometimes shift production of other device types to their memory device production lines. They crossassign personnel from commodity memory lines to other production lines, hold internal symposia and manufacturing and engineering councils, and internally disseminate weekly activity reports from the memory division to ensure that learning from the memory operation is diffused to other production areas. Semiconductor Industry Association, *Presentation to the White House Science Council*, January 16, 1987.

202   Chairman Karlheinz Kaska in *Frankfurter Zeitung/Blick durch die Wirtschaft*, February 4, 1987.

manufacturing, concentrating instead on research, development and design, and licensing their technology to firms which remain in manufacturing -- which increasingly means Japanese firms. In the short run, this may be the only way for a firm to survive, but over the long run, such strategies mean that the skills needed to manufacture semiconductors will be lost, a result which will inevitably lead to an overall loss of technological competitiveness. One U.S. semiconductor executive commented in 1986 that "we have sown well and are now failing to harvest."[203]

Investment. The commodity memory products have traditionally been the principal source of income for the U.S. semiconductor industry. The losses suffered by U.S. merchants in the commodity memory markets in the 1980s, coupled with their withdrawal from DRAMs and SRAMs, are making it far more difficult for remaining firms to raise the capital needed to remain competitive in the future.[204] A Dutch semiconductor executive, observing the depressed state of the U.S. industry, commented in 1986 that

> *You must be able to make chips in large numbers. Only in this way will you succeed in continuing to bear the enormous investments which are necessary for further development.*[205]

The U.S. merchants have traditionally funded R&D and capital investment largely through reinvested retained earnings and equity, but the events of 1984-86 eliminated profits for many producers and diminished equity investors' incentives for committing capital to this industry.[206] Declining levels of investment ultimately affects competitiveness; as Intel's Robert Noyce observed, his company's loss of $175 million in 1986

---

203 Irwin Federman, President of Monolithic Memories, in the *New York Times* (October 5, 1986).

204 The U.S. International Trade Commission observed in 1986 that "the DRAM industry, like other semiconductor producers, is extremely sensitive to declines in profitability. DRAM production is highly capital-intensive. Moreover, producers must continually invest large sums in research to develop the "next generation" DRAMs, to keep pace with demand for memory capacity on the part of end users. Consequently, declines in profitability are an extremely significant indicator of material injury to an industry." U.S. International Trade Commission, *64K Dynamic Random Access Memory Components from Japan*, p. 20.

205 R. Hamersona in *NRC Handelsblad* (December 3, 1986).

206 One financial analyst commented on semiconductor stocks in 1986 that "You look at return on assets in the business or return on capital over a cycle, and you see that you would be better off in T-bills". *Barron's* (June 16, 1986). Another counseled potential investors in 1985 that "[W]e would continue to avoid participation in the semiconductor group." John J. Laszlo, *The Semiconductor Industry: Grim Conditions Could Persist Through 1986* (Hambrecht & Quist, June 1985), p. 15.

[I]s a tax on our future. Our future products are not as good as they would have been. Our future manufacturing will not be as efficient.[207]

Upstream Implications. The loss of market position in the commodity memory product lines has resulted in a broader erosion of the U.S. microelectronics infrastructure, since the U.S. semiconductor, SME and materials sectors are mutually supporting and reinforcing.[208] Intensive capital investment by Japanese semiconductor device firms has primarily benefited the Japanese SME and materials industry. Figure 3.10 shows that at the same time that Japanese semiconductor device makers spending on plant and equipment was surpassing the U.S. levels, the market share of the U.S. SME firms in Japan was being cut in half.

As U.S. semiconductor device firms withdrew from DRAM and SRAM production, the SME firms which produced process equipment for DRAMs and SRAMs -- involving some of the most advanced technology used in the semiconductor industry -- experienced a dramatic and perhaps permanent contraction of their own market.[209] These firms have simultaneously come under strong competitive pressure from Japanese SME and materials firms,

---

207 *San Jose Mercury News* (December 1, 1986). A recent study by the Office of Technology Assessment observed that "Although R&D, a long-term investment, cannot solve industry's immediate problems, it is a crucial ingredient in industrial competitiveness. Without continued strength in R&D, solutions to the near-term problems will only delay the decline of U.S. companies. Yet microelectronics firms that are struggling to survive are likely to neglect R&D activity in the face of more immediate and pressing problems." Office of Technology Assessment, *Microelectronics Research and Development*, p. 4.

208 As the National Science Foundation observed in 1986, "Leadership in high volume semiconductor markets and leadership in SME technology reinforce each other: A Japanese lead in high-volume semiconductor products can contribute to a similar lead in SME, and vice versa. There are already reports that the U.S. lead in application specific integrated circuits (ASICs) and microprocessors is threatened by Japanese competition; there have also been reports of Japanese SME firms withholding advanced products from the U.S. market that are already in use in Japanese semiconductor companies." National Science Foundation, *Effects*, p. 3.

209 While U.S. semiconductor firms may or may not remain competitive in various low-volume "niche" markets, such activities are inadequate to support a viable domestic SME industry. The Defense Science Board concluded in 1987 that "In the absence of a domestic mass-production revenue base, which is needed to preserve a viable domestic production equipment industry, the specialty [semiconductor] producers themselves may become dependent on foreign supplies for their materials, equipment, and fabrication technology, and would then be at a disadvantage when under competitive assault." DSB, *Task Force on Semiconductor Dependency*, p. 4.

FIGURE 3.10

JAPANESE SEMICONDUCTOR CAPITAL SPENDING AND U.S. SME MANUFACTURERS' MARKET SHARE IN JAPAN

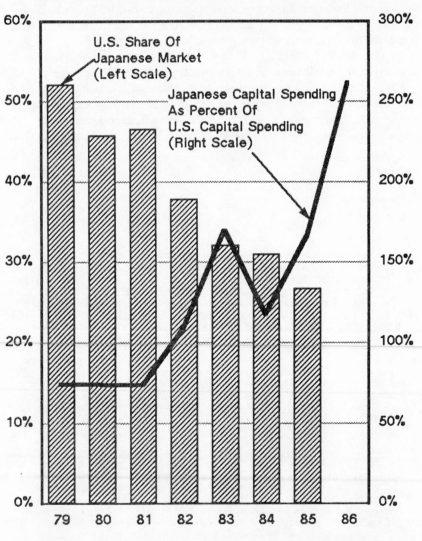

NOTE: U.S. SME market share for 1986 not available.

and confront some of the same structural problems as U.S. semiconductor device manufacturers.[210] Recent developments in the various subsectors of the SME and materials industries are largely a chronicle of U.S. competitive setbacks.

Wafer Steppers. Wafer steppers are a technology introduced in the late 1970s which permitted significant improvements in yields and quality. The Eaton Corporation, a U.S. manufacturer of steppers, dropped out of the market in 1986, saying that the business would never be profitable, and GCA, one of the last remaining U.S. producers of steppers, lost over $100 million in 1985-86 and has undergone financial restructuring. Meanwhile, two Japanese firms, Nikon and Canon, are rapidly moving toward a dominant position in this sector.[211]

Maskmaking. In 1985, three Japanese firms, Dai Nippon, Hoya, and Topan entered maskmaking and captured a major share of the world market. A number of U.S. maskmaking companies reported losses in 1985 and some may go bankrupt.[212] Glass blanks for photomasks are now virtually a Japanese monopoly.[213]

Lithography. Electron beam lithography will be crucial to the production of semiconductors with submicron circuit densities -- that is, the generation of VLSI devices. Eight U.S. firms entered the E-beam field, but by mid-1985 six of these had withdrawn, writing off more than $100 million in losses, and only one U.S. producer, Perkin Elmer, planned to sell E-beam equipment commercially. By contrast, three Japanese firms (including firms affiliated

---

210 Almost all of the companies in the U.S. semiconductor equipment and materials industry are small, entrepreneurial firms -- over two-thirds of the firms have sales of less than $10 million and fewer than 100 employees. The Japanese SME industry, in contrast, is comprised of large, multi-product companies that are often vertically integrated with semiconductor producers as shown in Table 3.11.

211 *New York Times* (January 19, 1987), p. D1; *Forbes* (April 7, 1986), p. 88. Perkin-Elmer and Ultratech, two U.S. firms, continue to produce steppers, but not "reduction steppers" which are particularly favored by producers of dense VLSI devices. Ibid. MIT's Ferguson commented in 1985 that "Nikon now dominates the world market for 5:1 direct steppers and has announced a 10:1 direct stepper. To [my] knowledge none of the American suppliers -- Ultratech, GCA, etc. -- offer 10:1 steppers." Ferguson, *American Microelectronics in Decline*, p. 83.

212 Ferguson, *American Microelectronics in Decline*, p. 82. The two largest Japanese companies have annual revenues over three times greater than the largest U.S. company. The National Science Foundation observed in 1986 that in maskmaking, "Capital requirements have increased, U.S. demand has grown less than Japanese demand, Japanese competitors have entered, and smaller American firms have failed or withdrawn. Corning was formerly a leader in glass; now Hoya dominates world markets."

213 Industry source.

TABLE 3.11

MAJOR TECHNICAL RELATIONSHIPS BETWEEN SEMICONDUCTOR PRODUCTION EQUIPMENT
MANUFACTURERS AND SEMICONDUCTOR MANUFACTURERS IN JAPAN

Equipment Manufacturer	Partner	Field of Cooperation
ULVAC	NTT	Implantation
ANELVA	Hitachi	Dry Etching
Kokusai Electric	Hitachi	Diffusion
Nippon Kogaku (Nikon)	VLSI Laboratory	Wafer Stepper
JEOL	VLSI Lab/Fujitsu	E-Beam Exposure
Tokuda	Toshiba	Vacuum Apparatus
TEL/Thermco	Mitsubishi	High Pressure Furnace
Kaijo Electric	NEC	Bonder
Ando Electric	NEC	Test Equipment
Takeda Riken (Advantest)	NTT & Hitachi	100 MHz Tester

with Hitachi and Toshiba) have entered the E-beam market, and are expected to dominate the world market in the future.[214]

Testing Equipment. In automated semiconductor testing equipment, Japanese firms are making rapid gains at the expense of U.S. producers. Takeda Riken (Advantest), a Fujitsu affiliate, currently holds the largest share of the world tester market and its sales are expanding, as are those of Ando Electric, an NEC affiliate.[215] Some U.S. makers of testing equipment (Varian, GenRad) lost money and announced layoffs in 1985 and others went out of business altogether.[216] The National Science Foundation reported in 1986 that

Terradyne is now effectively the only U.S. supplier of technically competitive memory testers in the United States. [Another U.S. firm] is steadily losing both market share and technical competitiveness.[217]

Materials. A similar story is unfolding in the industries which produce raw materials for semiconductor manufacturing. These U.S. firms now have virtually no remaining market position in Japan (less than 5%) and are coming under heavy competitive pressure from Japanese firms in world markets as shown in Table 3.12. Japanese materials firms held over half the world market by the end of 1985. Some key materials areas, such as high quality fused quartz, are already a Japanese monopoly.[218] In silicon wafers -- the basic building blocks of semiconductors -- Japan already possesses more capacity than U.S. and European producers combined, and Japanese firms are rapidly absorbing important segments of what remains of U.S. industry.[219] The National Science Foundation commented in 1986 that

---

214 Ferguson, *American Microelectronics in Decline*, pp. 81-82.

215 *Electronics* observed on October 16, 1986 that "Unanimous choice for the survivor list are two Japanese outfits: Advantest Corp. and Ando Electric Industrial Corp. Not only have they grabbed leadership roles in their important home market, but their ties to giant industrial companies ... lend them the financial stability they need to go the distance."

216 *Electronics* (October 16, 1986).

217 National Science Foundation, *Effects*, p. 14.

218 An NEC affiliate controls 85% of the world market for fused quartz. The only other firm that makes quartz of comparable quality is also Japanese. Ibid., p. 16.

219 In 1986, Japan's Osaka Titanium acquired U.S. Semiconductor Corporation, a U.S. manufacturer of silicon wafers which had been suffering operating losses, and in 1987, Japan's Mitsubishi Metals agreed to purchase Siltec, the only American manufacturer of silicon wafers remaining in Silicon Valley. *San Jose Mercury News* (December 23, 1986); *High Technology* (January 1987).

TABLE 3.12

THE JAPANESE INDUSTRY'S GROWING DOMINANCE IN SEMICONDUCTOR MATERIALS

Material	1985 Market ($Millions)	Japanese Share of World Mkt.			Major Japanese Suppliers
		1975	1985	1990e	
Wafers	$ 1060	15	40	54	SEH, OTC, Mitsubishi, Steel Firms
Photolithography	884	20	44	54	Hoya, Dai Nippon Paint, Tokyo, Ohka, Toray
Wet chemicals	166	20	38	58	Kanto, Sumitomo, Hitachi
Gases	161	20	36	42	Daido, Nippon, Osaka, Teikoku
Ceramic packages	260	72	92	88	Kyocera, NTK, Narumi, Showa Denko
Lead frames	335	30	76	80	Mitsui High-Tech, Shinko, Sumitomo, Enamoto
Encapsulation resins	140	12	74	80	Nitto, Sumitomo, Hitachi, Toshiba
Bonding wire	96	32	60	70	Tanaka, Sumitomo, Furukawa
Thick film pastes	220	6	14	26	Sumitomo, Tanaka, Toshiba
Hybrid packages	70	28	38	46	Kyocera, Shinko, NTK

Source: Electronics Materials Report

The number of U.S. firms in this business is decreasing, the remaining suppliers are experiencing loss of market share to Japanese competitors, and large operating losses are common in the industry. The Semiconductor Equipment and Materials Institute (SEMI) maintains that the result of these conditions is that the United States no longer has a fully integrated self-sufficient electronic materials industry and faces the prospect of total reliance on foreign supplies of some key strategic electronic raw materials.[220]

Downstream Implications. The disappearance of U.S. vendors in key "midstream" (semiconductor) and "upstream" (SME and materials) product areas inevitably affects "downstream" OEM firms -- and the erosion of the OEMs' domestic vendor base is already leading to a growing dependency on Japan for the components, tools and materials which these industries need to remain competitive, and which the U.S. armed forces need in order to maintain the U.S. defense posture.[221] While downstream firms can produce some semiconductors, materials and SME internally, even the largest of these firms lacks the resources to produce all of the components which it needs or to create the necessary level of upstream SME and materials production to remain self-sufficient.[222]

A number of U.S. downstream sectors confront direct Japanese competition in end markets, and are now beginning to experience strategic withholding of critical components by their Japanese competitors.[223] Three Japanese firms (Fujitsu, Hitachi and NEC) control over 80 percent of the world market for ECL RAMs, which are essential components of

---

220 National Science Foundation, *Effects*, pp. 15-16.

221 The Defense Science Board commented in 1987 that "[T]here are important areas of dependency, including field effect transistors, ceramic packages (available from virtually a single producer in the world -- a firm in Japan) and precision alignment manufacturing equipment. A National Academy of Engineering Study recently concluded that in the case of the missile system it had investigated, it would take 18 months to replace foreign parts content with domestically supplied hardware." DSB, *Task Force on Semiconductor Dependency*, p. 67.

222 The Defense Science Board concluded in 1987 that "[T]his dilemma confronts not only the U.S. merchant industry but the large captive firms as well, since it is very difficult for even this latter group to support an entire equipment industry and at the same time remain price competitive in the world market." Ibid. p. 72. Similarly the National Science Foundation observed in 1986 that "Although firms, including IBM, have developed specialized semiconductor production equipment in-house when such equipment could not be purchased outside the company, it would be difficult even for IBM to internally develop and produce the wide spectrum of SME equipment needed for an integrated manufacturing operation." National Science Foundation, *Effects*, p. 13.

223 Similarly, Siemens has complained of "an embargo policy on the part of the competition....Japan is no longer delivering certain components for solid-state lasers today." *Handelsblatt* (March 17, 1986).

supercomputers and mainframe cache memories.[224] In 1985, an executive of a U.S. supercomputer hardware firm complained that

> *It has been our experience that the Japanese vendors do not make their advanced products available for use in the U.S. until they are in full production assuring them of a substantial lead in the end products.*[225]

A White House Panel which monitors the state of the U.S. supercomputer industry reported in 1987 that U.S. supercomputer firms complained that

> *Japanese companies were not shipping their latest high performance components to outside markets until their needs for their own products are satisfied. This represents a serious problem to U.S. companies who may be forced to use components that are a factor or two lower in their performance than their Japanese competitors.*[226]

Only one U.S. merchant firm "remains even marginally competitive" in the ECL gate array market,[227] and its position is eroding relative to that of four Japanese firms; the National Science Foundation commented that

> *There are already indications that Japanese firms, particularly NEC, are now reserving their best technology for their own machines for significant periods of time before commercializing it. The inevitable result is that Japanese computers will enjoy increasing price/performance advantages over their American competition.*[228]

---

224 Cray and ETA Systems, two U.S. manufacturers of supercomputers, must purchase their bipolar memory devices, including ECL RAMs, from their direct Japanese competitors in the supercomputer market. 100 percent of the memory capacity of Cray's most advanced supercomputers must be acquired from Japanese sources. DSB, *Task Force on Semiconductor Dependency*, p. 71. National Science Foundation, *Effects*, p. 21.

225 L.M. Thorndyke, ETA Systems, Inc., "Supercomputer Systems Markets" (October 28-29, 1985).

226 Federal Coordinating Council on Science, Engineering and Technology (FCCSET) Committee on High Performance Computing, *Annual Report* (January 1987), p. 2.

227 The central processing units of most custom and semi-custom logic devices, primarily minicomputers and mainframes, depend on gate arrays, and mainframes and supercomputers usually use ECL gate arrays.

228 National Science Foundation, *Effects*, p. 21. Potentially even more serious is a looming U.S. dependency on Japan for CMOS ASICs, which are becoming increasingly important components in computers. The National Science Foundation observed in 1986 that "The potential dependency issues arising from Japanese control of CMOS ASIC markets are quite serious, because ASIC customers must disclose their designs to ASIC vendors and thereby risk industrial espionage and possible losses of national security secrets in defense applications." Ibid., pp. 21-22.

Summarizing the implications of Japanese gains in the components markets for the telecommunications industry, a Stanford scientist commented in 1986 that

> *If present trends continue, the component technologies upon which the information age depends will be dominated by Japan. It may then also follow that Japanese companies will ultimately dominate the design and manufacturing of the telecommunications systems that are based on these technologies. In that case, economic leadership in the "information age" will belong to Japan.*[229]

THE U.S. POLICY RESPONSES

The sheer magnitude of the U.S. competitive reversals in microelectronics markets in the 1980s has called into question the continuing viability of traditional U.S. policy responses in this key industrial sector. The U.S. Government's intervention in the problems of specific sectors has been largely limited to the sphere of trade policy, and in such cases, the government has generally made equity, rather than the promotion of U.S. commercial interests, its principal concern.

In the trade arena, the U.S. Government has pursued a policy designed, above all, to achieve a "level playing field" -- free from government intervention at the border or at the point of manufacture -- through a program of trade agreements designed to reduce trade barriers and by making available to U.S. industries a variety of quasi-adjudicatory trade remedies directed at specific "unfair" foreign practices.[230] Thus, the U.S. trade policy response to Japanese practices in the information technologies has consisted of (1) bilateral negotiations to secure agreements designed to mitigate the effects of Japanese Government intervention, and (2) the adjudication of trade complaints filed by beleaguered U.S. producers with respect to specific problems.[231] While it is too early to evaluate whether

---

229 Turin, *JTECH Panel Report on Telecommunications*, p. 6-25.

230 This system is described in Office of U.S. Trade Representative, *Annual Report of the President of the United States on the Trade Agreements Program* (Washington, D.C., 1985).

231 Prior to the 1980s, U.S. trade policy toward Japan in the advanced electronics sectors placed emphasis on the negotiated elimination of formal Japanese barriers to U.S. imports and investment in Japan. These efforts produced agreements which removed formal impediments to imports of U.S. consumer electronics products, semiconductors, computers, and telecommunications equipment. However, the elimination of formal

these policy responses will have a significant effect in the trade sphere, it is unlikely that these actions alone, even if effective, will reverse the shift in the overall competitive balance in Japan's favor in the information industries.

In semiconductors, the U.S. Government has sought to negotiate agreements with Japan to achieve meaningful market access in Japan and to curtail Japanese dumping, thus far with only limited success. In 1983, after a wave of low-priced Japanese 16K and 64K DRAMs had inflicted heavy losses on U.S. producers, a U.S.-Japan bilateral working group concluded a series of joint "recommendations" to promote U.S. access to the Japanese market and forestall dumping.[232] These accords collapsed in 1984-85 as U.S. market share in Japan began to decline rapidly and Japanese firms began dumping massive quantities of DRAMs and EPROMs in the U.S. market.[233]

In 1985, U.S. producers and the Department of Commerce commenced a series of antidumping actions against Japanese firms (which eventually resulted in affirmative findings of dumping), and the Semiconductor Industry Association filed a petition with the U.S. Trade Representative pursuant to Section 301 of the Trade Act of 1974.[234] These actions, which raised the prospect of retaliatory sanctions against Japanese products, resulted in the negotiation of a more comprehensive agreement with Japan in 1986, containing specific commitments by the Japanese Government with respect to market access and dumping.[235] However, it became evident by late 1986 that the Japanese commitments with respect to market access and dumping were not being met.[236] As a result, the U.S. Government imposed tariffs on

---

barriers was in some cases accompanied by "liberalization countermeasures," designed to offset the practical effect of liberalization, and in no case was the "liberalization" of the Japanese market followed by a substantial increase in U.S. participation in any advanced Japanese electronics sector. When Japanese dumping emerged as a prominent problem in the 1980s, U.S. trade policy efforts sought to curb dumping as well as to secure market access in Japan.

232   This agreement, which was adopted by the U.S. and Japanese cabinets, provided commitments by Japan to improve U.S. access to the Japanese market, established a system of trade data collection to provide "early warning" of export surges, and provided commitments to prevent predatory and anticompetitive practices in the semiconductor market.   "Recommendations of the U.S. Japan Work Group on High Technology Industries" (November 2, 1983).

233   The breakdown of the 1983 accords is described in Alan Wolff, Michael Gadbaw, Thomas Howell and Timothy Richards, *Japanese Market Barriers in Microelectronics* (San Jose, California: Semiconductor Industry Association, June 14, 1985).

234   Petition of the Semiconductor Industry Association, filed June 14, 1985.

235   "Arrangement Between the Government of Japan and the Government of the United States of America Concerning Trade in Semiconductor Products" (September 2, 1986).

236   In January 1987, U.S. officials charged that Japan's four largest semiconductor producers were continuing to dump their products and warned that the U.S. might cancel the agreement. *San Jose Mercury News* (January 17, 1987). In the fall of 1986, reports were received of extensive dumping by Japanese firms in East Asia, and a survey of U.S.

a number of Japanese electronics products (including televisions and laptop computers) to induce Japanese compliance with the Agreement.[237] It remains uncertain, at this writing whether such compliance will be forthcoming. Perhaps more significantly, during the period of this series of disputes (1983-87), U.S. semiconductor firms suffered major losses and some left the market altogether. The series of trade policy measures taken by the U.S. Government did not halt this process, and during this period, the Japanese competitive position has dramatically improved.

Several conclusions emerge from this record. First, the U.S. trade policy structure has to date proven inadequate to deal with the problem of systematic Japanese dumping to achieve longer run strategic industrial objectives. Table 3.13 shows that many of the Japanese firms which engaged in dumping EPROMs and DRAMs in 1984-86 were the same companies that dumped television receivers and a variety of telecommunications products in the U.S. market between 1970 and 1984. While dumping by these firms has produced a welter of antidumping cases and antitrust litigation, in each case, the Japanese producers were ultimately able to secure a substantial -- and in some cases dominant -- share of the U.S. market. The application of U.S. trade remedies has had little, if any, deterrent or restitutional effect.

Second, U.S. trade policy has not been able to resolve the problem of access to the Japanese market for U.S. semiconductor producers or, in most cases, for U.S. OEMs. The formal governmental obstacles to U.S. semiconductor sales and investment in Japan have largely been removed, but the Japanese market structure remains resistant to foreign penetration. No effective policy response to this intractable and increasingly critical problem has yet been devised.

---

semiconductor firms in Japan indicated that no progress was being made in expanding U.S. sales in Japan. See General Accounting Office, *Observations on the U.S.-Japan Semiconductor Arrangement* (Washington, D.C.: General Accounting Office, April 1987).

237 Proclamation by the President, *Increase in the Rates of Duty for Certain Articles from Japan* (April 17, 1987). Some of the tariffs were lifted in June 1987, reflecting evidence that dumping had diminished (but not halted) in some product areas. The U.S. Government has not imposed import restrictions (in the form of tariffs or quantitative restrictions) on semiconductor imports.

TABLE 3.13

DUMPING IN THE U.S. MARKET BY JAPANESE ELECTRONICS PRODUCERS
(Margins of Dumping)

Case	Hitachi	Toshiba	Fujitsu	Mitsubishi	Matsushita	Oki	NEC
Large Power Transformers (1970)	21.4	51.4					
Black & White TV (1971)	43.4	38.8		81.7	55.2		
Color TV (1971)	58.4	32.3		52.7	74.0		
High Power Amplifier Assembly & Parts (1981) (two types)							25.4
							41.4
High Capacity Pagers (1982)					109.1		70.4
Cellular Mobile Phone (1984)	3.0		57.8	87.8	106.6	9.7	95.6
64K DRAM (1986)	11.9	20.8	20.8	13.4	20.8	35.3	22.7
EPROM (1986)	85.2	21.8	103.0	93.9	93.9	93.9	188.0
256K DRAM (1985)*	19.8	49.5	74.4	108.7	39.7	39.7	108.7

Margins rounded off to nearest tenth of percent

* Preliminary margin.
Source: *Federal Register*

JAPAN'S EMERGING TECHNOLOGICAL EDGE

The erosion of the U.S. market position in semiconductors has serious implications for U.S. industry competitiveness in microelectronics and related upstream and downstream industries, and has received widespread attention and comment. However, a phenomenon equally significant, but less well recognized, is the fact that Japan is rapidly achieving a technological edge in a wide range of emerging VLSI process and device technologies which will be critical to competitive success in the early and mid-1990s. Here, as in the market, government policies have played a critical role.

The evidence of Japan's move toward leadership in future semiconductor technologies comes from many sources. The Defense Science Board concluded in 1987 that Japan held a "clear and increasing lead in most silicon product technologies," with the exception of design intensive custom logic and microprocessors; maintained a similar lead in nonsilicon products (such as optoelectronics and high speed digital devices); and was "pulling ahead in a number of key process technologies." [238] The Japanese Technology Evaluation Program ("JTECH"), a series of studies sponsored by the Commerce Department involving surveys of Japanese R&D by leading U.S. experts,[239] has produced a series of startling findings that Japan is leading, and pulling away from, the U.S. in a number of microelectronics and microelectronics-related technologies.[240] Similarly, a panel of the U.S. National Materials Advisory Board commented in 1986 that

It appears that Japan is taking the lead in several key areas of electronic materials fabrication. This subject is rapidly evolving, and its outcome is

---

238   DSB, *Task Force on Semiconductor Dependency*, p.9. The DSB noted that the Japanese were rapidly eroding the U.S. lead in microprocessors. The United States retained a lead in linear compound devices, "largely because of military interest in fast and radiation-hard circuits for satellite and radar applications."

239   The JTECH program selected panels of U.S. technical experts in fields such as optoelectronics, telecommunications, and biotechnology. Selection was based on three criteria: (1) leading authority in the field, (2) technically active with recent "hands on" experience, and (3) knowledge of Japanese and U.S. research programs. Members of each panel were selected from industry, academia and government. The JTECH panels conducted substantial fieldwork in Japan, and reviewed and assessed current technical literature.

240   For example, one JTECH panelist found that Japan had established a clear leadership position in the development of high-speed SRAMs, "the vehicle by which semiconductor technology is advanced to its highest levels of performance." Turin, *JTECH Panel Report on Telecommunications*, pp. 6-9, 6-10.

of major importance to the U.S. scientific and industrial position.[241]

The emerging Japanese technological edge in microelectronics is all the more remarkable because technology and innovation have long been the Japanese industry's weakest area. For many years the Japanese industry relied heavily on technology drawn from the United States, and while the Japanese industry was able to make incremental improvements on U.S. process and device technology, it generated few wholly new technologies. Japan's lagging technological position was attributed to structural factors such as domination of the Japanese industry by a few large OEMs, the low employee turnover rate (which limited "cross-pollination" of firms), and the "group mentality" prevailing in Japan.

However, while structural impediments to innovation exist in Japan, some aspects of the Japanese industrial structure are proving conducive to the development of new technology in the VLSI era. For example, as VLSI devices become more complex, vertical relationships within the Japanese industrial groups facilitate the development of components closely linked to end-system requirements.[242] Similarly, the large Japanese OEMs possess the financial resources necessary to sustain the high R&D investments which have become necessary with VLSI.[243]

Nevertheless, the principal factor underlying the Japanese technical gains which are being achieved in microelectronics and related information sectors is the Japanese Government's implementation of a coordinated strategy designed to transform Japan into an "information- based society" by the 21st century.[244] This effort involves, among other things, the channeling of

---

241 Panel on Materials Science, National Materials Advisory Board; Commission on Engineering and Technical Systems; National Research Council, *Advanced Processing of Electronic Materials in the United States and Japan* (Washington, D.C.: National Academy Press, 1986), p.8.

242 "The Japanese semiconductor industry, according to Toshiba, has the advantage of being a tripartite system composed of semiconductor manufacturers, users, and peripheral industries. Large companies such as Toshiba and NEC have several family companies manufacturing such products as household appliances and computers, and thus have a broad range of influence over the development and application of products that U.S. semiconductor companies could never enjoy." *Tokyo Business Today* (February 1986), p. 48.

243 *Fortune* commented on October 13, 1986 that "The scope, size and intensity of the Japanese effort in the development of new technologies for chip manufacture invariably startle visitors from the West...Work on [optical and x-ray lithography] techniques at all the Japanese companies, including NEC, Hitachi and Fujitsu, is now comparable in scope with that at IBM and AT&T's Bell Labs, long the leaders in chip technology."

244 See generally Tatsuno, *Japan's Technopolis Strategy*; Dataquest, *Building a Japanese Techno - State: MITI's Technopolis Program Underway* (San Jose, CA: Dataquest Incorporated, 1987).

massive public and private resources into R&D, particularly in three generic technology areas -- microelectronics, new materials, and biotechnology -- which are expected to provide the underpinning for Japan's "information-based" economy. Japan's recent technological gains in microelectronics are a reflection of this larger national effort.

To be sure, the U.S. Government also commits substantial resources to microelectronics R&D, and a superficial comparison of Japanese and U.S. Government actions in policy areas which affect microelectronics R&D reveals many apparent similarities between the two countries. Both the Japanese and the U.S. Governments conduct microelectronics R&D in their own laboratories, provide funding for industry-government joint R&D, and pursue a variety of other seemingly parallel policies to encourage microelectronics-related R&D. The source of Japan's advantage appears to lie in the differing strategic objectives pursued by the two governments and in the manner in which the respective governments' policies have been implemented in each subject area.

U.S. policies affecting microelectronics R&D have been implemented by a welter of federal and state agencies, as well as Congressional initiative, and have aimed at multiple objectives, including national defense, space exploration, regional development, and the stimulation of employment. The Office of Technology Assessment observed in 1985 that with respect to R&D in the information sector

[T]he environment is [often] affected by uncoordinated actions -- intended to serve other purposes -- taken by a variety of Federal entities including the Federal Reserve Board, the courts, regulatory bodies and a plethora of executive branch agencies including the Departments of Justice, Commerce, State and Defense, the National Security Council, and the Environmental Protection Agency.[245]

Conversely, two Japanese ministries, MITI and MPT, have been the driving force behind Japan's effort to create an "information-based society". Their objectives generally have been more narrowly focused on enhancing the commercial competitiveness of Japanese industry. While each of these rival ministries predominates in some policy areas which affect the information sector as illustrated in Table 3.14, they both exert a strong influence over the resources available to the information sector and the policies which will be employed. Their policies affecting microelectronics-related R&D have generally been more effective in fostering Japanese technological competitiveness than have corresponding U.S. policies.

---

245 Office of Technology Assessment, *Information Technology R&D* (Washington, D.C.: U.S. Government Printing Office, 1985), p. 28.

TABLE 3.14

GOVERNMENT ENTITIES HOLDING PRINCIPAL JURISDICTION
OVER POLICIES AFFECTING COMPETITIVENESS IN
MICROELECTRONICS

	Japan	United States
Information Industry Policy	MITI MPT	
Trade Policy	MITI	USTR Commerce USITC State
R&D Funding	MITI MPT	DOD DOE
Tax Policy	MOF MITI	Treasury OMB
Procurement	MPT	DOD
Antitrust	MITI JFTC	DOJ FTC
Telecommunications Policy	MPT MITI	FCC Federal Courts
Technology and Science Policy	MITI	NSF Commerce DOD NASA DOE
Regional High Tech Promotion	MITI MPT Prefectures	States Municipalities

Government-Funded Research and Development

Both the U.S. and Japanese Governments commit substantial funds each year to microelectronics R&D, but the manner in which these funds are allocated is fundamentally different. Table 3.15 shows that outside the Department of Defense, most U.S. Government aid to microelectronics is allocated to basic research. To the extent the U.S. Government funds R&D with respect to the application of this research to the development of generic technologies and ultimately, actual products, such support is limited to DOD programs designed to develop specific military products. In Japan, by contrast, MITI and NTT primarily direct their efforts toward advanced development -- the development of actual prototype production processes and products for the commercial market. (The products that were under development at the Musashino laboratory in 1979 are shown in Table 3.16.)

MITI places its research support on advanced development (which leads to the development of considerable proprietary innovations).... The U.S. government gives little support to the development of corporate proprietary interests. The major consideration is public domain development of basic and applied technology and defense.[246]

Perhaps not surprisingly, Japanese government programs have proven far more effective in enhancing the technological level of the national industry.

Direct Government Funding of Commercial R&D

In the United States, while the government funds basic R&D related to defense, space and energy concerns, direct government funding of microelectronics R&D for commercial purposes is nonexistent, and there is resistance to the concept both within and outside of the U.S. Government.[247]

---

246 D. Brandin, et. al., *JTECH Panel Report on Computer Science in Japan* (La Jolla, California: Science Applications International Corporation, 1984), pp. 1-2, 1-3; reproduced by National Technical Information Service, Document No. PB85-216760.

247 *Electronics* (March 31, 1986).

TABLE 3.15

U.S. GOVERNMENT FUNDING OF MICROELECTRONICS RESEARCH AND DEVELOPMENT IN FY 1987

AGENCY	ESTIMATED ANNUAL OUTLAYS ($Million)	TYPE OF RESEARCH	COMMENT
Department of Defense			
- Very High Speed Integrated Circuits	122	- Design and process techniques for military system ICs.	- Silicon based technology; emphasis on rapid insertion into specific military systems.
- Strategic Defense Initiative	60		
- Defense Advanced Research Projects Agency	16	- Long term research for military systems.	- Large-scale research efforts at U.S. universities. - Demonstration projects in GaAs.
- Manufacturing Technology	14		
- Microwave and Millimeter Wave ICs	10	- R&D to improve analog sensors.	- GaAs ICs for electronics warfare, communications, seekers for smart weapons.
- Defense Nuclear Agency	7		
- U.S. Air Force	60	- Basic research, emphasis on materials and device technology applicable to military systems.	
- U.S. Navy	28		
- U.S. Army	25		
Department of Energy			
- National Laboratories			
- Sandia	55	- Basic research, production of some specific ICs needed by military (at Sandia).	
- Lawrence Berkeley	4		
- Brookhaven	2		
- Other	2		
- Photovoltaic Research	15		
National Science Foundation	30	- Basic research at universities	- NSF responds to proposals from research community
National Bureau of Standards	4		
TOTAL	454		

Source: Adapted from Congressional Budget Office, *The Benefits and Risk of Federal Funding For Sematech* (September 1987), p. 60.

TABLE 3.16

COMMERCIAL SEMICONDUCTOR DEVICE PROTOTYPES UNDER DEVELOPMENT AT NTT'S MUSASHINO LABORATORY JANUARY 1979

(Devices Completed in Laboratory, Ready for Commercialization)

DEVICE	SPECIFICATION
NMOS Memory	64K ta 200us
NMOS Memory	128K ROM
NMOS Memory	256K, full wafer
CCD Memory	64K, 3.4 Mbit/s
Bipolar Memory	1K, ta 7.5 us
Bipolar Logic	200 gate, tpd
Microprocessor	8 bit slice ECL logic (1.5 kg)
CMOS Logic	16 bit multiplier

SOURCE: *Japan Telecommunications Review* (January 1979)

In Japan, by contrast, both MITI and MPT have well-established patterns of funding commercial microelectronics R&D, the most dramatic manifestation of which has been the funding of the large-scale joint R&D projects. In 1985, as a result of the perceived need to intensify government support of commercial R&D in the information sector, MITI and MPT jointly formed an institution dedicated to funding high-risk R&D by Japanese high technology firms for commercial purposes.[248]

In 1984, MITI unveiled a proposal to establish a new agency under its jurisdiction and funded, in part, by the Japan Development Bank to promote and finance high technology industries.[249] At about the same time, MPT, seeking a public agency to provide continuing support for NTT's joint R&D projects after NTT's "privatization," advanced a proposal to fund such an organization through the use of dividends paid on NTT shares still held by MPT. The Ministry of Finance ("MOF") proposed to fund the new entity by reviving the Industrial Investment Special Account, an unconsolidated account which had been used as an industrial promotional tool in the 1950s and 1960s.[250] Following a protracted and highly publicized wrangle between the three agencies over control of the new organization and the sources of its funds, the Japan Key Technology Center (*Kiban Gijutsu Kenkyu Sokushin Senta*) was born.[251]

The new center was established and funded pursuant to the *Basic Technology Research Facilitation Law* (June 15, 1985). The *Japan Times Weekly* reported on May 18, 1985 that the Center was

> to assure a low 7.1 percent interest rate on loans to companies successful in independently developing and marketing R&D projects. Companies whose R&D efforts fail won't have to pay back the interest. The center will also finance new joint companies for cooperative research and high-technology development schemes of public interest that could take long periods of time to start showing a profit. In addition, the promotion center will act as a go-between for private companies and the 16 laboratories managed by MITI and MPT in the hope of shoring up R&D cooperation between industries, academia, and the government.

---

248 *Nihon Keizai* (November 27, 1984) and (December 15, 1984).

249 *Nihon Keizai* (August 13, 1984); *Mainichi* (September 19, 1984).

250 MOF was extremely reluctant to leave NTT's shares under the "monopoly of a single ministry" (e.g., MPT). Johnson, *Telecom Wars*, p. 74.

251 *Nihon Keizai* (February 15, 1985); Johnson, *Telecom Wars*, pp. 72-77.

The Center is jointly administered by representatives of MITI, MPT, and MOF.[252] Its initial capitalization came from three sources:

- A 3 billion yen loan from the Japan Development Bank;

- 6 billion yen from the Industrial Investment Special Account (funded from dividends on NTT stock and funds raised from dividends paid on the government's shares of Japan Tobacco, Inc.);

- 4.5-5 billion yen from the private sector.

Thereafter, the bulk of the Center's funds were expected to be derived from dividends on NTT stock held by MOF.[253] For fiscal 1987, the Center's budget was 25 billion yen (17.3 billion for investments and 7.7 billion for conditional, interest-free loans).[254] The flow of funds for the Center is shown in Figure 3.11.

In May 1986, the Key Technology Center announced the formation of SORTEC (*Sorotekku*),[255] a ten-year industry-government project to develop synchotron orbital radiation (SOR) generation equipment, which will be needed to produce semiconductors of 16 megabit and above density. Thirteen Japanese companies are participating in SORTEC, virtually all of them participants in MITI's New Function Elements Project, which addressed related themes, such as ultra-fine processing.[256] As shown in

252 The Center was chaired by Yosihiro Inayama, the President of the Keidanren. The Chairman of the Board of Directors is a former MITI official; the Managing Director is an alumnus of MOF; and the Deputy Managing Director is a former MPT official. One of these officials commented when the center opened in October 1985, "Although this is a motley group drawn together from such diverse sources as MITI, MPT, and MOF, and the private sector, we must not fall into disarray but hang together as one and try to advance the cause of research in basic technology. We must forget who our parents are and just work together." Johnson, *Telecom Wars*, pp. 76-77.

253 *Kogyo Gijutsu* (August 1986). In addition, the Industrial Investment Special Account would provide 2 billion yen in working capital and 2 billion yen for research loans to private firms for high risk projects (no repayment if the projects fail). *Denshi Kogyo Geppo* (February 1985); *Nihon Keizai* (December 28, 1984); Johnson, *Telecom Wars*, pp. 72-77.

254 *Denshi Kogyo Geppo* (February 1987).

255 Hitachi, NEC, Fujitsu, Mitsubishi, Matsushita, Oki, Canon, Sanyo, Toshiba, Sharp, Sumitomo, Sony, and Nippon Kogaku.

256 *Nihon Keizai* (May 6, 1986).

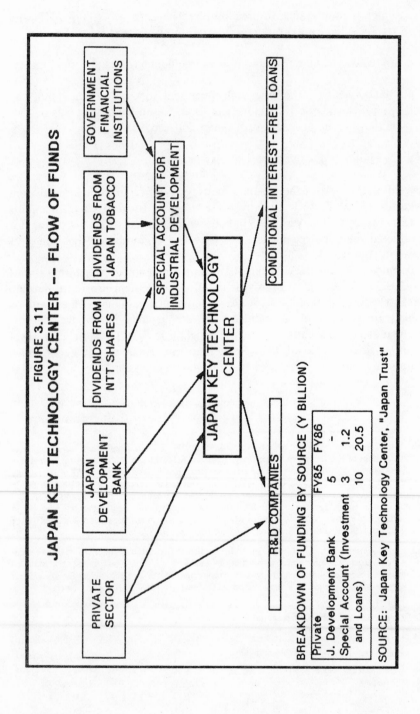

FIGURE 3.11

JAPAN KEY TECHNOLOGY CENTER -- FLOW OF FUNDS

BREAKDOWN OF FUNDING BY SOURCE (Y BILLION)

	FY85	FY86
Private	5	–
J. Development Bank	3	1.2
Special Account (Investment and Loans)	10	20.5

SOURCE: Japan Key Technology Center, "Japan Trust"

Figure 3.12, 70 percent of the project's estimated budget of 15 billion yen ($94 million at 160:1) will be provided by the Key Technology Center. The remaining 30 percent will be furnished by the private sector participants.[257] SORTEC is building a new synchotron facility in Tsukuba Science City which is expected to be completed in 1989.[258]

In the same month, another thirteen-firm consortium was formed to undertake a ten-year project to develop optoelectronic integrated circuits.[259] The consortium, "Optical Technology Research and Development," [260] will have a budget estimated at 10 billion yen; approximately 70 percent of its initial funding will be provided by the Basic Technology Research Promotion Center, the remainder by the participating companies.[261] As *Nihon Keizai* described the project on May 26, 1986.

> *The company will be located in Shimbashi, Tokyo, and a central research center is to be built. Each company will dispatch researchers to the central research center, where research will center on OEIC production methods. . . . Some 20 product development themes, such as super speed elements and photo emission development, are to be divided into thirteen groups and the participating companies will be assigned separate research themes. In other words, a branch of the Kogijutsu Kenkyu Kaihatsu company will be established in each company's research section and the participating companies are to exchange information.*

In contrast to these initiatives, the U.S. Government has never seriously considered establishing an institutional mechanism to fund microelectronics R&D for specific commercial purposes.[262] However in 1987, the government

---

257 *Nihon Keizai* commented on May 6, 1986 that "Nippon Telephone & Telegraph and Sumitomo Heavy Industries have already begun independent development of a smaller [synchotron] device and with the start of SORTEC, it would appear that the development of these devices will accelerate."

258 *Far Eastern Economic Review* (August 20, 1987).

259 The participants are Hitachi, Fujitsu, Oki, NEC, Mitsubishi, Matsushita, Sumitomo, Sharp, Sanyo, Fujikura Electric, Furakawa Electric, Toshiba and Nippon Sheet Glass.

260 *Kogijutsu Kenkyu Kaihatsu.*

261 The technological objective of this project was to increase the transmission speed of optoelectronic integrated circuits from the existing level of 1 G bit/s to 12 G bit/s. *Kogyo Gijutsu* (August 1986).

262 The U.S. semiconductor industry has formed the Semiconductor Research Cooperative ("SRC") to fund basic semiconductor R&D in U.S. universities, and the U.S. Government has begun to extend some funding to the SRC. However, the SRC is funded principally by the U.S. industry, not the government; its budget is dwarfed by that of the Japan Key Technology Center; and the SRC supports basic research, whereas the Key Technology Center was established in part to fund the development of specific high risk commercial technologies.

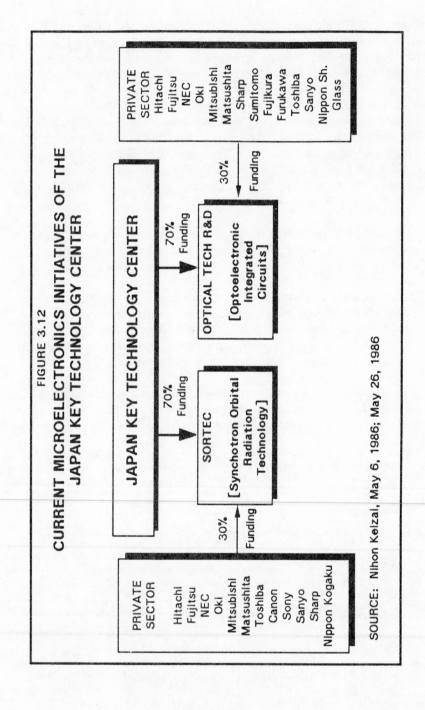

FIGURE 3.12

CURRENT MICROELECTRONICS INITIATIVES OF THE JAPAN KEY TECHNOLOGY CENTER

SOURCE: Nihon Keizai, May 6, 1986; May 26, 1986

began serious consideration of a proposal to fund commercial R&D in semiconductor manufacturing. The U.S. industry proposed that the government fund SEMATECH, the new semiconductor manufacturing R&D consortium, and by late 1987 legislation authorizing Defense Department funding of SEMATECH had passed both houses of Congress.

Large-Scale Joint R&D Projects

Japan's large-scale industry-government R&D projects, jointly funded by government and industry, have generally been recognized as a principal source of Japan's rapid gains in commercial microelectronics technology. The joint R&D projects have eliminated duplicative research efforts;[263] fostered a wider dissemination of technology throughout Japanese industry; shortened product development times;[264] and strengthened the microelectronics infrastructure. The MITI and NTT VLSI projects of the 1970s were the prototype for such efforts, and have been succeeded by a new generation of MITI and NTT projects, involving the development of ultra-fine processing technologies, optoelectronic devices, non-silicon based semiconductors, and high speed logic and memory devices -- all technologies with direct commercial application.[265]

In the United States, the only government-funded joint R&D efforts in microelectronics are those conducted under the auspices of the Department of Defense directed at developing technologies and products which are needed in specific military systems. These projects have undeniably had an impact in the commercial sphere,[266] but their effect has been substantially

---

263 An NEC executive commented in 1980 that without the MITI VLSI project (1975-79), his firm would have spent five times as much on the development of electron beam technology. *The Economist* (April 5, 1980).

264 A Japanese executive observed in 1983 that his firm's commercialization of the 64K DRAM would have been delayed by six months to one year in the absence of the joint VLSI projects sponsored by MITI and NTT. *New York Times* (May 18, 1983).

265 A Fujitsu executive commented in 1985 that the successful commercialization of an optoelectronic integrated circuit, a result of MITI's Optoelectronics Project, "could not have been done if one company had tried to do it alone." *Electronics* (March 17, 1986) and (November 18, 1985).

266 For example, in 1982, the Defense Advanced Research Projects Agency (DARPA) decided, on the basis of six years' research in GaAs technology, to fund a series of pilot lines to demonstrate the feasibility of using GaAs for semiconductors. Several defense electronics firms established a base of activities in GaAs grouped around the DARPA pilot lines, and a number of commercial ventures have been spun off from this work. Other U.S. companies have stepped up their GaAs R&D efforts as a result of the DARPA initiative. Office of Technology Assessment, *Microelectronics Research and Development*, p. 5.

less than that of the Japanese projects. Table 3.17 provides a comparison of the Japanese joint projects with the largest U.S. defense-related joint project, the Very High Speed Integrated Circuit Program ("VHSIC") -- a project which has proven highly successful in achieving its military objectives -- which illustrates the factors which underlie this disparity.

Commercial vs. Military Objectives

VHSIC was designed both to develop components which suited identifiable military needs and to ensure their rapid insertion into military systems,[267] an emphasis reflecting the fact that it has typically taken 10-15 years to adapt commercial semiconductor technologies to military applications.[268] The need for such a program had become critical because the pace of technological advance in the commercial market had become more rapid than in the military sphere. While it was envisioned from the outset that VHSIC would have commercial spinoff benefits, these were viewed as incidental to the fundamental military thrust of the program.[269]

267　The technological objective of VHSIC was to combine the density levels of commercial VLSI devices with characteristics of particular interest to the military, particularly speed of operation, but also radiation hardening, maintainability, low power consumption and built-in testability and fault tolerance. *Defense Electronics* (February 1985); Leslie Brueckner and Michael Borrus, *Assessing the Commercial Impact of the VHSIC (Very High Speed Integrated Circuit) Program* (University of California, Berkeley: BRIE Working Paper No. 5, December 1984), p. 9.

268　VHSIC is divided into three consecutive phases, with a fourth phase running concurrently during the entire length of the program. The ultimate goal is the development of production capability for submicron semiconductors, including lithographic and fabrication technologies, as well as design, architecture, software and testing technologies. Phase O (1980-81) was a planning phase to identify technologies needed for long-range VHSIC goals. Phase I was divided into parallel efforts: Phase Ia was directed at developing complete electronic brassboard systems within three years; Phase Ib was an initial effort to extend IC technology to submicron feature sizes and circuit complexities. Phase II was similarly subdivided: Phase IIa would provide subsystem demonstrations based on Phase Ia brassboards, and Phase IIb would continue the Phase Ia submicron development effort. Phase III, running the duration of the entire program, consisted of many smaller efforts designed to feed into the main program. National Materials Advisory Board, *An Assessment of the Impact of the Department of Defense Very High Speed Integrated Circuit Program* (Washington, D.C.: National Academy Press, 1982), p. 14.

269　The National Materials Advisory Board commented in 1982 that "The VHSIC program should not be misconstrued as the federal government's attempt to counter foreign commercial competition in integrated circuits or as a proposed remedy for the many serious problems that confront the nation's scientific and technical education establishment." Ibid.

TABLE 3.17

COMPARISON OF JAPANESE AND U.S. GOVERNMENT
SPONSORED JOINT R&D PROGRAMS IN MICROELECTRONICS

	JAPAN	UNITED STATES
Examples of Joint R&D Projects	Optoelectronics New Function Elements Supercomputers	VHSIC
Principal Objectives	Commercial Technologies	Military Technologies
All Participants Have Access to Results	Yes	No
Diffusion of Technology Within Participating Companies	Encouraged	Restricted
Diffusion of Technology Within Industry	Encouraged	Restricted
Commercial Sale of Device Technologies	Encouraged	Restricted
High Volume Commercial Products	Heavy emphasis	Emphasis on low-volume custom chips
Commercial Applicability of Technologies	Most have commercial applicability	Many have limited commercial value

In this respect, VHSIC stands in sharp contrast to the Japanese joint R&D projects, all of which are aimed at achieving specific commercial objectives.

This basic divergence in purpose between the Japanese and U.S. programs has in turn produced a series of divergences in the specific technological objectives pursued. The Japanese projects have placed heavy emphasis on the development of commercial device prototypes and process technologies that can be employed in the low-cost mass production of future generation semiconductor devices for the commercial market.[270] VHSIC, by contrast, emphasizes the development of customized devices which deliver a desired level of performance in specific military systems.[271] VHSIC research with respect to semiconductor design has emphasized fast turnaround time from design to production (to permit rapid insertion into military systems), an emphasis which tends to sacrifice chip performance, yields, and production cost -- all crucial factors in the commercial market.[272] Similarly, VHSIC research with respect to semiconductor production and device technology has emphasized one-of-a-kind solutions to specific military problems -- an approach which is wholly justifiable from a defense perspective but often inconsistent with commercial imperatives such as the need to increase volume and reduce production costs.[273]

Given the divergence in objectives and approach fostered by the Japanese and U.S. programs, the results produced by the respective projects are not particularly surprising. VHSIC is proving very successful in achieving its military objectives, and VHSIC microelectronics technologies are rapidly

---

270 For a summary of device prototypes under development in NTT's second stage VLSI project, see *Japan Telecommunications Review* (January 1979).

271 In Phase I of VHSIC, five of the six prime contractors pursued custom or semicustom development strategies with respect to components.

272 Brueckner and Borrus, *Assessing the Commercial Impact of the VHSIC Program*, pp. 48-49. One analyst comments that "As for those teams which take the custom design route, military requirements again skewed technological choices away from paths most relevant to commercial needs. . . . Efficient use of the chip's "real estate" may be less important for custom applications, where the number of custom designs available from a firm may be the crucial competitive variable. But in that case, VHSIC can have positive commercial effects only if computer-aided design tools developed by the military are characterized by open architectures that can be quickly and flexibly adapted to civilian uses." Jay Stowsky, *Beating Our Plowshares Into Double-Edged Swords* (University of California, Berkeley: BRIE Working Paper No. 17, April 1986), pp. 50-51.

273 As one U.S. merchant semiconductor executive commented, "the military is interested in ones and twos. We are interested in infinity." Brueckner and Borrus, *Assessing the Commercial Impact of the VHSIC Program*, pp. 49-50.

being inserted into a wide range of U.S. military systems.[274] VHSIC participation has also given rise to a certain number commercial "spinoff" benefits which are being exploited by U.S. firms, but which have not significantly affected the U.S.-Japanese competitive balance.[275]

The Japanese joint projects, by contrast, have had, and are having, a spectacular impact in the commercial market. To cite only one example, MITI's Optoelectronics Project (1979-86) has been credited with enabling Japan to achieve a world leadership position in optical semiconductor technology which will permit the production of devices with speeds hundreds of times faster than conventional silicon devices.[276] Over 300 patents were generated by the project, which has already resulted in the introduction of a number of commercial products:

- *Optoelectronic Integrated Circuits.* As a result of the project, Fujitsu has been able to commercialize an optoelectronic integrated circuit (OEIC) suitable for mass production, which combine single substrate multichannel devices that receive light signals from optical fibers, convert them to electrical signals, switch channels, and drive laser diodes. A Fujitsu executive has stated that the OEIC is the best single device to come out of the project.[277]
- *Laser-diode Driver Device.* As a result of the project, Hitachi was able to develop a device for a laser-diode driver that will form the basis of an experimental 1-Gb/s (e.g. very high speed) local area network.[278]

---

274 *Defense Electronics* commented in December 1984 that VHSIC "is dramatically improving the technology base for high performance integrated circuits to meet future defense requirements, and will soon be putting some of the most advanced IC technology available into the hands of the planners and designers of military electronics systems."

275 Honeywell, for example, has formed two venture business units to generate commercial products derived from Phase I technologies. One of these units has already generated an "outstanding" product, a DMOS gate array with 20,000 equivalent gates for use in supercomputers. *Electronics* (December 16, 1985), pp. 36-37. For an extensive survey of the commercial benefits being derived by VHSIC participants, see *Aviation Week and Space Technology* (July 30, 1984).

276 *Electronics* (March 17, 1986), p. 50; *Fortune* (October 13, 1986), p. 37.

277 *Electronics* (March 17, 1986) and (November 18, 1985); *Japan Economic Journal* (November 30, 1985). In the spring of 1986, Hitachi, another project participant, announced the development of an indium-gallium-arsenide-phosphide OEIC which incorporates different signal processing functions (semiconductor lasers and an optical switch) on a single chip. *Japan Economic Journal* (March 1, 1986).

278 *Electronics* (March 17, 1986).

- *Semiconductor Lasers.* The project enabled Japanese companies to develop visible light semiconductor lasers to replace the helium-neon model which requires a bulky glass envelope and high power supply.

Structure

From a purely organizational standpoint, both the Japanese and U.S. joint R&D programs have been widely praised, but their structure is substantially different, reflecting their fundamentally differing objectives.[279]   In the Japanese industry-government projects, MITI establishes "joint laboratories" with the leading Japanese companies, funded by a combination of government and company contributions.   The purpose of the joint laboratories is to explore generic technologies which are expected to be decisive in the next commercial product generation. Researchers from the participating companies work together in the joint laboratories and then return to their companies with the task of transferring the technologies to their companies for rapid commercialization.[280] This structure is intended to facilitate the diffusion of all the project results to all participating companies. The same leading Japanese firms participate in each successive generation of joint R&D projects.

By contrast, VHSIC is organized to achieve a completely different objective -- the development of components suited to the peculiar needs of

---

279 Two analysts commented in 1984 that "The current success of the VHSIC program indicates that its influence will reach beyond any immediate technological outcomes. The program continues to be hailed as an organizational triumph and will, in all likelihood, become the model for sustained government industry collaborative efforts in the future."   Brueckner and Borrus, *Assessing the Commercial Impact of the VHSIC Program*, p. 19. *Aviation Week and Space Technology* observed on July 30, 1984 that "there is general agreement, including sometimes vocal Pentagon critics in Congress, that the program has been well managed by a small central program office, headed by E.D. Maynard, Jr. . . . "

280 A Stanford scientist who visited and studied the Optoelectronics Joint Laboratory, commented in 1985 that "[t]he organization . . . goes from the most basic aspect, the growth of "ideal" large single crystals, to such advanced topics as Maskless Ion Beam Doping, and Compound Semiconductor Device Fabrication. . . . [emphasis is placed] on the generic problems of the technology with detailed development of systems to be manufactured being left up to the individual companies." Wieder, *JTECH Panel Report on Opto-& Microelectronics*, pp. 2-1 - 2-11.

specialized military systems. VHSIC is organized on a vertical "team" basis, with most major objectives pursued by a prime contractor (usually a systems company) working with a team of semiconductor company subcontractors to design components that meet the needs of the particular military system.[281] Semiconductor companies participating on one VHSIC team do not necessarily receive the results of the work of other teams and are, in some cases, not even the same companies from one phase of VHSIC to the next. Thus, while the net effect of the Japanese joint R&D programs is often the simultaneous commercialization of a new generic technology by five or more leading Japanese companies, it would be impossible for VHSIC to have such an impact on the U.S. industry even if commercial technologies were being pursued.

Controls on Technology

The Japanese joint R&D programs are designed to accelerate the diffusion of newly-developed technologies throughout national industries. A principle purpose of the joint laboratories is to assemble researchers from a number of companies in one project so that the results can be disseminated to (and within) all of their companies,[282] and "there appears to be a more robust exchange of information among the participants in Japan than there was in the United States".[283] NTT has also institutionalized the transfer of technology developed in its joint projects to second-rank Japanese firms which do not participate in the original projects.[284] Thus, while foreign access to the results of the joint projects is permitted only on a restricted basis, the results of the projects are rapidly diffused throughout Japanese industry.[285]

---

281 This structure was designed to introduce an element of competition (at the competitive bidding stage) but also fostered cooperation and synergy (at the team level).

282 For example, Dr. Hisao Hiyakawa, who heads MITI's Josephson Junction program (part of the Supercomputer Project), said that "he was having each of the MITI-supported companies send one or more engineers to [MITI labs] for an extended assignment to work on refractory technology. This assignment was ... necessary in order to develop more collaboration between the companies.... They tend to act too much like competitors." Wieder, *JETCH Panel Report on Opto-& Microelectronics*, p. 11-15.

283 Ibid., p. 11-29.

284 *Nikkei Sangyo* (July 9, 1981).

285 The Japanese government owns title to any patents developed during MITI-sponsored research, and can license (or refuse to license) them at its discretion. *Japan Economic Journal* (August 6, 1985). Wieder, *JTECH Panel Report on Opto-& Microelectronics*, p. 11-15.

By contrast, for national security reasons, VHSIC technologies are subject to elaborate government controls which will prevent many of them from being disseminated to other companies or even reaching the market at all.[286] To the current Administration, VHSIC "represents the preeminent technology to be controlled to prevent foreign transfer," [287] and this concern takes precedence over any potential for exploiting VHSIC technologies commercially.[288] The Department of Defense has stated that

> *[W]hile VHSIC is being developed and as long as the major needs and users of VHSIC lie in the military arena, the decision has been made at the Secretary of Defense level to protect the military advantages offered by the VHSIC technology and its application through adequate security measures.*[289]

In reviewing Phase I of VHSIC, *Electronics* commented on December 16, 1985 that

---

286 VHSIC technologies face several types of restrictions. The International Traffic in Arms Regulations (ITAR) require the issuance of a license by the Office of Munitions Control in DOD prior to the transfer of weapons-related hardware to all non-U.S. destinations, either via direct export or through disclosure to foreign nationals. In effect, ITAR restrictions, applied to semiconductor devices and device technology, operate to prevent their commercial introduction into international competition. ITAR controls are likely to be placed on all VHSIC dual use technology (e.g. usable for both commercial and military applications), devices designed for use in military systems, and design and manufacturing technology for advanced semiconductor production. In addition, the Export Administration Regulations (EAR) established a regulatory scheme designed to prevent the transmission of technology to the Eastern Bloc. The EAR will probably be applied to VHSIC in a manner which covers all technologies which are not already restricted pursuant to ITAR. Brueckner and Borrus, *Assessing the Commercial Impact of the VHSIC Program*, pp. 59-60.

287 M. Y. Yoshino and G.R. Fong, *Can the United States Conduct an Industrial Policy?* (Unpublished Monograph, Harvard Business School, February 1983), p. 9.

288 See generally C.W. Weinberger, *The Technology Security Program* (Washington, D.C.: Report to the 99th Congress, Second Session, 1986), pp. 25-26. A Pentagon committee was reported in 1985 to be studying the possibility of approving sale of some VHSIC semiconductors to nonmilitary customers because such sales would permit a reduction in unit costs. The Director of the VHSIC program office commented on the proposal for commercial sales, however, that "I don't think we perceive that as a necessary thing." *Electronics* (November 4, 1985), p. 18.

289 E.D. Maynard, Director VHSIC/ED, Office of the Undersecretary of Defense, Memorandum for VHSIC Contractors (February 28, 1984), cited in Brueckner and Borrus, *Assessing the Commercial Impact of the VHSIC Program*, pp. 72-73. One analyst reports that "Current Pentagon restrictions are so stringent . . . that VHSIC contractors are forbidden even to publish front-forward photographs of their chips. One story has it that, when the General Accounting Office insisted on such photos for an unclassified report on the program, VHSIC officials were directed to send, instead, an aerial photograph of a parking lot, reduced in size until the cars resembled a cluster of microcircuitry." Stowsky, *Double-Edged Swords*, p. 52.

Though there undoubtedly is a commercial market for Phase I chips, it is very unlikely that DOD will ever let these chips be sold to other than its suppliers [e.g., the prime contractors].

These controls substantially retard the ability of even directly participating firms to derive commercial advantage from VHSIC R&D.[290] Many companies fear that evidence of technology transfer within their company structure will subject their commercial products to DOD export controls under the ITAR and EAR.[291] As a result, most firms participating in VHSIC conduct their VHSIC and commercial VLSI development at separate corporate divisions.[292]

R&D in Government Laboratories

Both the U.S. and Japanese Governments conduct a substantial amount of microelectronics-related research and development in government laboratories. However, Japanese R&D is more directly related to commercial objectives, is better coordinated with commercial efforts, and appears to confer substantially greater commercial advantages on the Japanese industry than the R&D conducted in U.S. government laboratories.[293]

MITI, through its Agency for Industrial Science and Technology, operates nine laboratories at Tsukuba Science City, including the famous Electrotechnical Laboratory (ETL), and a substantial proportion of their activity is devoted to microelectronics R&D with commercial applications.[294]

---

290 *Defense Electronics* commented in December 1984 that "details about VHSIC circuits are probably the most closely held of any program that *Defense Electronics* regularly tracks, causing us to wonder if part of that secrecy is because DOD may have shot itself in the foot with VHSIC relative to commercial counterpart programs that accelerate the state of technology in dense circuitry."

291 One semiconductor executive from a company participating in VHSIC expressed concern in 1984 that his company would actually be disadvantaged because of its VHSIC role. He feared that VHSIC controls would prevent his firm from applying manufacturing techniques learned in VHSIC to commercial production. *Aviation Week and Space Technology* (July 30, 1984), p. 50.

292 Brueckner and Borrus, *Assessing the Commercial Impact of the VHSIC Program*, p. 73.

293 The Japanese national laboratories place a considerable emphasis on manufacturing as well as developing new technologies. MITI's Josephson Junction program, for example, from the beginning "has always been concerned with the manufacturability of Josephson circuits." Wieder, *JTECH Panel Report on Opto-& Microelectronics*, p. 11-16.

294 *Nihon Keizai* (August 2, 1984). The ETL in particular is contributing substantially to the development of leading-edge semiconductor technology for Japanese industry. It is

In 1986, for example, the ETL developed a prototype compact synchotron (which can be used in manufacturing semiconductors with submicron circuit widths) in conjunction with Mitsubishi, Toshiba, Sumitomo Electric and Shimadzu.[295] The ETL participates in and makes substantial contributions to the industry-government joint R&D projects in microelectronics.[296] An NEC executive commented in 1982 that

> *[T]his is not to flatter MITI officials, but having the group of technologists from the Electrotechnical Laboratory participating and furnishing outstanding and impartial leadership was tremendously effective [in the VLSI Project].*[297]

NTT possesses the foremost electronics research facilities in Japan and has been called both the "Bell Labs of Japan" and the "NASA of Japan." NTT spends an estimated $350 million per year on R&D, much of it in microelectronics and most of it undertaken jointly with Japan's leading electronics enterprises for the development of commercial device prototypes and process technologies for commercial manufacturing.[298] A Stanford University scientist who visited NTT's Atsugi facility in September 1983 commented that

> *I was impressed with the magnitude and focus of the electronics effort and the quality of the scientists and engineers at NTT. The only United States analogy I can think of is one that would have all the talent at Bell Laboratories sharply focused for the last twenty years into problems*

---

currently developing X-ray lithography techniques featuring a synchotron-storage ring system with a very intense beam. *Japan Economic Journal* (July 5, 1986). In 1984, it was able to create a gallium arsenide crystal through a technique controlling the formation of each atomic layer. The following year, it created a single crystal of silicon through the same technique. This method is expected to be instrumental in developing optoelectronic semiconductors and superlattice devices. *Japan Economic Journal* (June 15, 1985).

295 *Far Eastern Economic Review* (August 20, 1987).

296 Wieder, *JTECH Panel Report on Opto-& Microelectronics*, p. 2-1 - 2-11.

297 Atsuyoshi Ouchi in *Tsusan Janaru* (February 1982).

298 *Toki No Keizai* (January 1982); *Nihon Keizai* (May 12, 1982). *Nihon Keizai* observed on May 12, 1982 that "NTT is carrying out [development of advanced technology] jointly with domestic electronics manufacturers and influential research organs, and entrusting them with manufacture. By doing so, it is producing immeasurable benefits for the fostering of advanced industries in the form of eventually taking over the moving of advanced technology and expenses for research and development."

directly dealing with IC, opto-communication, and closely related areas.[299]

The NTT laboratories have been responsible for a number of major recent advances in semiconductor technology which will substantially benefit the Japanese industry.[300] NTT is currently making a significant commitment to synchotron R&D, and is currently building two synchotrons at its microelectronics laboratory at Atsugi.[301] A West German scientist commented in 1986 that

> *As far as I am concerned, the best and largest [microelectronics] research institute outside of the semiconductor industry is the Electro-Communication laboratory built by the Japanese telephone company NTT in Atsugi, just outside of Tokyo. Seven hundred people are already working there, and the next stage of construction is already under way. Once this stage is completed, one thousand people will be working there.*[302]

In the United States, a substantial proportion of total microelectronics-related R&D performed in government laboratories takes place in facilities operated by the Department of Defense and the Department of Energy, and is directed toward specific military applications.[303] Most of this research

---

299 Wieder, *JTECH Panel Report on Opto-& Microelectronics*, p. 2-11.

300 The 4-megabit DRAM will require circuits of less than one micron in diameter (0.7 microns). NTT has developed a high-speed electron beam device capable of etching circuits of 0.5 micron diameter, and has succeeded in 0.2 micron pattern transfer. *Jihyo* (November, 1985.) In the fall of 1984, NTT succeeded in the trial manufacture of a memory device with a speed of 0.85 nanosecond, the fastest speed yet attained in a silicon-based device. Devices made with gallium arsenide (GaAs) rather than silicon can attain much higher circuit speeds. NTT laboratories have been active in GaAs development, and NTT pioneered in the trial manufacture of a GaAs 16K memory device. *Nihon Keizai* (August 30, 1984); *Jihyo* (November 1985).

301 NTT is building a standard synchrotron ring in conjunction with Toshiba, and a synchotron using superconducting magnets in conjunction with Hitachi. *Far Eastern Economic Review* (August 20, 1987).

302 Dr. Anton Heuberger, Fraunhofer Institute for Microstructure Technology, in *Bild der Wissenschaft* (October 1986).

303 The Army, NASA, the Navy and the Air Force are all pursuing R&D into microelectronics technologies related to specific systems in use in their departments. The Navy's Office of Naval Research (ONR), for example, has been conducting R&D on ultra-submicron electronics, emphasizing non-silicon based device technology such as GaAs, development of gigabit logic capabilities, three-dimensional circuits, and optoelectronics. The Army is developing specific critical components needed in individual systems, such as signal processing and memory modules for electronic warfare, communications fire control, and data links. The Defense Advanced Research Agency

takes place under tight security controls and is unlikely to have a significant effect in the commercial market -- in fact, it is often specifically aimed at technologies, such as radiation-hardened ICs, which are of no interest to commercial producers and thus, cannot be supplied by them.[304]

At the same time, as shown in Table 3.18, a number of the U.S. National Laboratories conduct basic and defense-related microelectronics R&D which is of major potential value to U.S. microelectronics producers. In other industrial sectors, such as nuclear energy, the Labs have been given a mission and have played a major role in enhancing industrial development of a domestic commercial industry. However, for a variety of reasons, the National Labs and the U.S. semiconductor industry have not worked together to fully exploit the potential resource which the Labs represent for enhancing U.S. industry competitiveness.[305]   Oak Ridge National Laboratory commented in 1987 that

> *existing national laboratory/industry interactions in semiconductor processing lack several things, such as focus on industry needs, commitment commensurate with the magnitude of the problems, and appropriate involvement of the semiconductor industry.*[306]

A number of initiatives are under way to restructure the relationship between the industry and the National Labs. The *Technology Transfer Act of 1986* authorized the National Labs to enter into specific R&D agreements with private companies and to grant the patent to any invention made by a federal employee to a collaborating private party --

---

(DARPA) is pursuing an ambitious program designed to develop a CAD methodology for VLSI design, which also involves extensive R&D in the materials sciences. National Materials Advisory Board, *Assessment of VHSIC*, pp. 24-26.

304 The Department of Energy funds the Sandia National Laboratories, primarily to produce ICs needed by the military which commercial firms do not wish to produce. *Electronics Week* (February 4, 1985).

305 A panel headed by David Packard of Hewlett-Packard reviewed the work of the federal research laboratories in 1983 and concluded that "they perceived industry as an awkward partner with a different value system. . . . . The current federal procurement system discourages agencies and [government] laboratories from contracting with universities and industry. *"Report of the White House Science Counsel Federal Laboratory Review Panel* (Washington, D.C.: Office of Science and Technology Policy, May 20, 1983).

306 Manufacturing Studies Board and National Materials Advisory Board, Commission on Engineering and Technical Systems, National Research Council, *The Semiconductor Industry and the National Laboratories: Part of a National Strategy* (Washington, D.C.: National Academy Press, 1987), p.34.

TABLE 3.18

MICROELECTRONICS RESEARCH & DEVELOPMENT AT U.S. NATIONAL LABORATORIES
(Capabilities And Projects Proposed Or Under Way)

Los Alamos National Laboratory

* Ultra-high speed electrical measurements
* Theoretical modeling of semiconductor superlattices
* Theoretical modeling of impurities in semiconductors
* Non-steady-state transport measurements and modeling
* Finite elements modeling of thermo-mechanical coupling effects in diffusion
* Single event upset transient measurements
* Ion beam analysis of semiconductors
* Laser processing of semiconductor materials
* Beam-induced crystallization
* Advanced ceramics development

Sandia National Laboratories

* Silicon IC processing
* IC design
* Testing and assembly
* IC production operations
* Robotics and automation
* Engineering modeling
* Processing science and modeling
* Diagnostics and materials
* Compound semiconductor research

Brookhaven National Laboratory

* Synchotron X-ray lithography
* Superconducting storage rings

Oak Ridge National Laboratory

* Ion implantation and ion beam processing
* Ion beam deposition
* Pulsed laser annealing
* Laser photochemical vapor deposition
* Neutron transmutation doping of silicon
* High efficiency solar cell fabrication
* Supersaturated substitutional alloys of silicon and germanium
* Active optical device fabrication
* Microwave plasma processing
* Electronic packaging research (ceramics)
* Robotics and intelligent machines

Ames Laboratory

* Amorphous semiconductors
* Growth kinetics and surface diffusion
* Theoretical models of defect states

Source: National Research Council, *The Semiconductor Industry and the National Labs: Part of a National Strategy* (Washington, D.C.: National Academy Press, 1987); *DOE National Laboratories and the Semiconductor Industry: Continuing the Joint Planning* (Albuquerque, N.M.: Sandia National Laboratories, May 26-29, 1987).

measures which are expected to stimulate technology transfer to industry.[307] The Reagan Administration has implemented measures to encourage the Labs to transfer R&D results to the private sector.[308] In 1986 and 1987, representatives of a number of U.S. government laboratories met with U.S. semiconductor industry representatives in workshops held by the National Academy of Sciences to discuss the possible joint development efforts by the National Labs and industry, and a number of Labs have advanced specific proposals for supporting commercial microelectronics R&D.[309] However, these initiatives, while significant, are still in their incipient stages, and at present, while the need is increasingly recognized, few institutional mechanisms exist for coordinating the developmental efforts of the National Labs with those of the U.S. microelectronics industry.

Government Funding of University Research

The U.S. has a superb system of research universities, a number of which have established special microelectronics-related research centers.[310] Most observers regard the overall quality of U.S.-based university R&D to be far superior to that of Japan.[311] Both the federal and state governments, recognizing the universities as a national asset, have provided a substantial amount of funding for basic microelectronics R&D.[312] A substantial

---

307 In order to facilitate transfer of technology, the Act made the Federal Laboratory Consortium (a liason coalition of approximately 300 federal laboratories and 11 agencies) a permanent body within the National Bureau of Standards.

308 Executive Order 12591 of April 10, 1987, 52 F.R. 13414.

309 National Research Council, *The Semiconductor Industry and the National Laboratories*; National Research Council, Commission on Engineering on Technical Systems, Manufacturing Studies Board, and National Materials Advisory Board, *DOE National Laboratories and the Semiconductor Industry: Continuing the Joint Planning* (Workshop Materials, Sandia National Laboratory, May 26-29, 1987).

310 These include Cornell's National Research and Resource Facility for Submicron Structures; Stanford's Center for Integrated Systems (CIS); the University of California's Center for Robotic Systems in Microelectronics (Santa Barbara); and the University of Minnesota's Microelectronic and Information Sciences Center.

311 Okimoto, "Regime Characteristics of Japanese Industrial Policy," p. 60.

312 The National Science Foundation provides a substantial amount of funding for microelectronics R&D at U.S. universities. For example, the NSF has budgeted $14 million to the University of California at Santa Barbara's Center for Robotic Systems in Microelectronics, which is concentrating on automated semiconductor manufacturing techniques.   (Office of Technology Assessment, *Microelectronics Research and Development*, p. 22). An example of an ambitious state program is North Carolina's establishment of the Microelectronics Center of North Carolina (MCNC), an organization designed to link the research activities of North Carolina's Universities with

proportion of federal spending has involved DOD funding of defense-related projects in U.S. universities, and while these programs are not without some value to the U.S. industry, their significance is diminishing. While a decade ago many of these programs involved silicon-based research of substantial interest to the commercial industry, in recent years DOD funding has concentrated on non-silicon technologies aimed at niche applications for specific military purposes.

A major element of the U.S. semiconductor industry's strategic response to the Japanese challenge has been the funding and coordinating of basic microelectronics R&D in U.S. universities through the industry's research consortium, the Semiconductor Research Corporation (SRC), which currently channels approximately $20 million annually in industry funds into the universities.[313] The SRC was formed, in part, as a response to the U.S. Government's shift in funding of university-based R&D from an emphasis on silicon to non-silicon based technologies. By funding silicon-based R&D in the universities, the SRC is helping to ensure that sufficient numbers of students are graduated with skills which can be utilized by U.S. industry. In 1986, three agencies of the federal government became participants in the SRC and contributed $1.2 million for research, and in 1987, that funding was increased to $10 million over the next three years.[314]

The U.S. commitment to basic microelectronics R&D in the universities is important for two fundamental reasons. First, these programs are necessary to educate and train the young people who will provide the basis for U.S. microelectronics capability in the future. The U.S. semiconductor industry has expressed concern for a number of years over the shortage of trained electrical engineers graduating from U.S. universities, a shortage which such programs are designed to address. Second, basic scientific and technological

---

industry efforts. At the beginning of 1985, the State had committed over $75 million to the establishment and operation of MCNC.   Office of Technology Assessment, *Information Technology R&D*, pp. 184-89.

313 The SRC was created in 1982 by 11 semiconductor firms, and has grown to 35, including one member which is an association of 33 manufacturers of SME and materials. Its principal objectives are to undertake basic research and to increase the number of trained graduates coming from U.S. universities. It has dedicated an increasing proportion of its funding to R&D in the manufacturing sciences. Under the SEMATECH proposal, the SRC would coordinate manufacturing R&D efforts in support of SEMATECH by universities, national laboratories, and other public research institutions. Testimony of Larry W. Sumney before the Subcommittee on Commerce, Consumer Protection and Competitiveness of the House Energy and Commerce Committee, June 9, 1987.

314 These agencies (Department of Defense, National Security Agency, National Science Foundation) participate in the SRC through a Memorandum of Understanding with the National Science Foundation. The NSF authorized an increase in this funding to $2.4 million in FY 1987 and in the subsequent two fiscal years with a three-year limit of $10 million.

questions must be pursued to enable the U.S. microelectronics industry to remain competitive technologically over the long run -- the United States cannot rely on an uncertain ability to secure such knowledge from other countries.[315]

However, basic R&D in the universities, while important, does not by itself translate into immediate international competitive advantage for U.S. microelectronics firms. The results of such research generally enter the public domain and are available to anybody -- including foreign firms interested in commercializing it.[316] Any suggestion that this practice should be modified is inherently controversial, since it raises basic questions about the appropriate role of a university.[317]
Because the knowledge generated by the U.S. university R&D programs diffuses rapidly to other countries, U.S. investment in university R&D cannot by itself reverse the eroding U.S. technological edge.

Research and Development Tax Policy

While both the United States and Japan have adopted tax policies designed to stimulate research and development, Japanese tax incentives have been more precisely directed at specific sectors, such as microelectronics, which are deemed vital to the national interest. The U.S. Congress has generally granted across-the-board R&D tax incentives which

315 For example, while Japan conducts a substantial amount of basic microelectronics-related R&D in its universities, U.S. access to Japanese universities and research institutes has been restricted (although the Japanese government has given recent assurances of liberalization). The problem has been exacerbated, to be sure, by the U.S. lack of Japanese language skills and inadequate U.S. programs to translate and disseminate Japanese technical papers -- with the Japanese language operating as a barrier to outflow of technical information. Conversely, most Japanese students, scientists and engineers speak sufficient English that they can freely obtain U.S. technology which is in the public domain.

316 A Keidanren official commented in 1986 that "In the American university system, Japanese enterprises are paying out some 30 billion yen, none of which is earmarked for any specific project.... If some success is achieved, the enterprises that were the donors over that period may be given some priority privileges, but otherwise the project becomes a scholarship paper for public consumption. If there is no patent involved, the contents of the paper become public property and merely contribute to overall "know-how." Isamu Yamashita in *Kogyo Gijutsu* (January 1986).

317 The Office of Technology Assessment noted in 1985 with respect to Stanford's Center for Integrated Systems that there was "concern that there will be pressures to keep research secret. Such pressures are likely to be strongly resisted; the number of seminars, publications, and open meetings have demonstrated the University's and the Center's intent to maintain openess." Office of Technology Assessment, *Information Technology R&D*, p. 183.

apply to all industrial sectors, seeking to "avoid the appearance of playing favorites because of its commitment to the principles of equity and impartiality." [318] In Japan, the dispensation of tax incentives is structured to permit MITI to allocate those incentives to designated industries as it sees fit, a practice which tends to favor the high technology industries.[319]

In 1981, the U.S. Congress enacted the Research and Development Tax Credit, which originally allowed companies to claim 25 percent tax credits for qualified R&D expenditures in a given year which exceed their average expenditures for the prior 3-year period. The R&D tax credit, a temporary measure, was extended for three years in 1986, but the credit was reduced to 20 percent. Although it applies to all industries, the R&D tax credit has been particularly beneficial to the semiconductor industry, which maintains an extraordinarily high level of R&D expenditures.

Japan has "at least 19 different tax incentive systems to encourage technological innovation." [320] It has an R&D tax credit very similar to that of the United States.[321] The Government is currently seeking to expand the credit from 20 percent to 30 percent of the increase of R&D expenditures over a specified level.[322] In addition, it has established the Key Technologies Tax Credit, equal to seven percent of the acquisition 'cost of assets used in specified technologies or 20 percent of the corporate income tax, whichever is greater, with a one-year carryforward of any leftover amount.[323] The Key Technologies Tax Credit, effective between 1985 and 1988, is not available for R&D generally, but rather the development of expressly specified technologies which the government seeks to foster, including many types of semiconductor device, materials, and process technologies, and computer technology. Examples of specified technologies are given in Table 3.19. The Key Technologies Tax Credit credit has no U.S. counterpart.

---

318 Okimoto, "Regime Characteristics of Japanese Industrial Policy," p. 71.

319 Each year, the Ministry of Finance and MITI negotiate an aggregate ceiling for special tax measures. MITI is then free to grant tax incentives to industries of its choice, within the limits of that aggregate ceiling. Ibid., p. 71.

320 Stern, "Japan's R&D Tax Credit System," p. 20.

321 Japan's R&D credit is equal to the lower of (a) 20 percent of the excess of R&D and testing expenses for a given year over the largest amount of such expenses incurred in any preceding tax year since 1967; or (b) ten percent of the corporate income tax. Ibid., p. 21.

322 The new R&D credit will be included in the Government's special tax measure bill to be submitted to the Diet in mid 1987. *Japan Economic Journal* (June 27, 1987).

323 Stern, "Japan's R&D Tax Credit System," p. 21.

Antitrust Policy and Research and Development

The U.S. antitrust laws have long served as a deterrent to collaborative research and development efforts by U.S. firms.[324] In the 1980s, changes in U.S. antitrust law and antitrust policy have substantially diminished the antitrust exposure of firms engaging in joint R&D, but U.S. firms still confront greater antitrust inhibitions than their Japanese rivals. Japan's large-scale joint R&D projects generally involve the largest producers in a highly oligopolistic industry -- collaboration which would be severely inhibited, and in some cases blocked altogether, if Japan had an antitrust regime comparable to that of the United States.

Japan's Antimonopoly Law was adopted during the U.S. occupation at the end of World War II and was modeled on the U.S. antitrust laws. Since its enactment, however, numerous exceptions and exemptions to its application have been enacted, and MITI has engaged in a series of confrontations with JFTC designed to deter interference by that agency in the industrial sectors whose promotion was sought by MITI. One observer concluded that the basic intent of the Antimonopoly Law

is respected only as long as it does not stand in the way of Japan's industrial policy, especially the activities of the largest firms that are viewed by the LDP, MITI, the large firms themselves, and by many Japanese as being essential in increasing the productivity and international competitive abilities of Japanese industries. MITI's joint research projects, along with NTT's family-oriented research programs, are overt evidence that the Antimonopoly Law occupies such a position in Japan.[325]

The JFTC has never challenged any of the joint microelectronics projects conducted by MITI and NTT in the 1970s and 1980s. The special promotional laws governing microelectronics and related sectors authorized MITI to secure formal exemptions from the Antimonopoly Law after consultation with the JFTC, but these were

---

324 U.S. antitrust policy also led to the breakup of the AT&T System in a manner which did not give regard to the impact on U.S. international competitiveness. The manner in which the divestiture was implemented has worked to the disadvantage of U.S. firms relative to their foreign competitors.

325 Kozo Yamamura, "Joint Research and Antitrust: Japanese vs. American Strategies", in *Japan's High Technology Industries*, p. 198.

TABLE 3.19

EXAMPLES OF TECHNOLOGIES ELIGIBLE FOR JAPAN'S KEY
TECHNOLOGY TAX CREDIT, 1985-88

- Semiconductor clean rooms in which particles 0.5 microns in diameter
  or larger are kept to below 100 particles per 28, 316. 8 cubic meters.

- Computer controlled automatic ion implantation devices capable of
  acceleration energies of 1 million eV or more with currents of 12mA
  or more, that can handle up to 9 wafers.

- Measurement systems in which a dedicated computer and measuring
  device automatically tests

  - logic integrated circuits at speeds of 50MHz or greater, or

  - memory integrated circuits at speeds of 40 MHz or greater.

- Computers with at least 32 MB memory, capable of operating a
  program and computing at speeds of at least 400M FLOPS, that can
  be equipped with additional memory and with dedicated input and
  output devices such as keyboards, digitizers, tablets, OCRS, audio
  sources, display terminals, reading and printing devices.

Source: *Kampo* (March 30, 1985), cited in J.P. Stern, "Japan's R&D Tax
Credit System", *Journal of the American Chamber of Commerce in
Japan* (April 1987).

never invoked in the semiconductor industry. The JFTC has apparently never scrutinized joint activities in semiconductors because of the close involvement of MITI and NTT. The result is that these projects enjoy "de facto total exemption from antitrust concerns":

> *In pursuing its declared goal of strengthening Japan's high technology capabilities, MITI not only has shown little concern for the substantial antitrust concerns that are... raised by joint research projects and especially by the way they are carried out, but has also chosen to take an active and leading role in advocating the national necessity to engage in the joint research projects.*[326]

U.S. antitrust law and doctrine has always recognized that joint interfirm activity may generate economic advantages, particularly increased efficiency. However, because such activities may have anticompetitive effects, they are always subject to antitrust scrutiny; if a company has engaged in proscribed conduct, it may be held liable for treble damages. Some combinations are "illegal per se" -- that is, illegal by definition regardless of any procompetitive intent or effects.[327] Other types of cooperative arrangements are subject to scrutiny under the "Rule of Reason" -- in effect, a case-by-case factual determination of whether the arrangement significantly reduces competition, what the justification is, and whether that purpose could be achieved in a less anticompetitive way.

The constraints which these rules placed on U.S. industrial innovation led to the enactment of the *National Cooperative Research Act of 1984*, which reduced some of the antitrust inhibitions on joint R&D. The *Cooperative Research Act* provides that certain types of joint research specified in the Act are subject to scrutiny solely under the rule of reason standard -- that is, they cannot be deemed illegal per se. Joint R&D which falls outside the scope of the *Cooperative Research Act*'s coverage is subject to normal antitrust scrutiny. These changes facilitated the formation of the Microelectronics and Computer Technology Corporation (MCC), an R&D joint venture owned by approximately 20 U.S. computer and semiconductor firms to explore the technologies which would be needed in the next generation of computers.[328]

Despite these changes, U.S. electronics firms still confront substantially greater antitrust constraints than their Japanese counterparts. Some of the

---

326 Ibid., p. 193.

327 U.S. v. Socony Vacuum Oil Co., 310 U.S. 150 (1940); *Arizona v.Maricopa County Medial Soc.* 457 U.S. 332 (1982)

328 MCC, funded at $50-60 million annually, conducts R&D in four areas; packaging, software, CAD/CAM and advanced computer architecture.

joint activities which have been undertaken by Japanese electronics companies would at least raise questions -- and perhaps be held illegal -- under the U.S. antitrust laws as modified by the *Cooperative Research Act*.[329] More importantly, no U.S. joint R&D combination is exempt from antitrust scrutiny, and because the Rule of Reason standard requires a case-by-case balancing of facts, it is not always possible to predict with certainty whether a given joint activity will survive antitrust attack.[330] The risk of antitrust suit, particularly by private plaintiffs, increases the business risks associated with participation in a joint R&D project, and in some cases, may deter participation. In Japan, the risk of such a private suit is virtually nonexistent.[331]

Telecommunications Policy

The development of the semiconductor industry in both the United States and Japan has been significantly influenced by national telecommunications policies. In the United States, AT&T's Bell Laboratories were instrumental in the early development of semiconductor and computer technology; Bell Labs was required by the terms of a 1956 consent decree to license this technology for a reasonable fee to all applicants -- U.S. and foreign -- which proved a powerful stimulus both to the infant U.S. semiconductor industry and to the Japanese industry.[332] In Japan, NTT's R&D efforts have played a

---

329 For example, products are sometimes developed by the NTT family and their production allocated "so that several companies are not producing the same product." *Technocrat* (September 1976), p. 6. A number of Japanese joint semiconductor R&D projects were intended "to provide a division of labor in the production process, and to coordinate in sales." Mitsubishi-Oki joint development of microprocessors reported in *Nihon Kogyo* (February 19, 1974).

330 The legislative history of the *Cooperative Research Act* sets forth a number of factors to be weighed in evaluating a given transaction. While some types of joint R&D activity would almost certainly survive virtually any antitrust scrutiny, that is not always necessarily the case. See Conference Report on S.1841, 98th Cong., 2d Sess. (September 21, 1984), pp. 9-12.

331 In the U.S., over a thousand antitrust actions are filed each year. In Japan, by contrast, from the inception of the Antimonopoly Law through 1984, only forty-two private actions were filed. I. Hiroshi, "Antitrust and Industrial Policy in Japan," in *Law and Trade Issues of the Japanese Economy*, p. 62(n21).

332 One Bell Labs executive commented in 1982 that "without Bell Labs there would be no Silicon Valley." Vice President Arno Pensizas in *Fortune* (July 5, 1982). By the terms of the 1956 consent decree, AT&T was prohibited from entering lines of business such as computers and solid state components. It was permitted to develop Bell Labs technology in these areas, but could not market them to the public; it was required instead to license them to all applicants. The availability of licenses and technology "greatly speeded up

similar role in stimulating the development of the semiconductor industry, although NTT technology has not -- like that of Bell Labs -- been made freely available. One observer commented in 1986 that

> *[T]he bilateral implications of divergent U.S. and Japanese telecommunications structures ... were entirely fortuitous but far-reaching .... AT&T's structure and the international diffusion of Bell Technology kept the barriers to new entry low not only for U.S. companies but also for Japanese and other foreign latecomers .... Japan as a latecomer happened to be the beneficiary of America's open structure and strict antitrust enforcement. Had the situation been reversed, with Japan and NTT the pioneer and the United States and AT&T as latecomer, the U.S. information industries would have had a much harder time overtaking the Japanese frontrunners ....* [333]

In the 1980s, both the United States and Japan have engaged in major restructuring of their telecommunications systems which will affect the semiconductor industries of each country. In Japan, telecommunications restructuring has been undertaken with an eye toward its effect on the international competitiveness of its information industries, while in the United States, this was not the case.

- In the United States, in 1983, pursuant to the settlement of an antitrust investigation by the Department of Justice, the AT&T System was broken up, and the seven Regional Bell Operating Companies (RBOCs) became independent. AT&T continued to provide long distance service and remained affiliated with its manufacturing arm, Western Electric, and with Bell Labs. The AT&T divestiture was undertaken pursuant to U.S. antitrust standards, which do not emphasize strengthening U.S. industries in international competition.

- In Japan, in 1985, the NTT system was restructured rather than broken up. NTT's monopoly over some types of telecommunications services was terminated, and provisions were made for the gradual sale of a portion of its stock by MPT to the public (but not foreigners).

---

the development of the microelectronics industry." Office of Technology Assessment, *Information Technology R&D*, pp. 112-113.

333 Okimoto, "Regime Characteristics of Japanese Industrial Policy," p. 57.

The "privatization" of NTT has not had a significant impact on the benefits Japanese firms enjoy as a result of their joint development projects with NTT.[334] The NTT laboratories have not been significantly affected; their joint development projects are continuing after "privatization" and are still virtually entirely limited to Japanese firms.[335] While the family firms were worried about loss of support for joint R&D by the "privatization", they have been reassured by the establishment of the Japan Key Technology Center, funded by dividends paid on NTT stock.[336]

By contrast, in the United States, the AT&T divestiture has cast substantial doubt on the future technological benefits which the microelectronics industry can expect to enjoy from Bell Labs. The removal of the RBOCs from the Bell System substantially reduced the revenue and asset base available to support Bell Labs R&D activities, and raised questions about the stability of the future funding for research.[337] Bell Labs was reduced in size by about 7,000 employees.[338] The smaller AT&T was expected by "concerned observers" to be

forced, because of competitive pressures, to invest more of its R&D funds in developing salable products, and correspondingly, less in funding research projects that may lead to future scientific breakthroughs.[339]

Finally, as the Office Technology Assessment noted in 1985,

---

334 The *Japan Economic Journal* observed on April 5, 1986 that "Unlike AT&T's Bell Laboratories, which have undergone traumatic realignment since the divestiture of the regional operating companies, NTT laboratories are left largely as they were before privatization."

335 NTT has, however, broadened its activities to include firms such as Matsushita which were not traditional members of its "family." In 1986, NTT and Matsushita announced a technical cooperation arrangement providing for the joint development of 4 megabit and above memory devices. Matsushita and NTT will share each other's patented technologies, utilize each other's research facilities, and exchange engineers and technicians. *Japan Economic Journal* (January 25, 1986).

336 Johnson, *Telecom Wars*, p.59.

337 The predivestiture AT&T had a book value of $150 billion and annual revenues of $69 billion. AT&T, after divestiture, had an asset value of $34 billion and forecast annual revenues of about $57 billion. A significant part of the research budget of Bell Labs was funded from license contract revenues from the RBOCs which were allocated to research and system engineering. These fees, which "provided a steady income for Bell Labs, will no longer be available, and ... research funding will depend on yearly corporate decisions." Office of Technology Assessment, *Information Technology* R&D, pp. 123, 126.

338 Prior to divestiture, Bell Labs had 25,000 employees, including 3,000 with doctorates.

339 Ibid., pp. 125-126

*Even if Bell Laboratories continues to perform research at current levels,
it has fewer incentives to make the results available to others . . . . Now,
according to Bell Labs Vice President Arno Penzas, AT&T will have the
opportunity and motive to use our own technology."* [340]

Telecommunications restructuring in the United States and Japan also has
had a negative impact on the relative competitive posture of U.S. electronics
firms in the market.[341] In Japan, the NTT system was restructured in a
manner which did not lead to a significant increase in foreign penetration of
the Japanese telecommunications equipment market[342] -- in fact, the
restructuring was initially accompanied by measures which the U.S.
Government regarded as establishing new barriers to foreign sales.[343] By
contrast, the 1982 consent decree which broke up the Bell system terminated
the traditional Bell-Western Electric supply relationship, and the former Bell
operating companies began rapidly turning to foreign sources to supply their
equipment.[344] Thus, in effect, the United States unilaterally threw open its
huge telecommunications equipment market without securing reciprocal
market access in foreign telecommunications markets. Japanese and other
foreign telecommunications equipment firms moved quickly to capitalize on
this opportunity, and, inevitably, a massive trade deficit developed in
telecommunications equipment.[345] The loss of these OEM markets will
inevitably   affect   U.S.   semiconductor   producers   since   Japanese
telecommunications equipment firms overwhelmingly utilize domestic
components in their end products.

---

340   Ibid, p. 130.

341   See generally, T. Howell, S. Benz and A. Wolff, "International Competition in the
      Information Technologies," *Stanford Journal of International Law* 22 (1986).

342   The U.S. Trade Representative commented in 1985 that "[t]he 'privatization' of NTT on
      April 1, 1985 did not directly affect the structure of the so-called "Denden [NTT] family."
      Letter from USTR Clayton Yeutter to Senator Lloyd Bentsen (October 15, 1985).

343   M. Foster, *Telecommunications Equipment Standards and Certification Procedures for
      Japan* (Tokyo: Foster Associates International, October 1984). The Japanese draft
      legislation and its implementing ordinances would have established a regulatory body
      consisting of NTT and the leading Japanese telecommunications equipment producers
      which would test, register, and certify -- and thus effectively approve or disapprove -- all
      foreign telecommunications equipment for use in Japan. These plans were changed in
      the wake of strong U.S. government protests.

344   *Computerworld* (March 12, 1984); *Fortune* (June 25, 1984); *Telephony* (July 21, 1986) and
      (August 11, 1986).

345   The Subcommittee on Trade of the House Ways and Means Committee estimated the
      deficit at $1.3 billion in 1985. Staff of the Subcomm. on Trade of the House Ways and
      Means Comm., 99th Cong., 2d Sess., Comprehensive Trade Policy Reform Act 58
      (Comm. Print 1986).

As Table 3.20 illustrates, the net effect of restructuring the Japanese and U,S. telecommunications systems is likely to be enhanced competitiveness of the Japanese microelectronics and related information sectors relative to the U.S. industry.

Regional High Technology Development

An important element in the innovative dynamism of the U.S. information sector has been the "Silicon Valley phenomenon" -- the clustering of high technology enterprises around leading research university centers, as in Silicon Valley itself, North Carolina's Research Triangle, and Boston's Route 128. Such high technology centers foster an interplay between research scientists, engineers and entrepreneurs, dramatically enhancing the diffusion and rapid commercialization of information technology. An increasing number of U.S. state and local governments have taken policy measures to encourage new high technology centers in their own regions,[346] and some of the newer state programs (notably in Texas, Florida, Arizona, and Colorado) have been highly successful.[347]

MITI has been interested for a number of years in the dynamics of Silicon Valley and has attempted to discern how a geographic concentration of high technology companies and universities has spawned a continual stream of new product and process innovations. In the early 1980s, MITI adopted ambitious policies designed to create replicas of Silicon Valley throughout

---

346 State government initiatives generally involved broad infrastructural measures -- strengthening of local universities, implementation of training programs, and coordinating existing state programs in a manner designed to encourage innovation and entrepreneurialism. Substate and local governments offered assistance in land use planning and zoning; vocational and technical training; assistance to universities; marketing programs; and in some cases the provision of physical capital such as buildings and land. These efforts have been supported in many cases by federal regional development funding. An extensive survey of state, local and federal regional high technology assistance is set forth in Office of Technology Assessment, *Technology, Innovation and Regional Economic Development* (Washington, D.C.: U.S. Government Printing Office, July 1984).

347 Austin, Texas, for example, undertook a major effort to lure the Microelectronics and Computer Technology Corporation (MCC), donating a building site and investing $55 million in professorships, research facilities, graduate fellowships, and home mortgages. "In other cases, such programs are little more than faltering economic development programs repackaged as high-tech initiatives. In most areas, competition for high tech companies has heated up into a war among the states. . . ." Tatsuno, *Technopolis Strategy*, pp. 232, 234.

TABLE 3.20

TELECOMMUNICATIONS DEREGULATION IN THE U.S. AND JAPAN

	Japan	United States
Principal Source of Telecom Research and Development	NTT Laboratories	Bell Laboratories
Deregulation Measure	NTT "Privati-zation"	AT&T Divestiture
Breakup of Main Domestic Telecommunications system	No	Yes
Deregulatory Mechanism	Legislation	Judicial Consent Decree
Will Diminish Resources Available for R&D	No	Possible
Will Diminish Technology Flow to Industry	No	Yes
Opens Major Procurement Opportunities for Foreign Firms	Possible	Yes
Ends Preferential Procurement Relation-ship with Principal Suppliers	No	Yes
Has Resulted in Surge in Imported Equipment	No	Yes

Japan and to encourage the type of entrepreneurial innovation associated with it.[348]

In 1984, MITI began designating cities throughout Japan, ultimately numbering 19, each of which was to become a "technopolis" -- a city of approximately 200,000 residents consisting of research parks, universities, corporate R&D facilities, and venture businesses.[349] MITI estimates each technopolis will require infrastructural investments of $2-2.5 billion, or a total investment of between $38 and $57 billion. Each technopolis is eligible for low-interest loans from the Japan Development Bank, research and development subsidies, and tax breaks. In addition, regional development funds (loans, tax breaks, and subsidies) are being provided to each technopolis site. Finally, the prefectural governments are providing their own assistance, including loan guarantees, low-interest loans, and training. One analyst commented that in light of this assistance, "Technopolis is synonymous with pork-barrel spending for large high-tech companies, construction outfits, and consulting firms. . .".[350] He noted that

> *Since 1985, Japan's Technopolis regions have been working like people possessed. They are busy building new university complexes, research parks, highways, airports, and information networks, and organizing joint R&D projects and technology centers . . . . Governors have set up special Technopolis offices to coordinate the efforts of local universities, industry associations, chambers of commerce, and MITI's regional testing labs. Companies are operating technopolis research centers and staffing software design houses. Universities are inviting top professors from Tokyo to lecture on new technologies, while prefectures are sponsoring Technopolis fairs to drum up interest among local residents.*[351]

By fiscal 1986, there were 255 joint research projects underway among the Technopolis regions, involving applied research and technology transfers from Japan's national laboratories; a number of these projects are forecast to have a major impact on the semiconductor industry.[352]

---

348   "The idea of technopolis was formulated in order to create a high technology area like Silicon Valley or the North Carolina Research Triangle."   Ken-ichi Imai, "Japan's Industrial Policy for High Technology Industry," in *Japan's High Technology Industries*, p. 154.

349   S. Tatsuno, *MITI's Take Lead Strategy Shifts into High Gear* (San Jose, CA: Dataquest Incorporated, 1984).

350   Tatsuno, *Technopolis Strategy*, p. 132.

351   Ibid.

352   Dataquest cited six projects under way in January 1987 which were expected to affect microelectronics, including R&D projects involving automotive electronics and

The U.S. approach to high technology regional development has been completely decentralized, and has had mixed results. The Japanese approach has been systematic, and has been guided and funded by the national government. It is probably premature to assess which approach will prove more successful.

---

production technology; optoelectronics for factory and office automation; electronic controls for new materials production; fine ceramics; vision and sensor technology; and semiconductor applications.

4

NATIONAL MICROELECTRONICS
PROGRAMS IN OTHER COUNTRIES

The principal axis of international rivalry in microelectronics has been the competition between the United States and Japan. This pattern is beginning to change, however, as other industrialized and semi-industrialized nations recognize the overriding importance of this industry to their long-run national well-being, and implement ambitious national efforts to establish and expand their own capability in microelectronics. These national commitments are channeling enormous resources into the commercial microelectronics industry and will alter the international competitive environment in a manner which could be detrimental to the U.S. industry.

THE NEWLY INDUSTRIALIZING COUNTRIES

A large number of newly industrializing countries (NICs) have aggressively entered traditional manufacturing sectors like steel and textiles using a combination of protection, restrictions on investment, acquisition of foreign technology and massive government subsidies to build a modern industry. Several NICs, notably Korea, are employing similar methods in the information sector at present and the success of such methods is being noted with considerable interest by other NICs.[353] U.S. companies are playing a significant role in enabling the NICs to enter the information sector and many technological alliances have been formed between U.S. and NIC producers. However, the methods being employed by the NICs to promote their national industries raise several important long-run concerns: the danger of spreading protectionism; the prospect of overcapacity and dumping; and the misappropriation of U.S. intellectual property.

Protectionism

The NICs are major markets for U.S. OEMs and semiconductor producers. Many NICs, however, share the view that "without protectionism there is no local industry,"[354] and are imposing restrictions on foreign products as their own indigenous production comes on stream.   In 1986, China decided to adopt an "appropriate protectionist policy" on minicomputers, components, and integrated circuits because of its growing domestic production capabilities.[355] In Brazil, the beneficial effects of protectionism on the national computer industry have been widely hailed by government officials and the business and scientific communities.[356] These policies, should they continue to spread, will eventually foreclose important NIC markets to U.S. products.[357]

---

353 A recent Brazilian analysis noted the success of Korea in fostering a indigenous information industry: "South Korea, with an industry historically more backward than that of Brazil, is the third country in the world to produce 256K chips.... South Korea has legislation reserving the market for its national producers in the area of microcomputers and microelectronics....   [I]n South Korea, protectionism and interference by the state in the sector is extremely emphatic....   It was the South Korean Minister of Trade and Industry who synchronized the activity of the electronics industry, following a plan carefully explained in three basic plans: Long Range Plan for the Electronics Industry (1982); Long Range Plan for the Semiconductor Industry (1982) and Master Plan for the Creation of the Computer Industry (1984)."   Mario Fonseca in Sao Paulo *Dados et Ideias* (April 1986), pp. 48-49.

354 Paolo Tigre in *Dados et Ideias* (April 1986).

355 Vice Premier Li Peng in *Zhongguo Xinwen She* (January 23, 1986). *Xinhua* reported on June 24, 1986 that the Chinese State Council had decided to limit imports of integrated circuits in order to develop China's own products.

356 *O Estado de Sao Paulo* (May 20, 21, June 11, 1986); Sao Paulo *Istoe* (May 28, 1986).

357 Brazil's Secretary General of the Ministry of Science and Technology commented in 1986 that "[E]nterprises of 100 percent Brazilian ownership will take over all segments of the [informatics] market in the measure that they become technologically qualified. Foreign industries that find themselves in market segments that have recently been taken over by Brazilian industries will keep their products on the market, but may not introduce new products into that market segment."   *O Estado de Sao Paulo* (June 11, 1986), p.22.

Overcapacity and Dumping

In other industrial sectors, market entry by the NICs has been characterized by rapid installation of massive production capacity with little or no reference to international market conditions and the result has often been the bringing onstream of huge "white elephant" plants for which little domestic or foreign demand exists.[358] There is already some evidence that this pattern is being followed in the information sector and is likely to become more prevalent as more NICs enter the field.[359] In other sectors, dumping, export subsidies, and the subsidization of uneconomic production, and other export-forcing techniques, have been a natural consequence of such expansion practices and are likely to occur in the information sector as well.[360]

Misappropriation of Intellectual Property

The NICs must acquire the technology necessary to launch indigenous information industries from the advanced nations. Much technology transfer to the NICs takes place through normal channels, such as licensing arrangements with U.S., Japanese, and European electronics companies. The U.S. university system is freely open to students from the NICs and in many cases these students return to their home countries having acquired a technological education in the United States. However, companies in a number of NIC countries have also misappropriated a substantial amount of U.S. technology.[361] The NICs have very limited laws protecting intellectual property and tend to view such laws as an unfair mechanism employed by

---

358 Some noteworthy examples of this phenomenon include Brazil's ACOMINAS steel mill ("an embarrassing and hugely expensive white elephant" -- *Latin American Weekly Report*, November 2, 1982) and Venezuela's SIDOR steel mill ("a white elephant" -- *Zeta*, September 5, 1982.)

359 In 1985-86, after "feverish" investment, South Korean producers brought massive 64K DRAM capacity onstream in a depressed world market, with disastrous results. *Sanop-Kisul Yonghyang* (May 1985); *Maeil Kjongje Sinmun* (September 5, 1985); *Wolgan Chonggyon Munwha* (July 1985).

360 The fact that newly-installed production facilities may prove uneconomic is sometimes a secondary concern. A Brazilian observer noted approvingly in 1986 that the Korean "conglomerates can devote themselves to the production of chips with monetary losses in the short term, but in the future they will have in their hands a basic component...which is microelectronics." *Dados et Ideias* (April 1986).

361 *PC Week* (January 29, 1985) and (June 17, 1986); *Byte* (December 1985).

developed countries to impede their progress.[362]   The misappropriation of U.S. information companies' intellectual property is a serious problem for these firms, since it destroys the value of the investment they have committed to the development of new technologies.[363]

CASE STUDY: KOREAN GOVERNMENT PROMOTIONAL EFFORTS IN MICROELECTRONICS

Table 4.1 shows that in the space of five years, Korea has dramatically emerged as a major international competitor in semiconductors. Until the early 1980s, Korea possessed little indigenous microelectronics manufacturing capability and its domestic activities were restricted primarily to assembly of semiconductors and electronics products for foreign firms.[364] Such assembly operations, however, stimulated the rapid growth of an electronics sector,[365] the development of a manpower base with technological skills in electronics, and perhaps most importantly, fostered an awareness of the significance of microelectronics to industrial growth.[366]

In 1982, the Korean government announced a "Semiconductor Industry Promotion Plan," which featured a variety of measures designed to encourage the development of an indigenous manufacturing capability in semiconductors.[367]   The following year, three of Korea's largest *chaebol* (industrial groups), Samsung, Lucky-Goldstar and Hyundai, made a massive

---

362   *Chonja Chinhung* (January 1984).

363   See generally M. Gadbaw and T. Richards, *The Protection of Intellectual Property Rights in Developing Nations* (forthcoming, Westview Press).

364   Domestic wafer fabrication facilities were established in the mid-1970s to produce integrated circuits for watches and other consumer electronics products. *Kisul Kwanli* (July, 1985).

365   By the early 1980s, Korea had over 900 companies in the electronics industry, although over half of these were small firms with under 50 employees. World Bank, *Korea: Development in a Global Context* (Washington, D.C.: The World Bank, 1984), p. 71.

366   A Korean analyst commented in *Wolgan Chonggyong Munhwa* (July 1985) that "through these foreign semiconductor businesses, semiconductor assembly technology was introduced to our country, and the importance of the semiconductor has begun to be recognized in our society. . . . [T]hey never taught us the technology-intensive design or inspection processes. . . . [But] they have trained a good number of technical personnel in the semiconductor field, and as far as the assembly technique itself is concerned, they have brought the technical level up to the standard of the advanced industrial nations. The foreign businesses might also be credited for the broadening understanding of the semiconductor in our country as a result of those processes."

367   Korea Exchange Bank, *Monthly Review* (May 1985), p. 2.

TABLE 4.1
SOUTH KOREAN SEMICONDUCTOR PRODUCERS, 1986

FIRM	WAFER FAB FACILITIES	FOREIGN TECHNOLOGY TIES	PRINCIPAL TARGETED SEMICONDUCTOR PRODUCTS	WILL MAKE 1M DRAM	U.S. SUBSIDIARY
Samsung Semiconductor &	Yes	ITT Hewlett-Packard	64K DRAM 256K DRAM 16K EPROM	Yes	Samsung Semiconductor Inc.
Telecommunications (SST)		Rolm Micron Technology Excel Microelectronics	16K EPROM 16K EPROM 256K ROM 8-bit Microprocessor 16-bit Microprocessor		
Hyundai Electronics	Yes	Inmos Texas Instruments	64K DRAM 256K DMOS DRAM 16K SRAM 64K SRAM 128K ROM	Yes	Hyundai Electronics America (HEA)
Lucky-Goldstar	Yes	Zilog AMD AT&T Technologies	64K DRAM 256K DRAM 64k SRAM Gate Arrays 8-bit Microprocessor	Yes	United Microtech Inc. (UMI)
Hangkuk Electronics	Yes	Toshiba	Bipolar ICs Diodes		
Anam Electronics			Custom ICs		
Daewoo		Northern Telecom	Discretes Linear ICs		ID Focus

commitment to enter semiconductor manufacturing. These firms bought the technology for current generation technology-driver semiconductors,[368] and invested in a "stupendous" sum (estimated variously at $1-2 billion) in establishing domestic manufacturing facilities including large-scale wafer fabrication and test facilities.[369] A number of second-ranked Korean firms entered semiconductor "niche" markets.[370] While this huge commitment was recognized as extraordinarily risky, the Korean industry was swept by what was characterized as a "fever" for investment in microelectronics production.[371] By early 1985, four Korean firms had established domestic wafer fabrication facilities.[372]

The entry of the Korean *chaebol* into the semiconductor field was regarded by observers as significant because these diversified firms possessed the resources to incur sustained losses, if necessary, in their semiconductor divisions, without being driven from the market. Table 4.2 illustrates the large, diversified nature of the Hyundai *chaebol*.

Like Japan, Korea is characterized by large, vertically integrated corporations; they can use their semiconductor production to manufacture their own consumer products if the external market for their chips is weak.[373]

---

368 Hyundai purchased 256K DRAM technology from Inmos for $6 million. *Chugang Ilbo* (December 15, 1984). Lucky-Goldstar acquired 256K DRAM technology from AMD. *Wolgan Chonggyong Munwha* (July 1985).

369 A fourth *chaebol*, Daewoo, wavered on the brink of a major commitment to microelectronics. In 1984, Daewoo made a bid to take over a semiconductor production facility operated by the government Korean Electronics and Telecommunications Research Institute (ETRI) in Gumi. This initiative collapsed when Daewoo failed to meet its payments on the Gumi facility, and the government sold the plant to Goldstar in 1986. *Business Korea* (March 1986). Daewoo announced plans to acquire Zymos, a Silicon Valley producer, in early 1986. *Business Korea* (April 1986).

370 *Hanguk Kjongje Sinmun* (July 17, 1985). Hanguk Electronics has acquired wafer fabrication facilities and is producing ASICs, communications circuits, and discrete semiconductors. Anam Electronics produces ASICs.

371 Ibid.

372 *Sanop-Kisul Yonghyang* (May 1985). By mid-1985, for example, Hyundai had established or had under construction two wafer fab facilities, one capable of producing 20 thousand 5-inch wafers per year, the other, 300 thousand 6-inch wafers per year. *Chonja Chinhung* (August 5, 1985), p. 9.

373 *Electronics* (April 7, 1986), p. 21. A 1984 World Bank study of Korea observed that "[H]igh development costs, short product life cycles, the need to finance costly research through stable sales and the advantages of producing custom-made electronics components for particular kinds of equipment, have begun to favor large, vertically integrated firms with diversified products lines." World Bank, *Korea*, p. 71.

TABLE 4.2
THE HYUNDAI CHAEBOL
Percent Ownership

Company	Chung Ju-Yong Family	Hyundai Construction	Other Hyundai Firms	Outsiders
Hyundai Construction	47.2	N/A	-	52.8
Hyundai Heavy Industries	27.9	2.8	70.2	-
Hyundai Motor	7.4	13.2	18.6	50.8
Hyundai Mipo	-	-	95.0	5.0
Hyundai Rolling Stock	4.3	1.5	94.2	-
Hyundai Electrical Engineering	3.5	8.3	85.7	2.5
Hyundai Engine Mfg.	4.4	10.5	85.1	-
Hyundai Precision	16.7	42.9	40.1	0.3
Hyundai Motor Service	46.7	-	-	53.3
Hyundai Pipe	5.6	70.0	22.3	2.1
Hyundai Cement	45.2	-	-	54.8
Hyundai Engineering	24.8	-	64.8	10.4
Hyundai Lumber	2.9	70.0	26.0	1.1
Hyundai Corporation	6.8	7.1	24.3	61.8
Hanlla Corporation	28.0	48.4	21.6	2.0
Korea Urban Development	34.3	52.3	-	13.4
Hankook Pavement Construction	17.2	74.0	-	8.8
Inchon Iron & Steel	1.4	9.1	86.2	3.3
Aluminum of Korea	-	-	50.0	50.0
Kukdong Oil	25.0	-	29.0	46.0

The Korean firms entered full-scale production of 64K DRAMS at the moment (late 1984 and early 1985) that the world semiconductor industry was entering a severe recession, and Japanese firms were implementing an aggressive pricing strategy in the technology-driver product areas where the Koreans had concentrated their resources. The price of 64K DRAMs "dropped to a miserably low level." [374] The Korean semiconductor producers found that Japanese 64K DRAM prices were less than half the Koreans' cost of production, and the Korean producers incurred substantial losses.[375] The Korean semiconductor producers were stunned by these developments, and the industry, "once feverish with the development of new products and the building of production lines . . . has recently been quiet as though lost in the fog." [376]

This sobering experience led to a reappraisal by the Koreans. They concluded that they needed to diversify into product areas where Japanese pricing would not destroy the prospect of profitability.[377] It was evident that a greater degree of interfirm cooperation was essential, and perhaps most importantly, that the Korean government must play a larger role in fostering the development of the industry. The Korean producers did not, however, abandon their commitment to microelectronics, and sustained a high level of

---

374 *Wolgan Chonggyong Munwha* (July, 1985).

375 *Maeil Kjongje Sinmun* reported on November 28, 1985 that Japanese 64K DRAM prices were 60 cents per unit. A manager for Lucky-Goldstar indicated that in order to recover production costs (including materials costs), his firm would need to sell 64K DRAMs at $1.30 or $1.40 per unit. In fact, the manager indicated, "The prices for orders that are currently coming in are only 70 to 80 cents so that even if they produce them they will just be piling up losses if they are manufacturing at prices that don't cover their variable costs."

376 *Maeil Kjongje Sinmun* (September 5, 1985), p. 6. *Wolgan Chonggyong Munhwa* commented in July 1985 that "the slump of the international price of the 64K DRAM has brought serious skepticism about the appropriateness of investing in the domestic semiconductor industry. Voices have been raised repeatedly that any further reckless investment should be stopped."

377 A number of Korean firms found export outlets for fabricated, unassembled wafers. *Maeil Kjongje Sinmun* (July 16, 1985). Samsung curtailed its production of 64K DRAMs and used its 64K DRAM production line to manufacture 16K SRAMs and 16K EPROMs. It also began volume production of an 8-bit microprocessor. *Maeil Kjongje Sinmun* (September 5, 1985), p. 6. Hyundai placed greatest emphasis on CMOS DRAMs, "for which there has been both less demand and less cutthroat pricing." *Business Korea* (October 1986), p. 70. *Hanguk Ilbo* commented on March 31, 1985 (p. 4) that "[T]o survive the Japanese manufacturers' extermination strategy, we must go beyond excessive and duplicative investment in the domestic industry and diversify investment, with specialization by the major companies. For example, we should not concentrate investment solely in the memory element field, on products like the 64K DRAM and 256K DRAM, but should diversify investment in middle-grade products such as chips for electronic calculators, circuits for electronic watches, gate arrays, and microprocessors."

investment through 1985 -- as one observer commented, "the Koreans have said there's no backing out."[378] The Government announced plans to fund a joint effort to develop and manufacture 1 megabit and 4 megabit DRAMs, based on technology acquired from U.S. companies.[379] An official from Korea's Ministry of Trade and Industry (MTI) commented,

> *There's no point in making a big deal out of the recent situation. The risk of chipmaking and the immediate loss were well conceived from the beginning.*[380]

The Industry-Government Relationship

The Korean government has played an important role in fostering and sustaining the country's plunge into microelectronics. As in Japan, the government has indicated that the principal responsibility for developing a competitive microelectronics industry lies with the private sector, but that the government will provide support as needed.[381] During the "start-up" period of 1983-85, when the Korean industry was installing an indigenous production base, the government provided a variety of financial and tax incentives to facilitate intensive investments, and undertook numerous initiatives to elevate the industry's technological level and manpower base. In the wake of the 1984-85 DRAM debacle, the government is assuming a larger role, reportedly planning a long range strategy for the industry and encouraging changes in the industry's structure.[382]

---

378   Ibid.

379   *Maeil Kjongje Sinmun* (September 5, 1985), p. 6.

380   *Business Korea* (August 1985), p. 62.

381   Commenting on the government's role, an official of the Ministry of Science and Technology commented in 1985 that "The development of a 256K DRAM and its advance to a mass production system represents a rapid growth of our semiconductor industry. . . . Enterprises which are the main actors in industrial technological development must respond effectively to the need of called-for technological development. And the government must provide the motive factor for technological innovation by providing the support measures for compensating for risks involved in such technological innovation and for proper recovery of investment costs in technological innovations." Kim Song-ch'ol in *Kisul Kwanli,* No. 2 (1985).

382   *Maeil Kjongje Sinmun* (September 5, 1985).

Capital

The Korean *chaebol* possess massive financial resources, and the Korean government's financial aid measures to the industry have been designed primarily to mobilize private capital rather than directly to underwrite the full cost of the necessary investments. Thus, in 1985, the Korean government indicated it was loaning $346 million to the semiconductor industry between 1984 and 1986, a not inconsiderable sum which was, however, greatly exceeded by the $2 billion in private capital which Samsung, Hyundai and Lucky-Goldstar were expected to commit to semiconductor plant and facilities during the same period.[383] Government funds were channeled to the industry through institutions such as the Korean Development Bank and the National Investment Fund (NIF), which provide the basis for investment decisions by Korean banks.[384] The government reduced tariffs on imported semiconductor manufacturing equipment and materials.[385]

The Korean government has established a large number of tax measures designed to encourage investment in research, development and production of new technologies.[386] These include:

- *Reserve Fund for Technological Development.* This program permits companies to write off as a loss, in advance, funds which will be used in the future for technological development.

- *Deduction for R&D and Manpower Costs.* A 10 percent deduction is allowed for R&D and manpower development.

---

383 *Business Korea* (August 1985), p. 62.

384 *Business Korea* (May 1985), p. 30. The Korea Development Bank (KDB) is a government-owned institution which makes so-called "policy loans" to industrial sectors whose development is sought by the government. In 1984 and 1985, KDB loans (which totaled 132 billion won) were the largest single source of government funding for the development of new technologies. *Kisul Kwanli,* No. 2 (1985). The NIF is a government fund established to provide subsidized medium-term credit to designated industrial sectors. NIF loans are a catalyst for lending decisions by Korean banks, which are owned or dominated by the government.

385 An MTI official commented in 1985 that "70 percent of [the semiconductor industry] investment is covered by imported equipment [and] in order to alleviate the burden of businesses for vast amounts of funds for plant and equipment, the government has reduced the high tariff rates (on the average 20 percent) which used to be imposed on 70 items of major equipment . . . to a 7 percent level on the average. . . ." Chong Chang-sup in *Kisul Kwanli* (July 1985).

386 These programs were summarized by the Director General of the Information Industry Bureau, Ministry of Science and Technology, in *Kisul Kwanli* (February, 1985).

- *Deduction for Commercialization for New Technology.* A 6 percent deduction is allowed for the cost of commercializing new technologies (10 percent if domestic equipment is used), or, alternatively, the investing company is allowed to write off 50 percent of the investment as a depreciation expense during the first year.

- *Depreciation Allowance for R&D.* Companies investing in equipment for R&D may depreciate 90 percent of the acquisition cost of this equipment during the year of acquisition.

Technology

A principal weakness of the Korean microelectronics industry is its dependency on foreign sources for leading-edge technologies. The assembly operations of the 1960s and 1970s did little to foster the development of indigenous scientific and design capacity,[387] and the Koreans have complained that advanced countries refuse to share the technology with them which is needed to compete effectively:

[T]echnologically advanced countries keep their advantage by failing to supply them to us or asking high prices for obsolete technology which restricts our own development . . . [T]he United States and Japan hold the most advanced semiconductor design technology in computer use. However, they are reluctant to transfer technology and strengthen the measures to prevent disclosure of design. Our situation is at such a stage that neither industry nor academic circles can establish independent design technology.[388]

As partial response, the Korean government has strongly encouraged the development of an indigenous technological base in the information industries. Choe Younghwan, Promotion Bureau Chief of the Ministry of Science and Technology, commented in 1985 that:

---

387 A report by the Korean Institute of Economics and Technology observed in 1985 that "Because our country's semiconductor production system has been based on simply assembly there has been no great need for R&D investment in the past, therefore the R&D investment in the semiconductor industry has been quite low." KIET, *Kukga Changgi Paljon Kusang* (December 1985).

388 *Chonja Chinhung* (January 1984).

The information industry is the area where government-led technological developments are concentrated, and it would not be too much even if I stress this fact 100 times.[389]

The government promotes domestic R&D through the activities of three principal government research institutes, the Korean Advanced Institute of Science and Technology (KAIST), the Korean Institute of Electronics Technology (KIET), and the Korea Electronics and Telecommunications Research Institute (ETRI). The government also funds joint industry-government research projects in microelectronics, new materials, basic science, and systems engineering.[390]

The Korean Electronics and Telecommunications Research Institute (ETRI) established a semiconductor production facility in Gumi in 1976 to stimulate the development of the domestic computer and semiconductor industries. ETRI decided to sell the Gumi manufacturing facility to the private sector in 1983 in order to concentrate fully on research and development.[391]

The Korean Institute of Electronics Technology (KIET), located in Gumi, is a governmental entity established to

function as a supplier of that high technology needed to develop our electronic industry into a strategic one for the export market as well as to provide research and development capacity for applying advanced technology to our domestic needs . . . [and] to search for a breakthrough toward the independence of electronic technology and in building an advanced fatherland.[392]

The KIET is a "central body for the development of microelectronics and software.[393] It is currently developing semiconductor device prototypes and process technology and is establishing a national center for automated semiconductor designing and a training center for electronics technicians. It provides maskmaking, wafer processing and epitaxial services to Korean semiconductor producers, and sells a small quantity of semiconductors. The KIET maintains an office in California (KIETUS) which is used for design

---

389 *Hanguk Ilbo* (August 17, 1985).

390 *Yonhap*, 12:27 GMT (Foreign Broadcast Information Service, September 13, 1984). In 1984 the government funding for these projects was 30 billion won (approximately $37 million at 815:1).

391 The Gumi plant was sold to Lucky-Goldstar in 1986. *Business Korea* (March 1986).

392 *Chonja Chinhung* (January 1984).

393 Ibid.

and liaison with VLSI Technology, a U.S. company. In addition to its in-house research efforts, the KIET sponsors additional industry-government development projects in the semiconductor, computer and software fields.[394] The KIET has also developed semiconductor manufacturing facilities which have then been acquired by private companies entering the field.[395]

Supplementing these efforts, the Koreans have made clear their intention to draw on the technology of the more advanced nations. All four of Korea's leading *chaebol* established subsidiaries or joint ventures in Silicon Valley when they made their initial commitment to microelectronics in 1983, because as a Samsung executive put it, "of a certain kind of talent [in California] not available in Korea," as well as the prospect of acquiring U.S. technology.[396] *Business Korea* reported in February 1986 that

Access to skilled personnel is the primary reason for Korea's venture into Silicon Valley. A close second is access to technical information . . . Goldstar has concluded some ten technology transfer agreements. The agreements have been negotiated out of Seoul, but Silicon Valley sources can be helpful as talent scouts. . . . [A]ll the technology transfer agreements include training for six months to a year.

In 1984 the KIET announced

a plan to send trainees to those companies in the United States which can design ICs from LSIs, and to acquire technology in return for work through which we can secure professional labor in the areas of MOS LSI, bipolar LSI and CAD software.[397]

The Koreans are also hopeful that alliances with U.S. manufacturers against Japanese competition will result in acquisition of U.S. microelectronics technology. In a 1985 interview with *Maeil Kjongje Sinmun* (July 3) President Chong Chu-yong of Hyundai said that

---

394 Ibid. Microelectronics R&D activities under way at the KIET in 1984 included development of a prototype 16-bit microprocessor, a mass production system for a 64K HMOS ROM, development of technology for polysilicon gate CMOS, and developing design technology for gate arrays. Ibid.

395 The KIET established wafer processing facilities which it then sold to Taeu Electronics, a second-rank Korean producer entering into production of custom ICs and communications circuits. *Hanguk Kjongje Sinmun* (July 17, 1984).

396 *Business Week* (February 1986), p. 52. A Lucky-Goldstar executive indicated that parallel developmental objectives were frequently established between the California subsidiary and the Korean parent. Coordination was achieved by arranging personal visits in which designers from the Valley work with developers in Seoul, and vice versa. Ibid.

397 *Chonja Chinhung* (January 1984).

[T]his Japanese dumping offensive will stimulate the United States, and when U.S. manufacturers start looking for other countries to cooperate with in maintaining their price competitiveness against Japanese manufacturers, our country will have the best prospects as a candidate. Accordingly [Chong] says that the semiconductor field has bright prospects, with anticipated U.S. technology transfer and cooperation and provision of markets.

The Koreans have viewed the implementation of chip protection legislation in the United States and Japan with concern. *Hanguk Ilbo* commented on March 31, 1985 (p. 4) that

The United States and Japan have prepared laws to protect semiconductor chips and there is evidently a move to block the spread of semiconductor technology so that foreign companies cannot copy designs created by their own domestic semiconductor companies and make new products. Should this happen, countries like Korea, which import basic product designs, to say nothing of designs for machines necessary in manufacturing semiconductors, from foreign countries, will experience a great shock.

Manpower. One of the most critical problems confronting the Korean microelectronics sector is the shortage of skilled manpower. While decades of assembly-type manufacturing has produced a base of skilled production workers, the country has far too few scientists and engineers to sustain the ambitious program the government and industry have mapped out. The KIET estimated in 1985 that Korea would need to increase the number of research positions tenfold between 1983 and 1993, and that in the following decade the number of such personnel would need to increase at an annual rate of over 13 percent every year as shown in Table 4.3. The KAIST has implemented programs designed to attract Korean scientists currently working abroad to return to Korea.

In 1985, Seoul National University established a Semiconductor Joint Research Center (SJRD), in which 57 professors of electronics, physics, computer science and controlled instrumentation from 17 universities are participating. The SJRD is acquiring state of the art design, production and test equipment, and will "conduct joint research in semiconductors with

TABLE 4.3

KOREAN SEMICONDUCTOR INDUSTRY
PROJECTED MANPOWER NEEDS, 1983-2000

(Persons)

Category	1983	1990	2000	Annual Rate of Increase 1984-90	1991-2000
Research Positions	220	2,350	8,280	40.3%	13.4%
Technical Positions	1,600	5,170	13,800	18.2	10.3
Skilled Workers	19,880	35,720	64,400	8.7	6.1
Office Workers	2,300	3,760	5,520	7.3	3.9
Total	24,000	47,000	92,000	10.0	6.9

Source: KIET Estimates in *Kukga Changgi Paljon Kusang*, December 1985

industrial organizations, universities, and the government, and will train semiconductor specialist manpower."[398]

Joint Development Efforts

The Korean government has sought to nudge the country's fiercely independent *chaebol* into a greater degree of cooperation in microelectronics. Until recently the issue was sufficiently controversial in that rumors of joint projects were heatedly denied by company officials.[399] An MTI official commented in 1985 that

> *We don't want to exchange top secrets. But it is necessary to establish an information exchange system under government supervision. Private firms may have limitations in getting access to the world semiconductor market, which the government can solve.*[400]

In mid-1985, despite denials by Korean executives, an MTI official commented that by 1988, "Korean chipmakers will be led to jointly develop the next generation of VLSI."[401] At length, in April 1986, the Electronics and Telecommunications Research Institute announced the industry-government "Korean Semiconductor Cooperative Research Project." As Figure 4.1 shows, the Project is divided into three Committees, each with a separate set of technological objectives. The Project's objectives include not only the development of 4 megabit memory technology, but a variety of nonmemory and "upstream" technologies. The Project's budget of $119 million will be equally shared by industry and government, although the industry portion will be heavily subsidized by government-guaranteed, low-interest loans.[402]

---

398 *Kwahak Kwa Kisul* (September 1985).

399 One report suggested that "the country's semiconductor industry be realigned according to individual manufacturers' strengths in a specific area of the industry: MOS memory ICs for "A" company, and gate arrays for "B" company." A Goldstar executive commented that "This idea is totally absurd," and the government "denied the scheme doggedly." *Business Korea* (May 1985), p. 30.

400 Ibid.

401 *Business Korea* (August 1985), p. 63. *Business Korea* observed that "[A]ll companies in the Korean semiconductor industry are in the same boat with the same goal to compete with advanced countries for the sake of the country's future. It is not important for one company to gain an edge over other members boarding the same boat since its competitors are in different boats in foreign nations. . ."

402 Dataquest, *Japanese Research Newsletter* (1986).

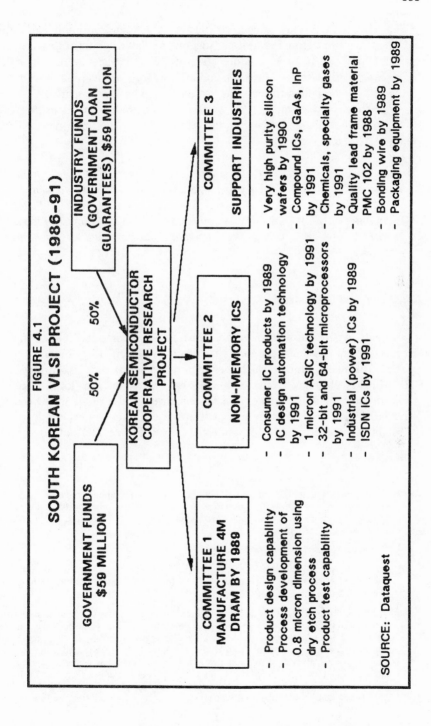

FIGURE 4.1

SOUTH KOREAN VLSI PROJECT (1986-91)

GOVERNMENT FUNDS $59 MILLION

INDUSTRY FUNDS (GOVERNMENT LOAN GUARANTEES) $59 MILLION

50%   50%

KOREAN SEMICONDUCTOR COOPERATIVE RESEARCH PROJECT

COMMITTEE 1 MANUFACTURE 4M DRAM BY 1989

- Product design capability
- Process development of 0.8 micron dimension using dry etch process
- Product test capability

COMMITTEE 2 NON-MEMORY ICS

- Consumer IC products by 1989
- IC design automation technology by 1991
- 1 micron ASIC technology by 1991
- 32-bit and 64-bit microprocessors by 1991
- Industrial (power) ICs by 1989
- ISDN ICs by 1991

COMMITTEE 3 SUPPORT INDUSTRIES

- Very high purity silicon wafers by 1990
- Compound ICs, GaAs, InP by 1991
- Chemicals, specialty gases by 1991
- Quality lead frame material PMC 102 by 1988
- Bonding wire by 1989
- Packaging equipment by 1989

SOURCE: Dataquest

The Koreans do not expect to achieve technological parity with the advanced nations during the next decade, but, as Table 4.4 illustrates, they do expect to be able to mass produce state-of-the-art devices before their life cycle has ended. Because the Korean market is comparatively small, Korean firms will be compelled to seek most of their sales in export markets,[403] and because they will be entering the market from a trailing position, they are likely to employ aggressive pricing tactics in order to capture a piece of the market. U.S. observers

cite Samsung's strategy of aggressively cutting prices to gain color-TV market share in the U.S. They predict Samsung will try the same tactic to get into the semiconductor market. "When there are 16 semiconductor companies lined up ahead of you, you're going to have to dump just to get noticed," says a leading semiconductor market analyst in San Francisco.[404]

Upstream and Downstream Sectors

Korea's upstream industries are thus far comparatively undeveloped. Korean producers must import virtually all of their raw materials and manufacturing equipment, which they regard as a substantial disadvantage.[405] The Ministry of Science and Technology has designated the "localization of semiconductor materials" as one of its objectives, and a number of projects have been sponsored by Government research institutes to develop domestic capabilities in semiconductor materials.[406]   The ETRI's Cooperative

---

403 "Our country's domestic demand is not large enough to support the semiconductor industry's continuous growth. Therefore, in the 1990s, the semiconductor industry has no choice but to rely on export for its growth just as in the 1980s." KIET, *Kikga Changgi Paljon Kusang* (December 1985).

404 *Electronics* (September 16, 1985).

405 Korea does not have indigenous silicon production, for example, and Korean producers must maintain six month's inventory, which imposes a substantial cost burden on them. Korea Exchange Bank, *Monthly Review* (May 1985).

406 In 1984, a Korean Institute of Science and Technology (KAIST) research team succeeded in developing single crystalline gallium-arsenide which is likely to form the basic material for optical semiconductors. *Seoul Sinmun* (October 21, 1984). In the same year, pursuant to a "national policy project," another KAIST team developed a new copper alloy, PMC 102, for use in semiconductor lead frames which has generated substantial interest among leading U.S. information sector companies. *Hanguk Ilbo* (July 14, 1984); *Business Korea* (July 1986). PMC 102 technology was licensed to a West German firm, one of the first examples of "reverse technology flow" from Korea to the West. Ibid.

TABLE 4.4

KOREAN SEMICONDUCTOR INDUSTRY--PROJECTED LEVELS
OF TECHNOLOGY

	Korea	Advanced Nations
1985	- 256 K DRAM mass production - Independent design capability - 64 K SRAM development	- 256 K DRAM mass production - 1 M DRAM development - 256 K SRAM development - 32 bit microprocessor mass production - PAL mass production
1986-90	- 1 M DRAM development & mass production - 4 M DRAM development - 16 bit microprocessor development	- 1 M DRAM mass production - 256 K SRAM mass production - 4 M DRAM and 1 M SRAM development - Inexpensive optical semiconductor
1991-2000	- 4 M DRAM mass production - PAL mass production - 16 bit microprocessor mass production	- Development of special components for artificial intelligence - 4 M - 16M DRAM mass production - Optical semiconductor mass production

Source: Korean Institute of Economics and Technology, *Kukga Changgi Paljon Kusang*, December 1985.

Research Project is placing emphasis, among other things, on the development of high purity silicon, chemicals and specialty gases, and a variety of process technologies.

In several "downstream" electronics industries, the Korean government has pursued a classic infant-industry policy designed to establish indigenous production. In 1982, the Korean Ministry of Trade and Industry issued regulations which effectively banned the import of mini and microcomputers, and contained provisions designed to encourage the transfer of foreign technology to Korean firms.[407] These measures were taken pursuant to the *Electronics Industry Promotion Law*, which gave MTI broad authority to "facilitate the promotion and technological upgrading of the electronics industry [in order] to enhance its international competitiveness and help develop the national economy."[408]

In addition to the market protection, the law authorized establishment of an "Electronic Industry Promotion Fund",[409] rationalization measures under MTI guidance, and the promotion of R&D projects.[410] Although Korea agreed to lift some restrictions on computer imports in 1987 following negotiations with the U.S. Government,[411] by the time this commitment was given, the Korean government's protectionist measures in computers had proven spectacularly successful, with Korean small computers making substantial inroads in the world markets.[412]

EUROPEAN PROMOTIONAL EFFORTS IN MICROELECTRONICS

The European information sector has trailed the U.S. and Japan technologically in computers and semiconductors. In the 1960s and 1970s, U.S. semiconductor companies established manufacturing facilities in Europe in order to penetrate high European Communities (EC) tariff levels, and eventually came to hold the largest share of the European market. Indigenous European computer and semiconductor companies, although

---

407 MTI Notice No. 82-28. The U.S. Embassy in Seoul commented that "the ROK wished to protect newly emerging local manufacturers from foreign competition by banning imports of any and all computer and peripheral units of a type made locally." (Unclassified cable, July 2, 1982).

408 Article 1.

409 Article 6.

410 Article 3.

411 Office of the U.S. Trade Representative, *Foreign Trade Barriers*, p. 169.

412 *PC Week* (February 4, 1986).

financially strong and backed by their governments, were nevertheless unable to mount a serious challenge to U.S. companies, largely as a result of their lagging technological level. European firms have retained a dominant position in the telecommunications equipment market, however, reflecting their preferential relationships with national telecommunications authorities, and several European firms (Philips, Siemens) also hold a strong position in consumer electronics markets.

In the early 1980s, a mounting sense of concern began to pervade Europe as policymakers, analysts, and industry executives grasped not only the extent to which Europe was falling behind in the new technologies, but the long-run implications of such trends for the European economy and European society. An intensive effort is now under way, both at the national and supranational levels, to catch up with Japan and the United States. This effort involves massive government investments in the information sector; efforts to enhance cooperation and standardization at the European level; and the aggressive acquisition of foreign technology through the formation of strategic alliances with Japanese and U.S. microelectronics firms.

While the prospects for the success of this effort are uncertain, it is significant from a U.S. perspective for several reasons:

- Europe has traditionally been a major market for U.S. information products, a situation which could change with efforts to "Europeanize" these industries.

- The Europeans possess outstanding scientific and technological ability, and are now devoting such substantial resources to the information technologies that they could well emerge as major competitors in a number of OEM and microelectronics markets by the early 1990s.

- European programs -- successful and unsuccessful -- may offer object lessons for the United States as it seeks the answers to its own difficulties in microelectronics.

The European Crisis

By the early 1980s, the deteriorating European competitive position in the information sector was becoming a subject of widespread concern within the Community. In 1983, the European Commission noted that during the past decade, the Community had moved from a trade surplus in information products to a deficit of over $10 billion; that the Community industry was increasingly dependent on importing technology or on licensed manufacturing and distribution for its profits; and that "the current rate of decline is fast and is accelerating."[413] A Viennese journal observed in 1985 that

> *Throughout Europe, the media are using the keyword Eurosclerosis, meaning that the technological level of the Japanese or the United States cannot be overtaken.*[414]

Europe faced a number of unique competitive problems. Unlike Japan and the United States, the European market is fragmented into a number of smaller national markets. National standards for electronics and information processing equipment frequently differ, and public bodies such as the Post and Telecommunications authorities (PTTs) aggravate the fragmentation of the market by pursuing explicit "buy national" procurement policies.[415] Thus, despite the huge size of the European market, European producers are often unable to achieve scale and learning economies commensurate with the size of that market.[416] Internal fragmentation has also led to duplicative R&D, the inefficient deployment of human and financial resources, and comparatively slow diffusion of technology.

While Europe possesses superb research capabilities,[417] European industry has been consistently slow in translating innovative research into

---

413 The Commission noted that the problem of the information sector trade deficit was compounded by the fact that Community imports tended to be state-of-the-art technologies, such as advanced semiconductors, whereas its exports tended to be "more mature, lower technology products." *Official Journal*, No. C.321 (November 26, 1983), pp. 9-10.

414 *Industrie* (June 19, 1985).

415 The Commission noted in 1983 that "Digital exchanges have required R&D investment of about $1 billion. To amortize this investment, $14 billion in sales are necessary, which exceeds the size of any one market of a Member State as projected for the next decade, a market for which there are many competitors." *Official Journal*, No. C. 321 (November 26, 1983).

416 Philips' President complained in 1986 that "There is one [carphone] system in the Netherlands, another in Belgium, another one in the FRG, and yet another in Denmark. . . . You will find at least nine tiny, horrid, complicated trademarks on a Philishave razor. . . . In order to sell a product that has been world famous for its quality for more than 50 years, we have to pass through nine quality checks. . . . In Bruges, we make 600 kinds of television sets. That is an embarrassingly high number, but we must because of all the possible variants in the various countries." Groot-Bijgaarden *De Standaard* (April 22, 1986), p. 17.

417 "Europe's best card is its long scientific tradition . . . The Old Continent still has a remarkable research potential. Its only problem is to use it effectively." *L'Expansion* (October 24, 1986).

commercially viable products.[418] This basic failing has been attributed variously to poor educational policy and university-industry cooperation,[419] resistance by the European social structure to technological innovations that may eliminate jobs,[420] and a mind-set which is not receptive to the commercial possibilities of innovation.

Examples of National Programs

The initial European response to the international competitive challenge in the information sector occurred at the national level, with several countries undertaking government-backed promotional programs between the late 1960s and the early 1980s. These programs, frequently tinged with an element of economic nationalism, in some cases emphasized the promotion of "national flagship" companies with heavy state backing (France, Britain) and in others, sought to stimulate a greater degree of entrepreneurial innovation by smaller companies (West Germany). However, it was evident by the early 1980s that these programs, by themselves, would not suffice to reverse the accelerating European decline, and that Europe's only hope of becoming competitive lay in a greater degree of transnational cooperation.

France

Curiously, France, whose national aspirations have frequently proven an obstacle to European unity, has become the driving force behind the emergence, in the mid 1980s, of the beginnings of a coherent Western European strategy in the information sector. By 1985, "nationalism coupled with pragmatism [had] made France the most important champion of

---

418 The EC Commission observed in 1985 that "it is clear that the Europeans do not have as good a grip on the innovation process as their main trading partners. These are often more efficient in turning scientific and technical results into commercial successes not only on their own marketplace but also on ours. . . ." Communication of the Commission to the Council, *Towards a European Technological Community,* Com (85) 530 final (September 30, 1985), p. 11.

419 Philips Chief Executive Officer Wisse Dekker in *Zero un Informatique Hebdo* (January 16, 1986). "Recently a French University researcher requested a waiver from a minister to join the board of directors of a high technology company. The best response he got was to send his wife in his place." *L'Expansion* (October 24, 1986).

420 The Essen *Elektro-Anzeiger* commented in February 1983 that "In the Federal Republic . . . so-called acceptance problems inhibit the successful introduction and expansion of microelectronics. The more and more frequently heard opinion [is] that increased use of microelectronics would lead to still more unemployment. . . ."

European cooperation in the field of new technology."[421] The unique role played by France reflects, in part, repeated failures which have forced it to confront competitive realities in the information technologies in a manner which is proving highly influential in the Community. The Rotterdam *NRC Handelsblad* commented on July 31, 1985 that

> *The electronics industry, too, has again and again received vital impulses from large-scale, state-subsidized projects. In France, this is sometimes perceived more clearly than in other European countries, if only because the country is more motivated than other nations to be among the leaders. Consequently, France's achievements in these fields are quite impressive, as far as technology is concerned. All too frequently, however, this is not sufficient to generate a flourishing industry. This, and the realization that going it alone no longer guarantees top performance, makes France more committed than other countries to finding Europe- oriented solutions.*

French policy in the information sector is implemented by several government entities. The Ministry of Industry is responsible for developing sectoral industrial policies, and its Directorate of Electronics Industries and Data Processing (DIELI) has implemented a number of promotional efforts in the computer and microelectronics sectors. Since 1982, the Directorate-General of Telecommunications (DGT) which administers the PTT, has been attached to the Ministry of Industry, a recognition of the important role played by telecommunications procurement in the development of the electronics sector.[422] Since 1981, the Ministry for Research and Technology has become heavily involved in implementing industrial policy in the high technology sectors.[423]

---

421 *NRC Handelsblad* (October 23, 1985).

422 The PTT conducts R&D through its Center for Telecommunications studies (CNET) at Grenoble, which places a particular emphasis on telecommunications applications of integrated circuits. The CNET's Norbert Segard Center (CNS) is devoted specifically to silicon IC R&D. *L'Echo des Recherches* (2d Quarter 1983.) CNET operates a pilot manufacturing facility for silicon integrated circuits; it has developed 1 micron technology for transfer to French industry in 1987, and plans to demonstrate an industrializable 0.7 micron circuit with 4 million transistors by 1990. *Electroniques Actualites* (September 12, 1986); *L'Echo Des Recherches* (4th Quarter 1985).

423 The Electronics and Data Processing Technology Laboratory (LETI), administered by the French Atomic Energy Commission, also conducts advanced microelectronics R&D with the results transferred to French industry. LETI carries out R&D in microelectronics materials technology, Josephson junction, sensors, display technology, ICs for infra-red imagery, and magnetic microelectronics, and is working with Thomson to develop ICs for application to industrial assembly lines. The Ministry of Economy and Finance channels government financial assistance to designated priority sectors, and the Armed Forces have provided support for the development of microelectronics,

The French government implemented a number of programs in the 1960s and 1970s to promote the development of an indigenous semiconductor capability.[424] Characterized by frequent industry reorganizations and the desire to foster national "champions" in the various information sectors, these programs fell far short of their objectives. In retrospect, their principle significance was that they enabled France to begin commercial production of information products and moved the French electronics sector toward consolidation into a few large, vertically integrated, diversified firms.

The Mitterand government, which came to power in 1981, made electronics its number one industrial development priority. Mitterand implemented a broad plan to promote the entire electronics industry (La Filiere Electronique), nationalized the major French-owned electronics producers, and undertook an industry rationalization which, by 1985, had resulted in the clear emergence of three "national champions" in the information technologies.[425] In 1982, the Mitterand government announced a new Microelectronics Plan (1983-86) which was far more ambitious than any of its predecessors. The Plan, drawn up by an Interministerial Group for Integrated Circuits (GICI), called for massive infusions of government funds to the semiconductor industry for R&D, new investments, and to subsidize the firms' operating losses.[426] Mitterand declared that his objective was to "win back" the French domestic market in key industries such as semiconductors, machine tools, and small computers. The overall goal of the new Microelectronics Plan was to have the French integrated circuit market

---

telecommunications, and computer systems. *Electronique Actualites* (June 14, 1985); *Bulletin de Liason de la Recherche en Informatique et Automatique* (June-July 1986).

424 The Plan Calcul (1967-71) was an unsuccessful subsidized effort to create a state-owned "flagship" computer company capable of competing with IBM. Two Plans des Composants (early 1970s and 1977-82) were implemented to promote the semiconductor industry. The second plan featured joint ventures between French and American companies and drew heavily on U.S. technology. By the end of the second plan, French firms had commenced low-volume production of semiconductors, but total French production capacity fell short of French domestic demand, and French firms were losing money and lagging technologically. *L'Usine Nouvelle* (March 18, 1982).

425 These were Bull in computers, Cit-Alcatel in telecommunications, and Thomson in semiconductors, consumer electronics products, and household appliances. In addition, Matra-Harris was an important producer of semiconductors. *NRC Handelsblad* (October 23, 1985). The nationalized electronics producers were organized as holding companies wholly owned by the government. The holding companies held between 50% and 100% of the operating companies, which were subsidiaries. *Electronics* (July 29, 1983).

426 *Electronique Actualites* reported on June 10, 1983 that "we believe that the entire envelope of aid scheduled . . . for French microelectronics during the 1983-86 period will be at least 4.500 billion francs. Of this figure, 2.550 billion will be used for R&D, 900 million will be used to cover losses, and 1.025 billion for investments for the nationalized companies."

covered by French production by 1986.[427] Underlying this extraordinarily ambitious objective was the new government's conviction that "without integrated circuits, the entire French electronics industry would crumble."[428] *L'Usine Nouvelle* reported on March 18, 1982 that

> *The government . . . will encourage [semiconductor] manufacturers to invest one-third of the Fr. 3.4 billion necessary for France to have true technological independence in 1986. And the state would thus be ready to pay the remaining two thirds. "It's a big bill, but independence comes at such a price," they say at DIELI. . . .*

Complementing this effort, the government electronics laboratories entered into comprehensive tie-up arrangements with French companies.[429]

Soon after the new microelectronics plan was launched, it became clear that the substantial resources committed by the government to this effort were nevertheless wholly inadequate to enable French firms to achieve Mitterand's objective. The new plan's subsidies permitted a substantial increase in investment levels, but, as one executive complained, "the subsidies allocated to research are not large enough; we are constantly running short of funds."[430] A French PTT official complained that "we have technological problems, problems with finding capable people and money problems."[431] The French were overwhelmed by the volume of investment undertaken by the Americans, Japanese, and Koreans in the boom years of 1983-4. *Electronique Actualites* commented on March 29, 1985 that

> *[T]he government did not anticipate in 1982 the formidable pressure that U.S. and especially Japanese investments would exert on semiconductors in 1983 and 1984, so that the amounts invested in this field in 1984 by*

---

427 *Electronique Actualites* (June 10, 1983).

428 *Le Monde* (September 22, 1983).

429 Under an arrangement between Thomson and LETI, a joint laboratory was established for the development of CMOS ICs with circuits as small as 1.2 microns. *L'Usine Nouvelle* reported on June 3, 1985 that "A total of 180 people (130 from LETI and 50 from Thomson) will be sent to the brand new LETI labs in Grenoble. They .. will relieve Thomson of all research worries, although it will still finance part of that research.... Actually, this agreement constitutes a localized merger of Thomson and LETI rather than a mere collaboration. It is quite natural since Thomson and [LETI] have the same majority shareholder, the State." A tie-up between CNET-Matra did not go as far, because the wholly state-funded CNS "had to keep its distance with a partner, 50 percent of whose stock is in private -- and U.S. hands." *L'Usine Nouvelle* (January 3, 1985).

430 *Le Monde* (September 22, 1983).

431 *NRC Handelsblad* (October 23, 1985).

predominantly French-owned companies represented only 1.4 percent of the amounts invested worldwide.

It was becoming apparent to the French that achieving international competitiveness in microelectronics would require investments on a scale which France alone could not match, forcing France to seek a European-scale effort. DIELI commented in 1984 that

Unfortunately, in the present context, we cannot afford to make the effort required. Certainly for the new [microelectronics] plan which will start in 1987, a European effort will have to be considered.[432]

By the spring of 1985, the Mitterand government had concluded that a pan-European electronics strategy would be required, and in April of that year, Mitterand unveiled his EUREKA proposal. The Rotterdam *NRC Handelsblad* commented on October 23, 1985 that

French nationalism, combined with probably somewhat less French pragmatism. The result: A European approach. In two fields: cooperation in the field of basic and applied research and, alongside this, the integration of the European market, so that products made in the one country are allowed into the other without difficulty and, for example, can be connected to equipment in the other country.

Certain parallels exist between the emerging French "national champions" and the large Japanese electronics firms. Bull, Thomson, and Cit-Alcatel are all vertically integrated and diversified, and have become more so since the Mitterand rationalizations. In addition, the priority assigned to microelectronics, coupled with state backing, has enabled them to expand their commitment to microelectronics regardless of operating losses.[433]

West Germany

West German industrial policy is generally characterized by reliance on the market, with government policy limited to broad macroeconomic

---

432 *Electronique Actualites* (March 29, 1985).

433 *Electronique Actualites* commented on June 10, 1983 that "[T]he most difficult thing still remains to be done: to take action so that the industrial complex created can balance its books. In 1982, losses of the French firms involved in [the Integrated Circuit Plan] reportedly reached 400 million francs. Losses will probably be about the same in 1983, since these companies will have to continue to expand, no matter what the current economic situation."

measures. It is noteworthy, therefore, that in the information sector, the Bonn government has felt compelled to implement an explicitly sectoral industrial promotion policy. Direct government aid to this sector -- particularly microelectronics -- has expanded dramatically in the 1980s as Germany has sought to enhance the international competitiveness of an industry regarded as essential to the future of the nation.

German industrial policy in the high technology industries has been implemented by several agencies -- the Ministry of Research and Technology (BMFT), the Ministry of Economics, and, to a lesser degree, by the Ministry of Labor.[434] The governments of some of the individual states *(Lander)* have also implemented programs to stimulate the development of high technology which have influenced industry growth.[435]

The German Ministry of Economics supports two dozen research institutes which form the Fraunhofer Gesellschaft (FHG), the Association of Institutes of Applied Research, a government-supported association which coordinates government-industry-university R&D. The FHG places a primary emphasis on the diffusion of technology from its research institutes to German industry. The institutes themselves are not basic research laboratories, but are oriented toward commercial technologies, including semiconductor technology. The FHG Institute for Solid State Technology, jointly funded by the government (BMFT) and industry, emphasizes semiconductor process technology, and has coordinated other government programs relating to microelectronics.[436]

---

434 In 1985, a Cabinet-level "Committee for Technology Policy" was established to coordinate technology policy between the various Ministries. Symbolizing the importance which the Bonn government placed on this issue, the new committee was established concurrently with the reduction of the number of such committees from 13 to 6. *VDI Nachrichten* (April 5, 1985).

435 The Deutsche Bundespost has also served as an instrument of German industrial policy in the information sector, both through its authority to set equipment standards and as a major purchaser of telecommunications equipment and computers. The Bundespost enjoys a legal monopoly on telecommunications and has the power to prohibit competing forms of business under a 1928 statute, the *Fernmeldeanlagengesetzt*. Its procurements of telecommunications equipment in 1984 were valued at DM 12.7 billion (over $4 billion), the bulk of which was purchased from German firms. U.S. International Trade Commission, *Changes in the U.S. Telecommunications Industry and the Impact on U.S. Telecommunications Trade* (U.S.I.T.C. Pub. No. 1642, June 1984), p. 71; Clayton Yeutter to Senator Lloyd Bentsen, October 15, 1984 (Attachment).

436 For example, the Bonn Government and the Land government of Berlin jointly constructed an electron accumulator ring for synchotron radiation (BESSY), originally planned for basic research in physics. The Solid State Institute's "Microstructure Technology Division" secured a commitment that one quarter of the Berlin synchotron laboratory space would be devoted to research on new process technologies for semiconductors. Coordinated by the Institute and funded by the State, representatives from four firms (Siemens, AEG-Telefunken, Valvo and Eurosil) have been participating in the "largest x-ray lithography research group outside Japan." The Solid State Institute

While the German government has never embraced the "national champion" philosophy, its initial efforts to foster its microelectronics sector, undertaken in 1974, centered on a comparatively small number of firms, most notably Siemens and Telefunken, and did little to enhance Germany's competitive position.[437] At the end of 1981, the BMFT launched a Special Program for the Application of Microelectronics which was designed to encourage wider use of microelectronics in German industry,[438] and which concentrated on smaller firms.[439] Through this effort, it was expected that "the German federal government will help German microelectronics make a decisive breakthrough."[440] Two surveys of the results of the program conducted for the BMFT concluded that it had been successful in accelerating the application of microelectronics by small and medium- sized companies,[441] and the program was extended in 1986.[442] Nevertheless,

---

also operates a synchotron R&D project in Hamburg ("DESY") which is concentrating on the use of x-ray lithography to manufacture electronic switching circuits. The work of the BESSY group has led to the formation of a new project, Compact Storage Ring for Synchotron Radiation (COSY), which uses superconducting magnets for an x-ray lithography technique utilizing eight beam lines. *Die Zeit* (March 23, 1984); *Technivisie* (November 19, 1986).

437 This program initially involved government funding of about $30 million per year. It was expanded in the 1979-82 period, with the government supplying about $300 million in funds which was matched by the private sector. *Elektronik Applikation* (September 1982). *Der Spiegel* observed on April 5, 1982 that "Eight years of [government] support has not made the FRG independent of foreign chip production. The result of millions in subsidies is very modest: "one or two production lines producing at world standards," according to [BMFT Uwe] Thomas."

438 The German economy lagged in the application of microelectronics to other industries, a fact which was adversely affecting the competitiveness of key German industries like machine tools and auto parts. Prior to 1981, the German government had withheld support for encouraging application of microelectronics because "with such funds we would have primarily helped only the foreign chip manufacturers." By 1981, with German export competitiveness jeopardized in a number of industries, the shortsightedness of this policy had become apparent. *Der Spiegel* (April 5, 1982); *VDI Nachrichten* (February 26, 1982).

439 Between 1982 and 1984 DM300 million were to be disbursed in the form of non-repayable grants to small firms for projects involving the application of microelectronics technology. "To prevent these subsidies from being funneled primarily to large companies, a cap of DM 800 thousand per company was established. The grants were disbursed with a minimum of bureaucracy." *Der Spiegel* commented (April 5, 1982) that "On the two-page application form, not much more than address and bank account number need be given.... Whoever fills out the forms according to instructions will have the support of money in his pocket almost instantly." The response from German industry was immediate: in the first two months after the program was announced, over 1000 applications were submitted to the VDI Technology Center. *VDI Nachrichten* (February 26, 1982).

440 *Frankfurter Rundschau* (December 5, 1981).

441 *Technologie Nachrichten -- Management Informationen* (November 17, 1986).

despite such efforts, microelectronics remained "the Achilles heel of the German electronics industry." [443]

Accordingly, in the spring of 1984, the German cabinet unveiled a report on information technology *(Informationstechnik)* outlining a much more comprehensive and ambitious government program to promote the development of the entire German information sector. The Minister for Research and Technology commented that

> *Our share of the world market in high technology goods is stagnating, while Japan's share in the last decade has doubled. We cannot overlook this, if we want to maintain our leading position in the 1990s as well . . . . One of the most important new priority areas for state support of research and technology is information equipment. To this end, the government has approved the comprehensive plan to support microelectronics, information and communications technology . . . . In this plan, we are documenting our determination to accept the challenges of information technology and to improve our competitiveness.*

The BMFT, which explained the new program to the public, indicated that among other things, the government would commit over DM 1 billion to promoting microelectronics technologies between 1984 and 1988. [444]

The Bonn government has also begun to contribute substantial sums to large-scale joint R&D projects. It is helping to finance the Mega-Projekt", a joint effort between Siemens and Philips to develop a 1 megabit SRAM and a 4 megabit DRAM. In 1986, the government indicated it would contribute DM 100 million to "Suprenum", a supercomputer R&D project involving three German firms.

The foregoing description of the recent French and German efforts under way in microelectronics is by no means a complete survey of European national promotional efforts. The government of virtually every large and small European country is supporting R&D in microelectronics, usually directed at commercial applications:

---

442 *VDI Nachrichten* (October 17, 1986).

443 *Suddeutsche Zeitung* (May 21, 1984), p. 25.

444 The planned expenditures included (a) DM 500 million for a "submicron project" designed to enable German companies to mass produce "internationally competitive" VLSI devices by the late 1980s; (b) DM 400 million for the development of microperipherals (components linking microprocessors to conventional machines); (c) DM 200 million for development of new component technologies; and (d) DM 120 million for the development of integrated optics. *Wirtschaftswoche* (March 9, 1984).

- The government of the United Kingdom established a "flagship" semiconductor company in 1978 (INMOS) and is currently funding two major microelectronics R&D efforts involving collaboration with British industry, the Alvey Programme and the Micro-electronics Industry Support Programme (MISP). The Alvey project involves 200 million pounds in government funds; its VLSI and CAD programme is designed to develop 1-micron technologies directly applicable to commercial production by 1989.[445] U.K. and Scottish government investment incentives have played an important role in establishing a "Silicon Glen" in Scotland.[446]

- The government of Italy has provided microelectronics R&D funding since the 1970s for Italy's largest electronics firm, SGS. It is currently supporting a major VLSI R&D program (involving Italian electronics firms, national research centers, and six universities) which "has a strictly industrial orientation." This effort will involve the development of commercial device prototypes, CAD design of semiconductors, and the use of a pilot production line (at SGS) to perfect new process technologies.[447] Government funding for the SGS VLSI effort consists of 13 billion lire in subsidies and 13 billion in "easy credit" at rates fixed by the Treasury Minister.[448]

- In 1986, the government of Belgium contributed $60 million to facilitate the establishment of IMEC, a research center which will promote microelectronics training, research and applications. IMEC -- Europe's largest independent research center -- will be staffed by 250 people and will concentrate on sub-micron technology, optoelectronics, and design procedure for VLSI systems.[449]

- In 1983, the government of Sweden launched a five-year program to support microelectronics R&D, providing 549 million kronor in financial support. The Swedish program featured a "niche" strategy, emphasizing R&D into gate arrays, gallium arsenide technology,

445 Alvey Directorate, *Alvey Programme Annual Report* (London: IEE Publishing Dept., 1986); Malerba, *The Semiconductor Business,* pp. 195-98.

446 *Daily Telegraph* (March 20, 1984); *Electronics* (May 5, 1986).

447 *Selezione* (February 15, 1987); Malerba, *The Semiconductor Business,* pp. 198-200; *Cronache del Gruppo STET* (May 1986), pp. 20-22.

448 *Gazzetta Ufficiale della Republica Italiana* (April 3, 1987).

449 *Frankfurter Allgemeine/Blick durch die Wirtschaft* (June 12, 1986).

optoelectronics, and customized ICs rather than high volume commodity products.[450] In 1987, this program resulted in the development of a complementary metal semiconductor (CMES) -- an alternative to CMOS technology -- which is the most advanced in the world. The Swedes were elated that they had "achieved these results before other teams of researchers at Stanford, in Silicon Valley, and elsewhere...." [451]

Cooperation at the European Level

The failure of national programs to narrow the competitive gap between Europe, on the one hand, and Japan and the United States, on the other hand, has led to the view that if the European information industry is to become competitive on a world scale, transnational cooperative efforts within Europe are essential. The form which such transnational efforts will take has proven a subject of continuing controversy, with the European Commission pursuing programs which feature a central role for itself, while industries and governments of several of larger member states are implementing transnational initiatives which relegate the Commission to a marginal role.[452]

European Community Policies

The Commission of the European Economic Community (EC Commission) has pursued a number of ambitious programs in the information sector in the 1980s. These programs have been designed (1) to fill gaps left by the various national programs under way in the member states, (2) to ensure coordination and information flow between the member states, and (3) to establish common Community standards in telecommunications and other information products, permitting the evolution of a common internal market.

The Microelectronics Program (Regulation 3744/81). In December 1981, the EC began a four year microelectronics program (the so-called "Regulation 3744/81 Program") designed to coordinate national activities in

---

450 *Teknik I Teden* (Winter, 1984); *Ny Teknik* (November 10, 1983); *Svenska Dagbladet* (October 25, 1983).

451 *Teknik I Teden* (Winter 1987).

452 For example, the governments of West Germany, France, the U.K. and Italy recently concluded an accord on the construction of a European Synchotron Radiation Source, a facility which could prove instrumental in the manufacture of submicron semiconductors. The EC Commission was not a party to this accord. Memorandum of Understanding reproduced in *Gazzetta Ufficiale della Republica Italiana* (July 25, 1986).

the field of microelectronics to stimulate research and development into production and testing equipment for VLSI manufacture.[453] The goal of the plan was to "make Europe independent of American and Japanese equipment and component suppliers."[454] The resources committed to this effort were comparatively small, and the Commission's assessment, as the project neared completion, was that the Community had not achieved competitive parity with the U.S. and Japan:

It may be appropriate here . . . to summarize the position of the Community in the two domains addressed by the programme (i.e. equipment and CAD for VLSI). The Community is still lagging considerably behind U.S. and Japan and is still dependent on imports for most of the state-of-the-art equipments that are used for the production and testing of VLSI circuits. It is also noted that neither the coordinated efforts (at national or Community level) nor the industry response on the equipment domain appear to be sufficiently intense.[455]

The Regulation 3744/81 microelectronics program, while modest in its accomplishments, helped to lay the groundwork for many of the microelectronics projects subsequently implemented pursuant to the much more ambitious ESPRIT program, which became operational in 1984.[456]

ESPRIT. In 1982, the European Commission made a series of major proposals for a strategic program in the information technologies, and in 1983, the Council of Ministers of the Member States adopted a Commission recommendation for a European Strategic Program for Research and Development in Information Technologies (ESPRIT).[457] The basic goal of

---

453 Council Regulation No. 3744/81 (December 7, 1981); *Official Journal*, No. L.376 (December 12, 1981), p. 38.

454 First Report by the Commission to the Council, *Community Projects in the Field of Microelectronics at July 15, 1983*, COM(83) 564 final (October 7, 1983). Pursuant to an open bidding procedure, the Commission made grants available for microelectronics R&D projects that involved participating companies or institutions from more than one member state. The majority of the proposals ultimately approved for Community funding under this program involved computer aided design (CAD) of VLSI circuits rather than device or process technology.

455 Third Report by the Commission to the Council and the European Parliament, *Community Actions in the Field of Microelectronic Technology*, COM(85) 776 final (December 23, 1985), p. 41.

456 The Commission commented that "the work carried out on microelectronics within the framework of the ESPRIT programme represents both a continuation and an expansion of the activities undertaken pursuant to Regulation No. 3744/81.... Some of the ESPRIT projects either are drawing on information from or are follow-ups of projects launched under Regulation No. 3744/81."

457 *Official Journal*, No. C. 321 (November 26, 1983).

ESPRIT was to provide the European information sector with the technology base needed to achieve competitive parity with Japan and the United States within ten years.[458] This was to be achieved by Community sponsorship of "pre-competitive" joint R&D projects in five designated areas of the information technologies: advanced microelectronics, CAD manufacturing, software, office systems, and advanced information processing.[459] ESPRIT was divided into two basic types of projects:

- *Type A projects:* large efforts aimed at specified objectives requiring major infrastructure, personnel and financial commitments, which would receive about 75 percent of total EC funding.

- *Type B projects:* smaller projects requiring fewer resources, which could range from long-term, basic, R&D to short-term specialized projects with immediate commercial applications.[460]

The Commission estimated that the first five-year phase of ESPRIT would require funding of 1.5 billion ECU, half of which would be provided by the Community.[461] ESPRIT was to take place in two overlapping "phases," with new projects (generally of several years' duration) being initiated each year. The cornerstone of ESPRIT was the annually-updated "Workprogramme," the technical content of which was prepared after consultation by the ESPRIT Advisory Board with "specialists drawn from all sectors of the [information technologies] research Community, both industrial and academic." The Workprogramme (divided into five "Sub-programmes" to reflect ESPRIT's five broad areas of inquiry) outlined broad technological goals and resulted in a call for proposals from industry and research institutes for specific projects. The projects chosen were then partially funded by the Community and periodically reviewed by Community officials.[462] In the first phase, three calls for proposals were made pursuant to successive

---

458 Ibid., p. 12.

459 Ibid., pp. 4-5.

460 *Official Journal,* No. C. 321 (November 26, 1983). The Type B projects were in part a political device to secure the support of the smaller member states for the project, ensuring that each nation would be able to participate in some aspect of the project. *L'Espresso* (July 1, 1984).

461 *Official Journal,* No. C. 321 (November 26, 1983), p. 32. The Commission proposed to fund 50 percent of the cost of Type A projects, with the balance supplied by industry. The norm for Type B project subsidies would also be 50 percent, but in individual cases this could be exceeded and might even result in a 100 percent subsidy in some cases.

462 Communication from the Commission to the Council, *The Second Phase of ESPRIT,* COM(86) 269 final (May 21, 1986), p. 17.

Workprogrammes in 1984, 1985, and 1986, each of which resulted in the initiation of new batches of Type A and Type B R&D projects.

Guidelines for the use of the results were to be agreed upon by the participants in each project on a case-by-case basis, "the Commission only ensuring that competition rules are not infringed." The Commission stipulated, however, that whatever arrangements were made, each participant in the project must have "guaranteed and privileged access to the results of the work done by the others."[463] The Commission required that "industrial companies in the Community" which did not take part in the products should have the opportunity to acquire the rights to the results under license.[464] The Commission also implemented a broad range of programs to encourage the sharing of information gained from ESPRIT within the Community and the application of ESPRIT results by Community industry.[465]

By the end of 1985, 173 R&D projects had been launched under ESPRIT, involving 263 industrial enterprises, 81 research institutes, and 104 universities, involving 1300 researchers.[466] The Commission committed a larger proportion of the ESPRIT budget to "Advanced Microelectronics" (24.2 percent as of the end of 1985) than to any of the other four project sub-areas.[467] The initial 1984 Microelectronics Sub-programme concentrated most resources on a few Type A projects devoted to silicon MOS and bipolar VLSI process techniques, and to CAD design of VLSI circuits.[468] In the 1986 Workprogramme, the main thrust of R&D in ESPRIT Microelectronics subprogramme was identified as pushing the silicon-based technologies

---

463 The Commission also provides that the results obtained by the ESPRIT working group "shall ... be arranged under privileged conditions" to research teams working on other ESPRIT projects.

464 Ibid., pp. 38-39.

465 Ibid., pp. 34-35. For example, the Community has established the ESPRIT Information Exchange System (IES), a data communications system for exchanging information between separated participants in various ESPRIT projects and Community and national authorities. Commission to the Council, *Draft Council Decision* (adopting 1986 ESPRIT Workprogramme), COM(85) 602 final (November 12, 1985), p. 0-5.

466 Answer by the Commission to Written Question from Mr. Vandemeulebroucke, No. 2261/85 (February 17, 1986).

467 The Commission commented that "Advanced Microelectronics ... [is] the hardware foundation of the Information Technology industry. This subprogramme concentrates on the priority areas needed to ensure that Europe maintains a competitive position regarding the supply of these essential ingredients for her IT manufacturing industry with the required capability, in sufficient quantity and at competitive prices." *Official Journal,* No. L. 365 (December 31, 1985), p. 8.

468 The Commission commented that "the importance of CAD for VLSI to the overall success of ESPRIT cannot be accomplished. Given good technology and outstanding CAD, the highly innovative European industry will be able to compete successfully in world markets." *Official Journal,* No. L. 55 (February 23, 1986).

(MOS bipolar) toward the limits of their capabilities while pursuing the possibilities afforded by compound semiconductor materials, such as GaAs. The largest number of new Type A projects under negotiation were in the area of CAD design of VLSI circuits.[469] A similar Community-administered program emphasizing R&D in advanced communications (RACE) was initiated· in 1985, featuring some microelectronics projects, and a close cooperation has developed between the ESPRIT and RACE microelectronics R&D efforts.

An initial wrangle over the funding of ESPRIT delayed its inception until early 1984, and budget controversies have been a chronic aspect of the program.[470] Nevertheless, by late 1985, after ESPRIT had been under way for 18 months, a number of analysts in Europe were cautiously characterizing it as a success:

> *According to [EC official] Mr. Carpentier, and to representatives from Thomson (France), ICL (Great Britain), and Philips (Netherlands), the ESPRIT program is progressing more rapidly than anticipated, and has already obtained positive results.*[471]

An independent body, the ESPRIT Review Board, assessed the project at the end of 1985, and concluded that ESPRIT had "been successfully established and is well on the way to meeting its objectives." [472]

ESPRIT also had numerous critics in the Community, who objected to its excessive bureaucracy; its exclusion of potentially valuable European partners outside of the Community; its requirements that small and medium enterprises take part in projects and share their results, and its emphasis on longer-term research to the detriment of immediate commercial opportunities.[473] The larger Member States objected to "the burden of a

---

469 *Official Journal,* No. L. 365 (December 31, 1985), p. 8.

470 Britain and West Germany argued that ESPRIT could not be funded unless the EC's broader budget problems were resolved, resulting in a delay in implementation of the project. A Greek Minister lamented, "how long are these programs supposed to continue to gather dust in Brussels file drawers?" *Wirtschaftswoche* (March 9, 1984); *NRC Handelsblad* (January 24, 1984).

471 *AFP Sciences* (September 26, 1985). *Electronique Actualites* commented on September 27, 1985 that "Eighteen months after its start, the ESPRIT program . . . is proving to be a success."

472 *NRC Handelsblad* (January 31, 1986).

473 *Le Monde Diplomatique* commented in August 1985 (pp. 18-19): "Three complaints [about ESPRIT] are frequently voiced: The program's industrial objectives are too far in the future; the profusion of subjects of research disperses the financial -- and above all, the human -- resources of the European teams . . . and lastly, the enterprises would prefer agreements between genuinely self-interested partners, which is in direct

European Commission that wants to stimulate technological cooperation with, for example, Greece and Portugal." [474] These criticisms resulted in adjustments to ESPRIT during its second phase (1987-91); however, they also added impetus to European transnational initiatives (such as EUREKA), which were designed to function independently of the Brussels authorities.

The Second Phase of ESPRIT. In 1986, the Commission, after extensive consultations with industry and the scientific community, established broad strategic guidelines for the second phase of ESPRIT (1987-91), taking account of "the changing environment and developments" which had occurred since 1982-84, and reflecting many of the criticisms of the first phase.[475] The second phase was to be based on a "demand-driven strategy," emphasizing the application of technologies developed in ESPRIT in a broad range of downstream industries where an established potential European demand base already existed. The Commission stated that

A multiplicator effect will be created, so the R&D will stimulate much greater investment and production activity by companies downstream, where EEC industrial and commercial potential already exists. Therefore the focus has been directed to enabling technologies, in particular advanced microelectronic and peripheral components and information processing systems design.[476]

The second phase carried forward many elements of the first, such as the effort to establish common European standards and the need to include small and medium enterprises in ESPRIT. In addition, in order to "take full

---

contradiction with the program's objective of systematizing the inclusion of each and every member of the Community in the joint pursuit of each and every subject of the program, while excluding participation by third countries, such as Switzerland or Sweden, for example." *Zero un Informatique Hebdo* (September 30, 1985).

474 *NRC Handelsblad* (December 6, 1986). A West German official commented in 1986 that "A much too large portion of [the EC] money has to be earmarked for the less developed member nations' attempts to catch up. You would do better to let that money be used by the member nations who are in the lead. Then you are doing something genuine about the Japanese and American threat. Not if you strive for a European mediocrity." Ibid.

475 The second phase, originally planned to begin in 1989, was initiated ahead of schedule because the budget for the first phase had been expended. *Nouvelles de la Science et des Technologies* (March 1986). The Commission noted in particular the growing spirit of cooperation with respect to high tech R&D within the Community; the increased resources being devoted to the information technologies in the U.S. and Japan; the new initiatives being launched within the Community (e.g., EUREKA); and the progressive fusion of the various information subsectors into a single interrelated industry. EC Commission, *The Second Phase of ESPRIT,* pp. 11-12.

476 Ibid., pp. 11-12.

advantage of the European dimension," the second phase would be open to participation by EFTA countries such as Sweden.[477] In microelectronics, three priority areas were identified for the second phase:

- *High Density Integrated Circuits.* The ESPRIT goal was to develop ICs of a density up to 4 million gates, particularly for use in parallel processing systems.

- *High Speed Integrated Circuits.* The objective was to fabricate devices for use where processing of large quantities of information cannot be assured through parallel processing.

- *Multifunctional Integrated Circuits.* The objective was to build a complete system on a single chip, with analog and digital functions, operating over a wide range of speeds, with a complexity of up to 1 million transistors.[478]

While ESPRIT continues to have many critics,[479] it is inevitable that the massive commitments of financial and human resources which ESPRIT entails are beginning to show results in the market. In 1986, for example, an ESPRIT project resulted in the development of a 10K array bipolar device which "compared with the best in the world" and which will be commercialized by Siemens.[480] In 1986, Thomson estimated that participation in ESPRIT had had a "multiplier effect" of 3 or 4 times on its R&D investments.[481] Another ESPRIT project resulted in successful development of a "silicon compiler" -- a software CAD system for designing VLSI devices.[482]

The EUREKA Initiative

The United States' decision to launch its $26 billion Strategic Defense Initiative (SDI) provoked widespread concern in Europe that commercial spinoffs from the U.S. program would lead to a widening of the U.S.

---

477 *AFP Sciences* (June 20, 1983).

478 ESPRIT projects in various areas of microelectronics are summarized in *Official Journal*, No. L. 365 (December 31, 1985).

479 *Technologie Nachrichten -- Management Informationen* (November 28, 1986).

480 EEC, *Information Memo*, No. P.-98 (December 1986).

481 *Le Monde* (December 19, 1986).

482 *Technivisie* (November 19, 1986).

competitive edge relative to Europe across a broad range of advanced technologies, reducing European companies to the role of subcontractors, and producing a "brain drain" of scientists to the U.S.[483] Most of Europe's large electronic firms saw little benefit to themselves from participating directly in SDI.[484] On the other hand, widespread interest existed in a European response to SDI -- a massive effort to mobilize European resources to develop advanced technologies with commercial applications.[485]

The initiative for such an effort came from French President Mitterand, who in April 1985 proposed to create a "technological Europe" through industry-led multinational R&D efforts in artificial intelligence, robotics, supercomputers, advanced microelectronics, new materials, optoelectronics, and high-powered lasers, a concept the French dubbed "EUREKA."[486] The European Commission, caught off balance by this proposal, prepared a parallel proposal for a "European Technology Community," which would place the Commission in a central coordinating role.[487] The differences between the French and Commission proposals were substantial; the French strategy was based on "demand pull" (develop products with immediate commercial applications), the Commission's on "technology push" (stimulate technologies for which future uses will be found).[488] With respect to program structure,

The French are opposed to EC structures, and even opposed to an agency operating independently of the EC . . . they want to leave the initiative entirely up to industry. The EC on the other hand does opt for its own structure, for "after all, it is there for a reason" as one official puts it. . . .

---

483 *AFP Sciences* (June 20, 1983).

484 Philips commented in 1985 that although some SDI money had been budgeted for research in Europe, "the Americans will primarily want to buy knowledge they don't have themselves." Moreover, in SDI there was "no connection between a research project and a potential order for production." Finally, "Philips considers the possibility very small that participation in SDI will lead to acquisition of knowledge from other parts of the program. The transfer of knowledge is not customary in such defense technologies." *NRC Handelsblad* (June 25, 1985).

485 *Neue Zurcher Zeitung* (June 8, 1985), p. 15.

486 The French government circulated a 77-page document outlining the EUREKA concept and detailing specific large-scale joint R&D projects, prepared by CESTA, the Center for Studies on Advanced Systems and Technologies. *La Renaissance Technologie de L'Europe* (June 1985).

487 EC Commission, *Toward a European Technology Community,* COM(85) 350 Final (June 25, 1985). The Commission officially welcomed the French initiative, but "behind the scenes," criticized it and engaged in "feverish efforts" to develop its own alternative proposal. *Neue Zurcher Zeitung* (June 8, 1985).

488 *NRC Handelsblad* (July 17, 1985).

[Under the French approach] cliques of large countries or companies can exclude small areas.[489]

Wrangling over the nature and form of EUREKA consumed most of 1985.[490] At length, agreement was reached on a program that would exist outside the framework of the Community institutions, governed only by a weak Secretariat, and which would include non-member countries such as Sweden.[491] Seventy-two projects were adopted in 1985-86, to bear the EUREKA label, budgeted at 3.2 billion ECU over a 10-year period.[492] The arrangement of financing for each project was left entirely to the participants, with the understanding that some projects would be state-subsidized[493] and

---

489   Ibid.

490   One observer commented that "the technological Renaissance of Europe . . . looks more like the Dark Ages." *Wall Street Journal* (November 5, 1985). The European Commission favored a EUREKA structure similar to ESPRIT, that is, organized and funded under the aegis of the Commission; the French proposed that the program be coordinated through a weak "Secretariat" in which the Commission would simply participate as a member. With respect to financing, Britain, Spain and Switzerland argued that the major role should be played by companies; the French and German governments stated their readiness to make major financial contributions. The relationship of proposed EUREKA projects with those already under way in programs like ESPRIT was unclear and substantial concern was expressed over the danger of wasteful duplication of effort. EC Parliament, *Working Documents,* Doc. A 2-52/86/Part II (May 28, 1986).

491   In June 1986, Ministers from 18 European nations and a representative from the European Commission agreed to the establishment of a permanent EUREKA Secretariat in Brussels. EUREKA was not an EC institution, and the "predominant coordinating role" the Commission had envisioned for itself was "whittled down to one place out of six within the Secretariat, and 19th member status within the EUREKA ministerial structure." The Secretariat was a relatively powerless entity whose principal function was to serve as a clearinghouse for information rather than to exercise central direction. EC Parliament, *Working Documents,* DOC. A 2-52/86 Part II (May 28, 1986), p. 18. The Secretariat was established at the behest of the smaller nations to ensure that "information is disseminated and the programme is transparent." *European Report,* No. 1174 (November 9, 1986).

492   Communication from the Commission to the Council, *EUREKA and the European Technology Community,* COM(86) 664 Final (November 20, 1986), p. 3.

493   In 1986, the commitments by national governments to EUREKA under discussion were: France, 1 billion francs; Germany, 300 million DM; Britain, 250 million pounds; Belgium, 500 million Bfs.; Netherlands, 25 million guilders. EC Parliament, *Working Documents,* Doc. A-2-52/86/Part II (May 28, 1986).

others wholly financed by the private sector.[494] The EUREKA projects differed from EC projects such as ESPRIT in several respects:

- *Emphasis on Advanced Development.* Community programs emphasized R&D with long lead times, while EUREKA was "closer to the market," stressing the rapid development of products with commercial potential. In contrast to ESPRIT, "the proportion of universities and public sector research centres is low."

- *Companies Provide Guidance.* EC programs were required to fit into a predetermined strategic framework, while EUREKA projects "come directly from companies, without reference to a strategic programme . . . apart from the broad reference made to the field of high technology."

- *Flexible Funding Structures.* EC projects were funded from the Community budget (usually covering 50% of the cost of the project), whereas the EUREKA projects' funding varied greatly from project to project, involving national government subsidies, private funding, and/or some mix thereof.[495]

From the outset, proponents of EUREKA placed heavy emphasis on microelectronics.[496] In 1985 and 1986, a number of major microelectronics programs received EUREKA designation, most notably European Silicon Structures (ES2), a joint venture for the design of integrated circuits using direct impression on silicon, and an Anglo-French project to develop gallium

---

494 The EC Commission noted that with respect to the approved projects, "the financing arrangements vary greatly from one country to another, so that it is difficult to determine the respective volume and breakdown of subsidies and repayable advances from government, of loans on ordinary or special terms and of the participants' own funds." Ibid., p. 5.

495 Ibid., p. 6.

496 Four of the twenty major projects advanced in the original French proposal were in the microelectronics field, each featuring heavy French participation and suggesting partners among the large European electronics producers (principally Siemens, Plessey, Philips, and INMOS): (a) development of a 64-megabit memory by 1995; (b) development by 1990 of a "Europrocessor", e.g., a high-end flexible microprocessor in submicron technology which would lead to the introduction of a standard and end the U.S. "de facto monopoly" in this field; (c) industrial development of high-speed gallium arsenide components and development of a GaAs pilot plant within five years; and (d) development of a prototype plant for making customized signal processing (MOS-type digital semiconductors). CESTA, *La Rennaissance Technologique de L'Europe.* The European Commission's proposal for EUREKA proposed projects which were similar if not identical. EC Commission, *Toward a European Technology Community,* pp. 1-4, 1-6.

arsenide design and manufacturing processes. Projects receiving EUREKA designation are listed in Table 4.5. In mid-1986, Siemens, Philips and Thomson announced a new joint R&D project to create a 64 megabit DRAM by 1995 -- "Chip 1995" -- an effort whose cost was estimated at FFr. 15 billion.[497]

It remains to be seen whether EUREKA will "become a shield against the American-Japanese technological invasion of European markets. . . . [or] not much more than a kind of industrial directory, handy for firms in search of international partners."[498] The continuing reluctance of Member States to provide funding at the levels called for poses the danger that "EUREKA will slowly suffocate" from lack of funds.[499] Some European governments and the European press have been skeptical of EUREKA, which has been characterized variously as "something that could have been born spontaneously from private initiatives,"[500] a "hot air balloon," and a "disorderly technological afterbirth."[501]

The Siemens-Philips Mega-Projekt

In 1984, Siemens and Philips, the Dutch electronics multinational, announced an ambitious joint effort to develop megabit memories, and approached their respective governments for financial support.[502] The driving force behind this effort was the impact of visits to Japan by German and Dutch scientists and engineers in the early 1980s.[503]

A joint voyage of discovery through the Japanese microelectronics industry in fall 1983 gave all the participants a great shock. Japan threatened to

---

497   The Germans advocated conducting this effort under the auspices of EUREKA; the French preferred ESPRIT. The 64 megabit project was to be kept separate from other ongoing joint projects, including the ESPRIT CAD VLSI projects and the Siemens-Philips Mega-Projekt. *L'Usine Nouvelle* (July 10, 1986), p. 19; *Bild Der Wissenschaft* (November 1985).

498   *Elseviers Weekblad* (July 5, 1986), p. 22.

499   *NRC Handelsblad* (December 6, 1986).

500   *Zero un Hebdo Informatique* (June 16, 1986), p. 7.

501   *Elseviers Weekblad* (July 5, 1986), p. 22.

502   *Frankfurter Allgemeine Zietung* (July 11, 1984), p. 16.

503   Elektrotechnische Studievereniging Delft, *Electrotechniek in Het Licht van de Rijzende Zon* (Netherlands: Three Dutch Technical Universities, April 1982).

TABLE 4.5

MICROELECTRONICS PROJECTS RECEIVING "EUREKA" DESIGNATION (AS OF NOVEMBER 1986)

Project	Partners	Objective	Cost (Million ECU)	Duration Years
European Silicon Structures (ES 2)	BEL, UK, FRA, FRG, SWE, SWI	Design and automatic production of ICs using direct impression on silicon	94	3
Gallium Arsenide	UK, FRA	Develop design and manufacturing processes for monolithic ICs for microwaves from GaAs	60	3
DIANE	FRA, SPA, UK	Nondestructive use of neutron beam for quality control in large, complex components made from new materials	15	4
DESIRE	UK, BEL	Development of an all-dry single layer photo-lithography technology for submicron devices	4	3
Sub 0.1-Micron Ion Projection	AUS, FRG	Increase level of integration in electronic components by reducing width of circuits capable of mass production, and by improving materials technology.	5	3-5
Fast Prototyping Service for Silicon ASICs	FRA, UK	Develop compatable design and manufacturing tools for ASICs	30	5
New Design Technologies for Power Semiconductors	SWE, SWI	Develop new techniques for designing high power semiconductors	5	2

Source: EUREKA Ministerial Conference, June 30, 1986, Communique of the Conference, "Nouveaux Projets Eureka"

gain an insurmountable lead over Europe. Only fast and united action could still save the day. . . . It was perfectly clear what had to be done. Siemens had to cooperate with Philips.[504]

The Bonn government initially extended a grant of DM 320 million; the Dutch government contributed 170 million guilders. Siemens and Philips contributed 2.2 billion DM and 2.5 billion guilders to the project, respectively.[505] The objective of the Mega-Projekt is to develop a 1 megabit static RAM (Philips) and a 4 megabit dynamic RAM (Siemens) by 1988.[506] This is illustrated in Figure 4.2.

The Mega-Projekt was widely hailed as Europe's opportunity to "get back in the race" with Japan in microelectronics. Dr. Hermann Franz of Siemens commented in 1985 that

This megabit project is Europe's last chance in the competitive battle against the Japanese chip invasion. If we in the chip industry do not enter the age of submicron technology at the same time as the Japanese firms in particular, then we will not survive the next decade.[507]

However, by mid-1985, it was apparent that Japanese DRAM technology was moving forward so rapidly that the Mega-Projekt's completion deadlines would be too late.[508] Accordingly, Siemens -- reportedly "limping 3.5 years behind the Japanese"[509] -- purchased the technology for a 1-megabit DRAM from Toshiba.[510] Phillips hedged its

---

504 *NRC Handelsblad* (November 5, 1986).

505 *Der Spiegel* (October 29, 1985).

506 *De Volkskrant* (October 5, 1985). Siemens hopes to ship samples of a 4-megabit DRAM in 1988 and go into full production in 1989. *Handelsblatt* (December 5, 1989).

507 *De Volkskrant* (October 5, 1985).

508 Siemens' Dr. Hermann Franz commented that "[O]ur Japanese competitors have sped up all their research and development. Our original plan, whereby we wanted to have the 1-megabit chip in mass production at the end of 1987, would simply have been too late." *NRC Handelsblad* (October 4, 1985).

509 *Handelsblatt* (March 17, 1986).

510 This arrangement annoyed the German government. One official complained that "Siemens doesn't need any research support if it just buys the expertise, does it?" *NRC Handelsblad* (October 31, 1985).

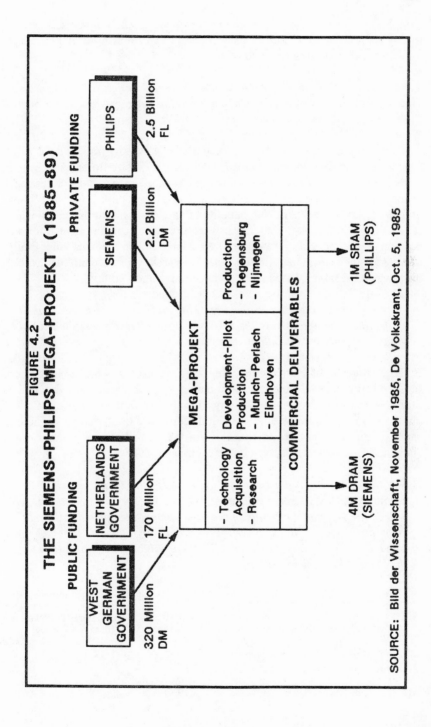

FIGURE 4.2

THE SIEMENS-PHILIPS MEGA-PROJEKT (1985-89)

PUBLIC FUNDING

PRIVATE FUNDING

WEST GERMAN GOVERNMENT

NETHERLANDS GOVERNMENT

SIEMENS

PHILIPS

320 Million DM

170 Million FL

2.2 Billion DM

2.5 Billion FL

MEGA-PROJEKT

- Technology Acquisition
- Research

Development-Pilot Production
- Munich-Perlach
- Eindhoven

Production
- Regensburg
- Nijmegen

COMMERCIAL DELIVERABLES

4M DRAM (SIEMENS)

1M SRAM (PHILLIPS)

SOURCE: Bild der Wissenschaft, November 1985, De Volkskrant, Oct. 5, 1985

bets by simultaneously pursuing the development of a 1-megabit SRAM through a joint venture with Matsushita.[511]   The Finnish journal *Helsingen Sanomat* commented on June 20, 1985 that

> *The experts indeed regard the Siemens-Philips project as a hopeless attempt to participate in a development that has managed to a great extent to slip out of European hands.*

This assessment was probably too pessimistic. At the end of 1986, following a crash program which featured parallel efforts in research, development, and preparation for production, Siemens and Philips were reportedly on schedule and would begin delivering samples of 1M SRAMs and 4M DRAMs in 1988. The benefits of cooperation had been sufficiently established that the two companies were preparing collaborative efforts to develop a 16 megabit DRAM.[512]   In March 1987 Siemens and Philips presented the German Minister for Research and Technology with a prototype 4 megabit DRAM, and he "declared proudly" that

> *According to all the information about the competition, amidst all their spectacular announcements, the FRG will be catching up with the leading nations, Japan and the United States.*[513]

Perhaps more fundamentally, the Mega-Projekt itself -- whether it succeeds or fails in its avowed objective of catching up with Japan and the United States -- has brought together a large number of European scientists and engineers for an intensive developmental effort, and by so doing, will help to maintain an infrastructure so that the Europeans will at least remain in the running. *Handelsblatt* observed on December 17, 1985

> *that the fact that development takes place in Munich and fabrication in Hamburg and Regensburg instead of perhaps California or Scotland, as well as the fact that the results of the development are applied in Europe, is at the disposal of technology in Europe, or rather in the Federal Republic. This is largely a matter of creating a high-tech infrastructure in the Federal Republic or Europe.*

---

511 The Rotterdam *NRC Handelsblad* reported on January 15, 1986 that "If Philips and Siemens are the first to produce the megabit [SRAM], MEC [the joint venture] might ask for help from the European connection, says A. Herada, the Matsushita vice president. The opposite is equally conceivable in his opinion."

512 *NRC Handelsblad* (November 5, 1986).

513 Dr. Heinz Reisenhuber in *Die Welt* (March 18, 1987).

Protectionism - Actual and Potential

It is perhaps inevitable that European efforts to establish a greater degree of technological independence have been accompanied by consideration of measures which would increase the level of protection of the European electronics market. The community market is already subject to high tariffs and voluntary restraint agreements on some electronics products, such as VCRs.[514] In addition, some national governments have concluded bilateral agreements with Japan establishing quantitative limits on their imports of Japanese electronics products. Italian quantitative restrictions on Japanese electronics products are presented in Table 4.6. At present, in assessing their strategic position, the nations of Europe are discussing the potential merits of protectionism as a means of enhancing their international competitive position.

France has been a prime mover in these discussions; in electronics, "protectionist leanings are an integral part of the French view of European industrial policy."[515] An important element of the original Mitterand program launched in 1982 was "recognizing their own French market with their own French technology."[516] It was believed by government authorities that this could be achieved only through a "circular flow" strategy:

It consists of producing, on a top-priority basis, the chips needed by French users, in exchange for a commitment from the latter to veer toward the French chip-production poles. A sort of interactive support between one and the other. . . . [F]or digital circuits, the idea would be to base production on the telecommunications, professional electronics, and data processing sectors, requesting these sectors to "buy French."[517]

As the French have shifted to a pan-European approach, these ideas have been pressed by the French within the Community as part of the basis for a

---

514 A European executive commented with respect to the VRA on Japanese VCRs that "perhaps it is nothing to be proud of, but it would be suicidal to let the Japanese plow right over us. When the scales are tilted so far one way, you cannot have an offensive strategy without a defensive one also." *Le Point* (October 15, 1984).

515 *Neue Zurcher Zeitung* (July 31, 1985), pp. 9-10.

516 *NRC Handelsblad* (October 23, 1985).

517 *Le Monde* (September 22, 1983), p. 34.

TABLE 4.6

ITALIAN QUANTITATIVE RESTRAINTS ON IMPORTS OF JAPANESE ELECTRONICS PRODUCTS, 1983-84

(Voluntary Restraint Agreement Between Italy and Japan)

Order Number	Tariff Item	Import Quota (Value in $USD 1000)
27	Electric Motors for Records and Tape Players	550
28	Electric Batteries	60
29	Automobile Radios	30
30	Hi-Fi Tuners and Receivers	50
31	Radio Receivers	80
32	Television Receivers	50
33	Television Video Recording Devices	270
34	Antennae	50
36	Cathode Tubes for Color TVs up to 18"	750
37	Cathode Tubes for Color TVs 20" and 22"	250
38	Mounted Piezoelectric Crystals	30
39	Diodes and Transistors	30
40	Electronic Microstructures	30
41D	Wafers Not Yet Cut Into Microchips	30
42	Wires, Plaits, Cables, Tapes and Rods	135
43	Electrodes for Ovens	340

Source: Government of Italy, *Giappone -- Norme Ministeriali Relative Aglie Scanbi Commerciali*, August 9, 1983

European strategy. Thomson has argued, for example, that tariffs on consumer electronics products should be raised substantially to compensate for the current lack of common internal Community standards,[518] and that by protecting the end-markets, a natural market will be created for European semiconductors:

> *The crucial question is whether Europe will fall behind in the field of technology, unless its industry is protected or subsidized. At Thomson, they feel that in information science the Europeans have already fallen behind and that the producers of electronic components therefore cannot expect any new ideas from them. This is where the entertainment electronics industry is supposed to step in: it will become the principal buyer of European components, thereby ensuring that Europe will remain competitive in electronics as a whole.*[519]

While it is unclear how this debate will be resolved, it poses risks to U.S. electronics firms, who are likely to lose markets in any comprehensive effort to "Europeanize" the electronics industries.

---

518 The *Neue Zurcher Zeitung* commented on July 31, 1985 that "one sometimes gains the impression that tariff protection is to take the place of a common market, or rather, that for the firms' top management, it is easier to urge Brussels to institute tariff protection than to come to an agreement among themselves on uniform standards and to obtain from the politicians genuine market integration."

519 *Neue Zurcher Zeitung* (July 31, 1985).

5

CONCLUSION AND POLICY
IMPLICATIONS

The difficulties encountered by the U.S. microelectronics industry in the mid-1980s have generated a lively debate over what should be done by the U.S. Government to address the problem. A number of observers have concluded that the U.S. Government should adopt measures to enhance the competitiveness of the U.S. industry, and some analyses, such as the recent Defense Science Board report, have set forth specific agendas for a government effort to foster U.S. industry competitiveness in microelectronics.

An alternative perspective sometimes offered is that the U.S. information sector is moving toward a consolidation into two or three large vertically integrated firms, such as AT&T and IBM, and that the best policy is simply to accept the inevitability of this process and allow it to unfold. However, even firms like AT&T and IBM will find it difficult to remain competitive when the upstream sectors which supply their basic tools, materials and components are dominated by foreign firms who are their direct competitors -- and these firms do not posses the resources both to replicate such an infrastructure and to remain internationally competitive. Moreover, it is noteworthy that countries like Japan, Korea and West Germany are committing substantial government resources to foster large numbers of new start-up companies in microelectronics -- recognizing the unique role played by such companies in the process of innovation. It would be extraordinary if the United States, the home of the original Silicon Valley, were passively to accept the disappearence of many of its small innovative firms at the very moment that its competitors, realizing their importance, are now seeking to create them, if necessary, through subsidies and other promotional measures.

However, if one accepts the notion that the relative international competitiveness of the U.S. industry has declined as a result of foreign government promotional policies -- and that a U.S. Government response is necessary -- an equally important issue is what type of government policy measures are needed.   The recent past is replete with examples of comprehensive foreign government initiatives in the information technologies which have failed to achieve their objectives, and which, in the process, have sometimes created significant market distortions.[520]   The nations of Eastern Europe, where government intervention in microelectronics is most pervasive, are also among the least competitive in the field, although their difficulties in this sector are certainly not solely attributable to government policy measures.[521]   At the same time, the government policies which have already been implemented in this sector -- both in the United States and abroad -- offer some guidance as to how a more effective industry-government relationship might be structured.

Perhaps the salient feature of the Japanese effort in microelectronics is not so much the role of the government, per se, as the extent to which individual actions of the government and industry have been directed toward achieving strategic goals. If the United States is to respond effectively it is essential to establish a greater degree of coherence between industry actions and government policies.   This need not and should not involve central direction by government institutions.   But it will require improved coordination between the public and private sectors to ensure that policies are implemented which enhance, rather than undermine, the U.S. industry's international competitiveness.

A number of the U.S. government policy measures which affect U.S. competitiveness in microelectronics have been implemented in response to U.S. industry initiatives, and such industry-driven policy actions may offer the best model for future industry-government cooperation. The Semiconductor Industry Association was formed in 1977 in part as a response to the Japanese government's increasing role in promoting the Japanese

---

520 Kenneth Flamm, *Targeting the Computer* (Washington, D.C.: The Brookings Institution, 1987), pp. 153-60.

521 An analyst in Hungary, one of the most technologically advanced countries in Eastern Europe, commented in 1986 that "If there is talk of microelectronics, or of the manufacture of parts used in the modern instrument and computer technology industry, in informatics, we always mention our years of backwardness, our "irretrievable disadvantage." Katalin Magos in *Nepszabadsag* (June 26, 1986.) "I would estimate our backwardness [in computers and electronics] at about five years overall." Janos Kazamer in *Nepszabadsag* (June 9, 1986).

semiconductor industry.[522] SIA was active in developing and proposing public policy responses to various aspects of the Japanese challenge, both in the area of trade policy and general industrial competitiveness. SIA played a major role in the enactment of legislation reducing antitrust inhibitions on joint R&D;[523] the establishment of intellectual property protection for semiconductor mask designs;[524] the extension of tax credits for research and development; the elimination of semiconductor tariffs;[525] and the establishment of a negotiating mandate for the U.S. Government to eliminate foreign barriers to U.S. high technology products and services.[526] SIA has developed a number of initiatives designed to promote enhanced industry cooperation, including the formation of the Semiconductor Research Corporation (SRC) and SEMATECH.

While the measures taken to date have been important from the perspective of the U.S. industry, their effectiveness and sufficiency cannot be evaluated without reference to their international context. Most of the policy measures adopted in the past six years by the U.S. Government have been modest by international standards. The R&D tax credit, for example, provides a significant stimulus to R&D, but it does not provide tax incentives for microelectronics R&D commensurate with those currently enjoyed by Japanese firms. Similarly, the *Cooperative Research Act of 1984* reduced antitrust inhibitions on joint R&D by U.S. firms, but in so doing simply removed impediments to joint research that foreign firms have never faced. Ultimately, the adequacy of U.S. policies must be measured not solely in a domestic context, but in terms of whether they are succeeding in sustaining U.S. industry competitiveness in a world market characterized by pervasive government intervention. The experience of the U.S. industry in the 1980s strongly suggests that U.S. policies have fallen short in this regard. The ways in which these policies could be further strengthened deserve close examination.

---

522 SIA currently consists of over 50 U.S.-based merchant and captive producers of semiconductors, which account for over 90 percent of U.S.-based production of semiconductors.

523 *Cooperative Research Act of 1984*, 15 U.S.C. 4301 et seq.

524 *Semiconductor Chip Protection Act of 1984*, 17 U.S.C. 900-914.

525 The U.S. and Japanese semiconductor tariffs were eliminated under a bilateral agreement with Japan negotiated pursuant to authority delegated to the President in the *Trade and Tariff Act of 1984*, 19 U.S.C. 2114a(c).

526 *Trade and Tariff Act of 1984*.

TRADE POLICY

To date the most visible and dramatic actions taken by the U.S. Government in the semiconductor field have been in the trade arena, where intervention has been required to prevent the outright destruction of some segments of the U.S. industry. A number of observers of the recent semiconductor trade dispute with Japan have commented that no series of trade policy measures, by themselves, will suffice to sustain U.S. competitiveness in this industry. While this is certainly true, without an effective trade policy, no effort to maintain and enhance U.S. competitiveness is likely to succeed -- much of the U.S. industry will be eliminated regardless of the level of technological excellence, productivity and efficiency it is able to achieve. The issues of trade and competitiveness are thus inextricably linked, with an effective trade policy a prerequisite to initiatives aimed at strengthening competitiveness.

At present, one of the most serious unresolved trade issues confronting U.S. firms is systematic dumping. The ability and willingness of large Japanese firms to sell semiconductors below cost on a protracted basis poses a fundamental competitive dilemma for companies which are organized under our own industrial system, and the United States has not yet been able to formulate a fully effective policy response.[527] Every U.S. company must make a profit over the long run in order to survive and to generate the investment capital needed to remain competitive. Sustained dumping destroys this ability, and if not checked, ultimately destroys companies, product sectors, and entire industries. The problem posed by Japanese dumping may soon be exacerbated as Korean and European firms enter the arena. Their governments and industrial groups may also be willing to underwrite massive loss operations in order to "buy" market share and to achieve long-run national objectives.

The current Semiconductor Agreement with Japan contains provisions which, by their terms, address the problem of dumping in a comprehensive manner.[528] The Agreement provides, in effect, that each company price at or above its allocated cost of production.[529] It does not establish a "price

---

527 The Contracting Parties to the General Agreement on Tariffs and Trade (GATT) provide that injurious dumping "is to be condemned." (Article VI). The Contracting Parties have entered into a separate accord on the procedures to be applied by individual countries in imposing antidumping duties (Agreement on Implementation of Article VI of the General Agreement on Tariffs and Trade, April 12, 1979).

528 Both governments reaffirmed the need to prevent dumping in accordance with the relevant provisions of the GATT. *Agreement*, Part II.1.

529 The Agreement provides for a monitoring of costs and prices to prevent dumping (e.g. below cost sales) (Part II.2.(2)), and establishes an agreed methodology for determining

floor" -- a Japanese company, for example, can price below all of its U.S. and Japanese competitors if its production costs are actually lower. While the dumping provisions of the Agreement have been criticized in some quarters as "protectionist," the phenomenon which those provisions are designed to address -- protracted dumping by large, state-backed firms to gain market share -- is itself antithetical to free-market principles and, if unchecked, will lead to greater distortions of the market. At the same time, the concept upon which the dumping provisions of the Agreement are predicated -- that competition should be based on relative efficiency and productivity -- is a basic feature of a market oriented economic system.

An equally important problem, related to dumping, is the continuing market access problems which U.S. companies confront in Japan. Japan is now the world's largest market for semiconductors, and U.S. firms' continuing role as residual suppliers in that market places them at a progressively greater disadvantage as the Japanese market grows in proportion to the world market. U.S. efforts to secure improved access to the Japanese market have been based on persuading the Japanese government to take steps to enhance market opportunities for foreign products. Many individuals in Japan's political leadership are committed to this end, and formal Japanese government barriers in the electronics industries have been virtually eliminated. The principal current obstacle to foreign sales is a complex web of relationships among Japanese companies which operates to exclude foreign sales, tolerated if not visably supported by elements within the government which remain resistant to the notion of a truly open market. This type of embedded market barrier cannot be removed through a relatively straightforward government action (such as the lowering of a tariff). Rather, it requires more fundamental measures, such as the vigorous enforcement of Japan's Antimonopoly Law in the electronics sector and the growth of a consensus within Japan that real market opening is in the long run national interest.

The Semiconductor Agreement contains provisions designed to provide for an improvement in foreign market access in Japan, based primarily on commitments by the Japanese government to encourage a shift from traditional procurement patterns.[530] While some progress is being made as

---

company costs, including the allocation of R&D, calculation of depreciation, valuation of materials, and so on. USTR Clayton Yeutter to Ambassador Nobuo Matsunaga (September 2, 1986), Attachment.

530 "[T]he Government of Japan will impress upon the Japanese producers and users of semiconductors the need to aggressively take advantage of increased market access opportunities in Japan for foreign-based firms which wish to improve their actual sales performance and position. In turn, the Government of the United States of America will impress upon the U.S. semiconductor producers the need to aggressively pursue every sales opportunity in the Japanese market." *Agreement*, Part I.1.

of this writing, it is too early to assess the success or failure of this effort. For the moment, the Semiconductor Agreement probably provides the best basis for resolving the problems of dumping and market access in Japan, and the most attractive policy, from a U.S. perspective, is thus to encourage the Japanese Government to implement its terms effectively.[531]

U.S. INDUSTRY COMPETITIVENESS

An effective trade policy can ensure that the U.S. microelectronics industry is not destroyed by dumping, and it can maximize U.S. market opportunities in other countries. These steps will ultimately be of little avail if the industry itself does not remain competitive in an environment where national governments are making major resource commitments to their own microelectronics industries.

Some of the principal problems which the U.S. industry confronts have already been identified. U.S. industry research and development efforts in microelectronics are duplicative and relatively inefficient compared with the focused cooperative efforts in Japan. For a variety of reasons, the U.S. industry is in danger of losing competitiveness in semiconductor manufacturing. U.S. government programs which affect U.S. microelectronics competitiveness are poorly coordinated and often counterproductive. Foreign producers enjoy government-sponsored financial and tax benefits which have no U.S. counterpart, and partly as a result, the U.S. industry is being outspent in capital and R&D investment. U.S. government R&D efforts in microelectronics are often of little assistance to the U.S. industry.

The U.S. semiconductor industry has taken a number of strategic measures on its own designed to enhance its international competitiveness. It consistently spends a higher percentage of sales on R&D than any other U.S. industrial sector. Through the SRC it commits substantial resources each year to fund university research and the training of engineers, scientists and physicists in U.S. universities. It has established a number of research consortia in to reduce duplicative R&D, enhance economies of scale, and

---

531 While the Agreement has encountered criticism, the policy alternatives to the Agreement are unattractive. If the Agreement is abrogated, either widespread dumping will resume, with the likelihood that at a minimum, traditional trade restrictions (such as antidumping duties imposed at the border) will be imposed on Japanese semiconductor products, or equally disruptive to normal trade patterns, "voluntary restraint" will be practiced. This will very likely encourage U.S. OEMs to move their production outside of the U.S. to avoid antidumping duties, a shift which is probably not desirable from the standpoint of the long-run national economic interest.

accelerate technology diffusion, most notably the Microelectronics and Computer Technology Corporation (MCC). While these measures are significant, the events of the present decade have demonstrated the need for government policies which support industrial competitiveness. An effective combination of government policies and industry initiatives is essential in order to address the challenge confronting U.S. industry. A number of potential policy initiatives deserve consideration.

Research and Development in Semiconductor Manufacturing

Two of the most significant recent proposals for sustaining U.S. competitiveness in microelectronics feature Department of Defense investment in an industry R&D consortium in the field of semiconductor manufacturing technology. Such a consortium would be designed to redress the current U.S. vulnerability in semiconductor manufacturing, strengthen the "upstream" SME and materials industries, eliminate duplicative R&D, improve technology diffusion within the U.S. industry, and provide a focus for the R&D efforts of U.S. universities and the National Labs.

The Defense Science Board (DSB), whose 1987 report detailed the growing U.S. dependency on foreign components, proposed the establishment of an industry-government supported Semiconductor Manufacturing Technology Institute to

develop, demonstrate, and advance the technology base for efficient, high yield manufacture of advanced semiconductor devices, and to provide facilities for production of selected devices for DOD needs.[532]

The semiconductor industry itself (including captive and merchant device makers and upstream suppliers) has adopted a plan for SEMATECH, a consortium which would

develop, demonstrate and advance the technology base for efficient, high-yield manufacture of state of the art semiconductor devices.[533]

Both the DSB and SEMATECH proposals call for investment in a consortium by the industry and the Department of Defense, participation by the national laboratories, and the use of a "vehicle" -- the actual manufacture of a technology driver -- to develop and prove process techniques.

---

532 DSB, *Task Force on Semiconductor Dependency*, p. 11.

533 SEMATECH, *Business Plan* (Washington, D.C., 1987), p. CD-1.

The SEMATECH proposal would involve the active participation of the majority of the U.S. merchant and captive producers of semiconductors, as well as the upstream SME and materials suppliers, in a joint effort to develop advanced semiconductor manufacturing processes, tools, and software. SEMATECH would (a) conduct R&D into advanced manufacturing techniques, tools and materials, (b) prove and demonstrate the techniques, tools and materials on an actual pilot manufacturing line, and (c) disseminate the results to members and license them to non-members. While the pilot line would produce a "technology driver" device to test its processes, SEMATECH would also develop software to permit the processes so developed to be applied to flexible manufacturing.[534] The organizers of SEMATECH are seeking government funding on a matching basis, at a total annual budget of $250 million.[535]

Several advantages of such a joint R&D approach are obvious. A project such as SEMATECH would reduce duplicative R&D and permit rapid diffusion of technology throughout the U.S. industry, and each participating firm would receive a far higher level of R&D results per dollar invested. SEMATECH would provide an obvious stimulus to the upstream producers of SME, and materials, since it will contract with the firms for R&D and equipment and provide them with a strategic direction which has generally been lacking in the relationships between device makers and tool and materials suppliers.[536]

The government-funded joint R&D approach would adopt a mechanism that is being used by virtually every industrialized nation to enhance national microelectronics competitiveness. Foreign joint R&D projects have been generally directed at areas of perceived weakness. In the case of Japan, this weakness has been in the area of innovation and development of advanced device designs and production processes. Similarly, the DSB and SEMATECH proposals are aimed at the U.S. industry's area of vulnerability -- manufacturing. The United States still leads Japan in most areas of device design, but the destruction of much of the commodity memory sector has dramatically reduced the U.S. industry's manufacturing base and threatens an overall loss of manufacturing competitiveness. SEMATECH is, in substantial part, a proposal designed to offset the effect of the loss of that business in the mid-1980s.

---

534 Testimony of Charles Sporck before the Subcommittee on Science, Research and Technology of the House Committee on Science, Space and Technology (April 29, 1987).

535 Ibid. The DSB recommended government funding at a level of $200 million annually.

536 Testimony of C. Scott Kulicke on behalf of the Semiconductor Equipment and Materials Institute (SEMI) before the House Subcommittee on Commerce, Consumer Protection and Competiveness, House Energy and Commerce Committee (June 9, 1987).

SEMATECH also offers an alternative to the consolidation of the U.S. microelectronics industry into a few large firms. The innovative ability of small firms has traditionally been one of this country's principal areas of strength. The increasing scale of R&D investments required to remain competitive has jeopardized the future of these firms and led to predictions that the industry must consolidate into several large firms. SEMATECH will make an enormous range of generic R&D available to all members, large and small, which they could not possibly achieve through the use of their own individual resources. In effect, cooperative R&D will secure the benefits of consolidation while at the same time preserving the entrepreneurial character of the U.S. industry.

Both the DSB and SEMATECH proposals envision the marshalling of existing U.S. technological resources in a concerted fashion -- something which has not occurred in microelectronics in this country to date. The National Laboratories and some university research would be committed to the support of the U.S. manufacturing consortium.[537]

A Department of Defense investment designed to foster generic R&D in semiconductor manufacturing would be consistent with past U.S. government efforts to support generic R&D in fields such as machine tools, aviation and agriculture.[538]   Each of those fields, like microelectronics, provide the underpinning for an entire industrial complex of many industries, which, taken together, constitute a major segment of the American industrial base.

From the perspective of the Department of Defense, an investment in SEMATECH would be justified on the basis of the need to preserve indigenous manufacturing capability for components which are critically important to the national defense. A recent study by the National Research Council concluded that "the U.S. defense industrial base is deteriorating," and that

---

537 SEMATECH, *Business Plan*, pp. HW-1-8.

538 In commercial aviation, the National Advisory Committee for Aeronautics (NACA), the forerunner of NASA, funded R&D in aviation technology. NACA built and operated the largest and most powerful wind tunnels in the country and was the first to have wind tunnels capable of simulating transonic and supersonic airplane speed. NACA-supported R&D gave a major impetus to the development of the U.S. commercial aviation industry. In machine tools, the U.S. Air Force sponsored R&D into the use of numerically controlled machine tools in maufacturing -- technology which spread throughout the U.S. machine tool industry, triggering one of the biggest surges in the U.S. productivity since World War II. In agriculture, federal funding of a nationwide system of experimental stations, as well as various R&D efforts of the Department of Agriculture, have played an important role in making the U.S. the world's most advanced agricultural economy.

*A primary cause of this decline is the failure of the Department of
Defense (DOD) and its contractors to invest sufficiently in manufacturing
technology.*[539]

The study recommended that DOD place a higher priority on developing
manufacturing and invest in innovative manufacturing technologies that will
be required to produce the next generation of advanced weapons systems.[540]
SEMATECH would represent such an investment.

One danger pointed out by a number of observers is that DOD investment
in an R&D consortium like SEMATECH would lead to excessive
government control over the management of the project and its technological
objectives. This would seem to be a real, but avoidable, danger. The
governments' role in such a project should be limited to that of investor in
generic research, rather than manager, and its concern should simply be to
ensure that its investment is realized, not to control the operational aspects of
the project.[541]

Coordination of Federal Policies

Over a dozen U.S. government entities implement policies which
substantially affect U.S. competitiveness in microelectronics. While these
policies are sometimes implemented in a contradictory and even
counterproductive manner,

> *demands for coherent Federal policy towards information technology
> R&D conflict with the traditional system of pluralist decisionmaking by
> various agencies and the private sector.*[542]

---

539 Committee on the Role of the Manufacturing Technology Program in the Defense
     Industrial Base, Manufacturing Studies Board, Commission on Engineering and
     Technical Systems, *Manufacturing Technology: Cornerstone of a Renewed Defense
     Industrial Base* (Washington, D.C.: National Academy Press, 1987), p. 1.

540 Ibid., p. 27.

541 The Department of Defense is the most likely potential large-scale investor in
     SEMATECH. Its investment would be based on its need to ensure that a capability
     exists within the United States to manufacture the semiconductors needed by U.S. armed
     forces in the future. This investment can be realized by securing at the outset an
     understanding that the manufacturing consortium will provide that capability. It need
     not (and should not) require actual management or control of the project by the
     government.

542 Office of Technology Assessment, *Information Technology* R&D, p. 290.

Nevertheless, the success of Japan, whose government policies affecting microelectronics are closely coordinated, has led to calls for a more systematic and rational application of government policy measures.

Virtually every analyst who has examined this issue agrees that a greater level of "coordination" is desirable, although the specifics of how this would best be accomplished are still a matter of debate:

> *Coordination is like motherhood; everyone agrees that it must be done but it lacks an operational definition. . . . A certain amount of coordination is good for the health of the Government, but like exercise, too much will cripple or kill.*[543]

Many U.S. observers in government and industry fear that the establishment of an excessively powerful government "coordinating" body -- such as an American MITI -- would stifle innovation and entrepreneurialism through excessive centralization and bureaucratic controls.[544] This concern is probably well founded.

However, a substantially greater degree of coordination of federal policies affecting microelectronics competitiveness could be achieved through measures which fall far short of an "American MITI."[545] For example, a national advisory council on microelectronics could be established, consisting of representatives of government, academia and industry, which could make long-run assessments of the factors affecting U.S. competitiveness in microelectronics; identify technological areas where the United States is deficient relative to other countries; identify important emerging technologies; and make recommendations for R&D strategies and other appropriate policy actions.[546] Such a body's powers would be limited largely

---

543 Hahn, Alberts and Lovelace, "Interagency Coordination: Workshop Report," cited in Office of Technology Assessment, *Information Technology R&D*, p. 291.

544 Such fears are not unique to the U.S. A Siemens executive commented in 1985 that "I don't think a ministry such as MITI is conceivable for the Federal Republic of Germany. We have a different conception of the roles of state and industry. Cooperation between state and business under the leadership of a ministry based on the MITI model cannot work in our free enterprise system." Karl-Heinz Beckurts in *Bild der Wissenschaft* (November 1985).

545 The Reagan Administration has established several ad hoc interagency working groups on microelectronics which serve as clearinghouses for information and debate on appropriate federal policies.

546 Several legislative proposals to establish such a coordinating body are pending before the 100th Congress. H.R. 2191, sponsored by Congressman Valentine of North Carolina would establish a 13-member national advisory council including the secretaries of Defense, Commerce and Energy; the Directors of the Office of Science and Technology Policy and the National Science Foundation; and eight Presidential appointees. Senators Sanford, Dodd and Durenberger are sponsoring similar legislation in the Senate.

to those of consultation and information exchange, but it could well be in a position to influence federal policy decisions with a direct impact on the U.S. competitive posture. The mere existence of an entity where factors affecting U.S. competitiveness in microelectronics are discussed by individuals representing a cross-section of government, academia and industry will mitigate some of the worst features of the present U.S. system. One of this body's functions, for example, would be to ensure that in the future, major regulatory actions (such as the AT&T divestiture) not be undertaken without discussion and analysis of their potential impact on U.S. international competitiveness in microelectronics.

Tax Policy

A fundamental problem confronting U.S. semiconductor producers is the fact that they are being outspent, dollar for dollar, by their Japanese competitors in the investments which they need to make in order to remain competitive over the long run. Comparative U.S. and foreign tax policies inevitably affect this process. While a number of U.S. tax policies have historically been implemented to encourage U.S. firms' capital and R&D investments, these are being curtailed or phased out at the time when foreign investment incentives are being expanded. These changes in U.S. tax law need to be reassessed in light of their international context.

While the U.S. tax system has traditionally served as a mechanism for achieving specific economic objectives, the tax reform legislation enacted in 1986 was designed to curtail this tendency. The 1986 Act has in fact had a negative impact on U.S. semiconductor industry competitiveness, reducing incentives for capital and R&D investments. Because of the high level of capital investment in semiconductors, the 1986 Act's elimination of Investment Tax Credits (ITCs) had a pronounced impact on the U.S. industry. The U.S. semiconductor producers undertook intensive investments in 1985-86 despite severe losses, building up ITCs which, because of their losses, they were unable to use in those years. The 1986 Act substantially limits the extent to which ITCs can be carried forward. The R&D tax credit was extended for three years, but it was reduced from the rate of 25% to 20% and remains a temporary measure.

The 1986 changes reflect a Congressional balancing of the desire to encourage R&D and capital investment against other national concerns. However, it is significant that a number of key foreign countries, including Japan and Korea, are substantially increasing their tax incentives for R&D and capital investment in microelectronics at a time when the United States is reducing them. This shift in relative tax treatment will work to the disadvantage of U.S. firms. Given the significant role played by tax policy in determining levels of capital and R&D investment, if the United States seeks to remain competitive in microelectronics U.S. tax policies which substantially affect U.S. competitiveness should be formulated with reference to comparable policies being implemented by major U.S. competitors.

In general, tax policies should be designed to put U.S. firms on an equal footing with their foreign competitors with respect to R&D and capital investment. Depreciation schedules for U.S. semiconductor producers, for example, should not be longer than those of Japanese or Korean producers. With respect to R&D, the President's Commission on Industrial Competitiveness recommended in 1985 that the R&D tax credit should be made permanent (which would enable companies to plan their investments with a greater degree of certainty); that the R&D tax credit be based on total R&D expenditures rather than incremental increases; and that a preferential tax credit be established to encourage further industry investment in university research.[547] These measures would be useful, although their adequacy would ultimately be a function of how they compare with the mix of tax measures employed by this country's principal competitors.

Protecting U.S. Intellectual Property Rights

The U.S. microelectronics industry's greatest remaining competitive advantage is its ability to innovate. The product areas where the United States retains market leadership are generally design-intensive segments where U.S. innovative ability can be most effectively brought to bear. However, the fruits of innovation in microelectronics can be dissipated with extraordinary rapidity. While the design of a semiconductor may cost tens of millions of dollars, that design can be copied in a matter of months for as little as $50,000. This problem has been compounded by the fact that until very recently, no country -- including the United States -- extended intellectual property protection to semiconductor designs.[548]

---

547 President's Commission on Industrial Competitiveness, *Global Competition: The New Reality*, Vol. 1, p. 51.

548 The lack of adequate international protection of intellectual property rights is pervasive in the information industries. The multilateral conventions governing intellectual property merely provide for national treatment and certain minimum reciprocal rights, and contain no dispute settlement provisions -- a wholly inadequate framework for preventing misappropriation of U.S. information technologies. See Howell, Benz and Wolff, *Stanford Journal of International Law*, pp. 256-258. Not until 1986 did a U.S. federal court hold that microcode, the computer code for most of the basic functions of information processing, was eligible for protection under the U.S. copyright laws. *NEC v. Intel*, 645 F.Supp. 590 (N.D. Cal. 1986).

In 1984, Congress enacted the Semiconductor Chip Protection Act, which extended the protection of the U.S. intellectual property laws to semiconductor designs.[549] Japan, which like the U.S., now has a substantial amount of semiconductor technology to protect, enacted similar legislation in 1985,[550] and several other countries have extended protection to semiconductor designs (the U.K., Australia and Switzerland). However, most nations of the world do not extend intellectual property protection to semiconductor designs and a number of these countries -- particularly NICs seeking to establish domestic information industries -- vehemently oppose measures which would restrict their ability to appropriate U.S. technology as needed.[551] As these nations, such as Korea, enter large scale semiconductor production, lack of protection for U.S. designs is becoming a major problem for the U.S. industry.[552]

A number of U.S. government policy measures may be taken which can partially alleviate this problem. The government can continue to press U.S. trading partners -- particularly NICs like Taiwan, Brazil and Korea -- to extend protection to U.S. intellectual property rights in the information field. Section 337 of the Tariff Act of 1930[553] provides a unilateral remedy for U.S. firms which have suffered infringement of their intellectual property rights, but under current law, this remedy is only available if the infringement destroys or "substantially injures" the U.S. industry -- a requirement that seriously limits Section 337's utility.[554] The repeal of the "injury" requirement would give U.S. companies a more effective remedy and would serve as a substantially more effective deterrent to foreign infringement.[555]

Over the longer term, success by the U.S. Government in negotiating a comprehensive intellectual property agreement in the new Uruguay Round of

---

549   17 U.S.C. 901-914.

550   Law No. 43 of 1985, the *Act Concerning the Circuit Layout of a Semiconductor Integrated Circuit.*

551   Gadbaw and Richards, *The Protection of Intellectual Property Rights in Developing Nations.*

552   A company which shoulders the cost of designing a new technology is at a disadvantage relative to a company which copies that technology once it is designed, since the innovating firm must recover its development costs in its sales, whereas the appropriating firm need not do so. This problem can become so severe as to constitute a disincentive to investment in development.

553   19 U.S.C. 1337.

554   See U.S. International Trade Commission, *Certain Optical Waveguide Fibers* (U.S.I.T.C. Pub. 1754, Inv. No. 337-TA-189, September 1985).

555   The Reagan Administration supports legislation which would eliminate the injury requirement, and appropriate legislation which was incorporated in the House and Senate omnibus trade bills in the 100th Congress.

Multilateral Trade Negotiations can provide an international mechanism for addressing such problems that is currently not available.

Export Controls

One of the most serious competitive handicaps the U.S. information industry confronts at present is the asymmetry between U.S. national security controls on exports of high technology products[556] and those which are maintained by U.S. allies such as Japan and West Germany. The maintenance of a system of multilateral controls on exports to the Soviet Bloc is conducted through the Coordinating Committee on Multilateral Export Controls (COCOM), consisting of 15 allied nations. COCOM has been characterized by a lack of consensus among its members as to the form and stringency of export controls which are required by Western security interests. As a result, major disparities exist between the controls enforced by the United States, on the one hand, and by its principal trading partners, on the other hand. These disparities are listed in Table 5.1. Export controls are principally an impediment to U.S. competitiveness in West/West trade -- in effect, U.S. firms face much more stringent restrictions on their exports to other Western nations than do Japanese and European firms with respect to comparable products. Because many U.S. export controls are ineffective, this imbalance does little or nothing to improve U.S. national security and ensures that many potential sales of semiconductors, SME and OEM products are lost to Japanese and European firms.[557]

---

556 *The Arms Export Control Act of 1976* requires U.S. government approval for the export of military weapons; the Act is implemented through the International Traffic in Arms Regulations (ITAR), based on the U.S. Munitions List maintained by the Department of Defense. The *Export Administration Act of 1979* controls the export of "dual use" goods and technologies -- products which have commercial applications but which could contribute significantly to the military capabilities of an adversary. This Act is adminstered by the Department of Commerce through the Export Administration Regulations (EAR).

557 A 1987 study observed that "if goods comparable to U.S. controlled products are available with little or no control from foreign sources, then a clear incentive exists for buyers to seek those sources. The trend toward non-U.S. sourcing or "de-Americanization" is already evident in Europe ... These actions stem not only from concerns about the additional costs and delays imposed by U.S. export controls but even more importantly from a view that the United States is not a reliable supplier..." National Academy of Sciences, *Balancing the National Interest*, p. 65.

TABLE 5.1

COMPARISON OF COCOM COUNTRY CONTROLS ON WEST/WEST EXPORTS

	United States	Japan	West Germany	Britain
Licence Required for Re-export from Another Country	Yes	No	No	No
Exporters Required to Screen Transactions Against List of Denied Parties	Yes	No	No	No
Prelicense and/or Postshipment Check of Consignees Conducted in Country of Destination	Yes	No	No	No
Applies Controls to Transactions Retroactively	Yes	No	No	No
Requires License for Export to other CoCom Country	Yes (except Canada)	No	—	No
Use National Security to Deny Licenses to Free World Destinations	Yes	No	No	No
Estimated Average Time for Licensing of West/West Exports (January 1985) (Weeks)	4	1	4	1

Source: Presidents' Council on Competitiveness, *Global Competition: The New Reality*, (1985); Exhibits 11 and 12; National Academy of Sciences, *Balancing the National Interest*, (1987); Table 6-1.

There is a growing consensus that the entire system of U.S. export controls needs to be rationalized to reduce the imbalance with other Western nations.[558] A 1987 study by the National Academy of Sciences concluded that most U.S. export controls were largely ineffective in preventing diversions of technology to the Soviet Bloc and only served to undermine U.S. competitiveness.[559] Rectifying this imbalance while preserving Western security interests will require the development of a greater degree of consensus within COCOM as to the form of export controls necessary to prevent diversion of sensitive technologies to the Soviet Bloc. In addition, some specific changes which could be considered by the U.S. Government are listed below:

- *West/West Foreign Availability.* Where comparable products are available from other Western allies, the U.S. Government should seek consistent application of export controls for such products by all COCOM members.[560] However, failing this, if a product is available outside of the United States without restriction on export to other Free World countries, then all similar products with lower technical parameters should be decontrolled by the U.S. government for export to Free World countries.

- *U.S.-Origin Components Controls.* Current U.S. unilateral controls on foreign products that incorporate U.S.-origin components create an incentive for foreign manufacturers to "engineer out" U.S.-origin components from their products. The late Commerce Secretary Baldrige recommended major reforms in the manner in which the U.S. controls re-exports of de minimis levels of components.

- *Re-export Controls.* Only the United States requires foreign resellers (including the closest U.S. allies) to obtain the prior approval of (or account to) the U.S. Government for re-export of U.S.-origin products, U.S. parts and components incorporated in foreign products, and foreign products manufactured with U.S. technology. Controls on re-exports to those western countries that have agreed to control exports of U.S.-origin goods and technology to the Soviet Bloc should be removed.

---

558 The President's 1987 Competitiveness Initiative contained seven recommended action items in the area of export controls, and both houses of the 100th Congress have been actively considering legislation to reform the existing export controls system.

559 Ibid.

560 See recommendation of President's Council on Industrial Competitiveness, in *Global Competition: The New Reality*, p. 59.

The National Laboratories

The U.S. National Laboratories constitute a national resource with major potential for enhancing U.S. competitiveness in microelectronics. The National Labs possess some of the most sophisticated instrumentation equipment in the world -- synchotrons, particle accelerators, supercomputers -- as well as major expertise in areas of engineering, science and physics which are of direct applicability to microelectronics. However, there is a general consensus that this resource is not being fully utilized to support the commercial competitiveness of the U.S. microelectronics industry.

In the 1940s and 1950s, the National Labs were given a mission to develop peaceful uses for atomic energy, and developed technology for nuclear ships, nuclear-powered civilian electrical plants, and breeder reactors, playing a major role in the development of the U.S. nuclear power industry. In the 1950s and 1960s, a group of federal aeronautical agencies and labs formed the institutional core of NASA, which was given a mission of achieving U.S. leadership in space and putting a man on the moon -- a mission which was accomplished with spectacular success and which has provided the impetus for a commercial space industry. In the 1970s, a number of National Laboratories were given the task of reducing U.S. vulnerability in the energy area, and have devoted their efforts to developing solar, wind, fusion, and fossil fuel energy sources. They have a statutory mandate to work in a number of other areas of commercial interest, such as automotive propulsion and electric vehicles.

The Reagan Administration has already developed initiatives to employ the resources of the National Labs to help the U.S. steel industry improve its productivity and meet foreign competition.[561] Given the importance of microelectronics to the economic future of the United States, it would be entirely appropriate to give the National Labs an explicit mission to support and enhance U.S. competitiveness in microelectronics. Implementing this mission would require a much greater degree of collaboration between the Labs and the U.S. industry than has occurred to date. A workshop held by the National Academy of Sciences in 1987 to assess the role of the National

---

561 The White House Office of Science and Technology Policy was the principal advocate of a new National Labs - Steel industry R&D program -- a partnership in which the steel industry, two national laboratories of the Department of Energy, and the National Bureau of Standards worked to develop "leapfrog" technology. According to White House Science Advisor, "One practical result is to marry the technical expertise of the labs with the needs of the steel industry." W. Henry Lambright, *Federal Laboratories and Federal Policies: Evaluation and Current Trends* (Testimony before U.S. House Committee on Science and Technology, October 2, 1985).

Labs in supporting the semiconductor industry concluded that

> *If the industry can articulate specific areas of generic research that conform to the capabilities of the national laboratories, and the laboratories can adjust their operations and mobilize their resources to address those research areas, the potential contribution of the national laboratories for future industry competitiveness can be realized.*[562]

At least four of the National Labs have already proposed major projects in microelectronics which would be undertaken in conjunction with the industry.[563] These and other similar proposals should be assessed in conjunction with the overall strategic objectives of the U.S. industry, and should be implemented as part of an overall effort to further those objectives. The SEMATECH proposal, for example, envisions the National Labs undertaking specific research projects in conjunction with the overall work of the consortium. Such an effort would probably require an increase level of federal spending at the National Labs on specific projects linked to microelectronics.

University-Based Research

The 1987 Defense Science Board report on semiconductor dependency recommended that federally-funded university "centers of excellence" be established at eight universities to develop innovative approaches to semiconductor device design and manufacturing technology.[564] Given the high quality of U.S. university-based R&D, an expansion of federal assistance would enhance the commercial strength of the U.S. industry, both by increasing the number of trained graduates and the store of basic technology available to U.S. industry. Such an effort should build upon the existing centers of excellence sponsored by the semiconductor industry through its research consortium, the SRC.

---

562 National Research Council, *The Semiconductor Industry and the National Laboratories*, p. 4.

563 Brookhaven has proposed to use its facilities and personnel to develop X-ray lithography; Sandia proposes a project for silicon process integration, including an automated pilot manufacturing plant; Oak Ridge proposes a project concentrating on processing and new materials technology; the Lawrence Berkeley Laboratory would establish a process analysis and diagnostics program concentrating on materials and process characterization.

564 DSB, *Task Force on Semiconductor Dependency*, p. 12.

Conclusion

The major industrial nations of the world and an increasing number of developing nations have concluded that they cannot prosper in the 21st century without a strong indigenous microelectronics capability. Their governments are aggressively moving to secure, maintain and expand that capability. The U.S. microelectronics industry provides the underpinning for much of the U.S. industrial base, and it is essential to this country's economic future and national security that the U.S. Government develop a coherent, pragmatic, and effective response.

Although the recent erosion of U.S. leadership in microelectronics is viewed by some observers as inevitable and irreversible, this is almost certainly not the case. The United States has great strengths -- an unsurpassed capability for innovation, a superb university system, a flexible work force and capital markets, and a technological edge in many of the information technologies. Japan itself has shown that by mobilizing its own national resources, it has been able to move from a trailing position in microelectronics to the point where it can now challenge U.S. leadership. The United States has repeatedly proven capable of marshalling national resources -- public and private -- to meet fundamental technological challenges in space, defense, and aviation. There is no reason why the challenge cannot be met in microelectronics.

APPENDIX A

STATISTICAL INFORMATION AND ANALYSIS

WORLD MARKET SHARE METHODOLOGY AND DATA SOURCES

The World Semiconductor Trade Statistics (WSTS) program is relied on as the primary statistical base for the world semiconductor industry. The WSTS data is obtained largely by compiling confidential data submitted by virtually all of the world's semiconductor companies.

Market share is the primary analytical means of determining competitive performance over a period of time. To measure market share over time, the WSTS follows these essential criteria:

- Products must compete in the market;

- Valuation must be at market and not at an intermediate level;

- Measurement must be applied consistently over time.

Substantial confusion has arisen over the years with respect to the treatment of "captive" consumption of semiconductors in calculating market shares. "Captive" consumption popularly refers to internal consumption of semiconductors, but refers to two types of internal transfers. Technically "captive" consumption is internal consumption of *nonstandard* devices which can be used only within the company and for which no outside market exists.

This should be distinguished from "in-house transfers" which refer to the internal consumption of *standard* semiconductors which other companies also use and for which, therefore, a market exists outside the company itself.

The WSTS program has always been operated on the concept of Total Available Market (TAM). Under TAM, the product which is relevant to a market analysis is that which can potentially be traded -- that is, a product which is fungible with devices made by other producers. Under this methodology, standard commercial products are included in the WSTS system, whether consumed in-house or sold on the merchant market, whether the producer is Fujitsu, Motorola, NEC or TI. AT&T standard products will be counted as AT&T standardizes its production to utilize commercial packaging.

On the other hand, nonstandard (captive) products are not counted because there is no market for them. The product cannot be assigned a clear value, nor does a clear reason exist even to collect the data. The test of whether a product is properly includable in the total available market is that of the burned-down factory: if the producer could buy a substitute product on the market if it lost its internal supply due to a fire, then the internal production should be counted as part of the market.

Thus, under the WSTS system, both Japanese and U.S. firms' in-house transfers of standard products are counted for purposes of market analysis. Only U.S. firms, like IBM, produce significant volumes of nonstandard products, but if NEC, Toshiba or other Japanese firms began producing nonstandard devices, those too should be excluded from compilations of data.[565]

WSTS only began reporting *world* market share data in 1982. Market share data for 1978 to 1981 has been based on data from Integrated Circuit Engineering Corporation after taking out ICE estimates of U.S. captive production and taking out ICE estimates of CMEA production in 1978 and 1979. The data in Table A.1 therefore, present an accurate time series portrait of world market share in semiconductors.

The data used in the study on capital spending and research and development are provided in Tables A.2 and A.3.

---

565 IBM does not make standard semiconductors, and has had a policy for 25 years of not selling any semiconductors on the merchant market.

TABLE A.1

SEMICONDUCTOR MARKET SHARE DATA
($ Billion)

	1978	1979	1980	1981	1982	1983	1984	1985	1986
U.S. Based Shipments	4.78	6.62	8.44	8.00	8.03	9.73	14.00	10.65	11.38
Japan Based Shipments	2.49	2.93	3.84	4.17	4.68	6.63	9.80	8.76	11.86
Europe Based Shipments	1.41	1.65	1.62	1.54	1.35	1.41	2.10	2.07	2.86
ROW Based Shipments	0.23	0.30	0.32	0.36	0.10	0.14	0.20	0.18	0.25
WORLD MARKET	8.91	11.49	14.22	14.07	14.16	17.91	26.10	21.66	26.35
Share of World Market (%)	100.00	100.00	100.00	100.00	100.00	100.00	100.00	100.00	100.00
United States Share (%)	53.61	57.55	59.35	56.86	56.71	54.33	53.64	49.15	43.19
Japanese Share (%)	27.94	25.49	27.00	29.64	33.05	37.02	37.55	40.46	45.01
European Share (%)	15.86	14.36	11.39	10.95	9.53	7.87	8.05	9.56	10.85
ROW Share (%)	2.59	2.60	2.25	2.56	0.71	0.78	0.77	0.83	0.95

SOURCE: 1978-1981, ICE Corporation; 1982-1986, SIA.

NOTE: ICE data adjusted by (1) deleting estimate for U.S. IC captive production, and (2) adjusting 1978 and 1979 ROW data to exclude CMEA estimates.

TABLE A.2

SEMICONDUCTOR CAPITAL SPENDING

U.S. MERCHANT SEMICONDUCTOR FIRMS AND
JAPANESE SEMICONDUCTOR FIRMS
(\$ Million)

	JAPANESE FIRMS		U.S. FIRMS	
	Capital Spending	% of Sales	Capital Spending	% of Sales
1976	\$238.6	21.3%	\$306.0	9.0%
1977	\$179.4	14.1%	\$413.4	10.6%
1978	\$453.2	18.2%	\$650.1	13.6%
1979	\$656.3	22.4%	\$887.1	13.4%
1980	\$956.2	24.9%	\$1,299.8	15.4%
1981	\$1,046.7	25.1%	\$1,424.0	17.8%
1982	\$1,301.0	27.8%	\$1,188.4	14.8%
1983	\$2,234.3	33.7%	\$1,323.3	13.6%
1984	\$3,508.4	35.8%	\$3,010.0	21.5%
1985	\$2,960.9	33.8%	\$1,789.2	16.8%
1986	\$2,585.5	21.8%	\$990.1	8.7%

SOURCES: U.S. Firms: (1976-1986); SIA
Japanese Firms: (1976-1984); MITI as reported in *Japanese Semiconductor Industry Yearbook 1985*, and in *The Japanese Semiconductor Industry 1981/1982*, BA ASIA, Limited, (1985-1986); ICE Corp.

NOTE: Percentage levels based on local currency.

METHODOLOGY: R&D as a percent of sales taken from indicated sources. Absolute R&D spending derived from WSTS sales data, using percentage shown.

TABLE A.3

SEMICONDUCTOR R&D SPENDING

U.S. MERCHANT SEMICONDUCTOR FIRMS AND
JAPANESE SEMICONDUCTOR FIRMS
($ Million)

	JAPANESE FIRMS		U.S. FIRMS	
	R&D Spending	% of Sales	R&D Spending	% of Sales
1976	$164.7	14.7%	$227.8	6.7%
1977	$199.8	15.7%	$300.3	7.7%
1978	$375.9	15.1%	$384.3	8.0%
1979	$427.8	14.6%	$470.0	7.1%
1980	$483.8	12.6%	$624.6	7.4%
1981	$621.3	14.9%	$776.0	9.7%
1982	$725.4	15.5%	$875.3	10.9%
1983	$941.5	14.2%	$943.8	9.7%
1984	$1,078.0	11.0%	$1,414.0	10.1%
1985	$1,314.0	15.0%e	$1,597.5	15.0%
1986			$1,581.8	13.9%

SOURCES: U.S. Firms: SIA (1976-1986)
Japanese Firms: MITI as reported in *Japanese Semiconductor Industry Yearbook 1985* (1976-1984); Japanese 1985 R&D% based on estimate from all electronics R&D spending. See Thomas M. Chesser, "The Electronics Industry Combats a Stronger Yen" (September 8, 1986), Smith Barney International.

NOTE: Percentage levels based on local currency.

METHODOLOGY: R&D as a percent of sales taken from indicated sources. Absolute R&D spending derived from WSTS sales data, using percentage shown.

EXCHANGE RATES AND WORLD MARKET SHARE MEASUREMENT

The yen/dollar rate of exchange, after having remained almost constant in 1983, 1984 and 1985, changed dramatically in 1986. The Japanese yen appreciated by 42% in relation to the U.S. dollar. Such a dramatic change in the exchange rate must be carefully evaluated with respect to the measurement of world market share expressed in U.S. dollars.

The change in the exchange rate in 1986 has distorted the measurement of the change in total world shipments and market share in 1986 compared to 1985 by inflating the size of Japanese shipments expressed in U.S. dollars. If one makes the simplifying assumption that the yen/dollar rate did not change in 1986 compared to 1985, but all other economic changes did occur, the U.S. position in world markets expressed in dollars would have improved and the Japanese position also expressed in dollars, would have deteriorated.[566] However, it would be an analytical error to interpret the constant exchange rate results in 1986 as an indication that the U.S. position in semiconductors relative to the Japanese has not worsened dramatically in the 1980s.

First of all, the market share trends showing a decline in U.S. share and an increase in Japanese share were well established prior to the dramatic appreciation of the yen in 1986. Figure A.1 shows OLS trend lines including and excluding 1986 as a data point. The trend lines only differ in the steepness of the slopes (the rate of change), not their direction.

Secondly, the U.S. dollar was clearly overvalued for the past 4-5 years relative to the Japanese yen. In effect, the weak yen has masked the share gains of Japanese semiconductor producers when expressed in U.S. dollars in the 1980s. If one makes another simplifying assumption to isolate the exchange rate effect on market share measurement and assumes the 1986 exchange rate had prevailed since 1982, Japan would have pulled even with the United States in world market share in 1984 and surpassed the United States significantly in 1985.

To sum up, the sharp appreciation of the yen in 1986 has *overstated* the relative performance of Japanese producers with respect to U.S. producers in 1986. Similarly, however, the relatively weak yen since 1982 has *understated* the relative performance of Japanese producers compared to U.S. producers since 1982.

---

566 Also, total world semiconductor shipments expressed in dollars would have increased only by 6 percent, not by 22 percent.

FIGURE A.1

SEMICONDUCTOR MARKET SHARE TRENDS

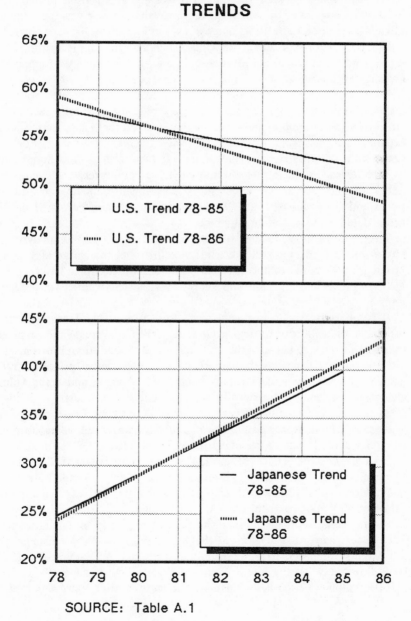

SOURCE: Table A.1

THE DETERMINANTS OF U.S.-JAPANESE TRADE IN INTEGRATED CIRCUITS: AN ECONOMETRIC ANALYSIS

This section analyzes the economic forces that influenced trade flows in integrated circuits between the United States and Japan from 1981 to 1986. It has been suggested by some that the overvalued dollar was the dominant force behind these trade flows and can even fully explain the large increases in U.S. imports of semiconductors from Japan, and the failure by the U.S. to expand into the Japanese domestic market. This analysis empirically investigates these assertions.

To properly evaluate how significant an impact the overvalued dollar had on these trade flows and to identify other relevant economic factors that affect trade, economic models must be constructed that can describe all the economic relationships underlying international trade. For the semiconductor industry these should include factors that affect supply, such as inventories, production levels and capital expenditures, and factors that affect demand such as consumption levels of downstream products, relative prices and the exchange rate. These models must then be tested utilizing actual data for the period under study.

Two econometric models have been constructed, one to analyze U.S. imports of Japanese integrated circuits, and the other to analyze U.S. exports of integrated circuits to Japan. These models, which are described below, incorporate various demand and supply variables as well as the exchange rate.

It has become vogue in recent years to attribute all international trade problems for U.S. firms to the exchange rate of the dollar. While changes in the rate of exchange between the U.S. dollar and other national currencies do affect economic decisions through changes in the relative prices of traded goods, the correlation between exchange rate changes and trade volume changes is far from unity and differs significantly from industry to industry. Even at a macroeconomic level, the effect of exchange rate changes on aggregate trade flows has not been well understood in recent years, especially with respect to the time lags and elasticities involved.

In assessing the effect of exchange rate changes on U.S. trade in semiconductors, this section will focus on U.S. exports and imports of integrated circuits with Japan. The rationale for this focus is that Japanese firms are the major competitors of U.S. semiconductor firms and U.S. losses in various semiconductor markets have been primarily to Japanese firms. The basic analytical question is the significance of ¥/$ exchange rate movements compared to other economic factors in explaining changes in trade flows between the United States and Japan. It is generally assumed that the volume of exports to Japan should decrease with appreciation of the dollar relative to the yen. [567]   The empirical task is to estimate the importance of the ¥/$ rate on trade volumes relative to other economic variables affecting the trade flows.

To capture the effects of changes in the ¥/$ exchange rate on trade flows it is necessary to link functionally the changing value of the ¥/$ exchange rate with U.S. exports to Japan and Japanese exports to the United States. Proper specification of the functional form is essential to determining a statistically significant result.[568]

A proper understanding of the effects of exchange rate movements on U.S. semiconductor trade must place exchange rate effects in the context of all other important economic variables affecting semiconductor supply and demand decisions in the United States and Japan.

On the supply side the following economic variables are important: capital expenditures, R&D expenditures, inventories, costs for factors of production, and relative price of semiconductors in each market.

On the demand side the following economic variables are important: relative consumption levels of downstream products in the United States and Japan, relative prices in each market, and any trade barriers that would affect semiconductor trade between the two countries.

The other important factor to understand is the behavior of U.S. and Japanese semiconductor firms competing in the market and their response to changes in such macroeconomic variables as the ¥/$ exchange rate. Because learning and other scale economies are so important in semiconductor production, semiconductor firms are very concerned with maintaining volume and market share. Movements in exchange rates are thus unlikely to alter long term strategies with respect to market share. Gains in market share by individual companies reinforce those share gains through cost economies.[569]

---

567 In markets that are not perfectly competitive, such as semiconductors, the volume effects will be significantly affected by how firms respond to exchange rate movements. To the extent that firms, because of competitors' actions, adjust import and export prices to maintain constant foreign market prices, the volume effects will be negligible. For example, in the face of dollar appreciation since late 1985, Japanese firms have the option of taking lower profits, changing sourcing decisions or other actions depending upon the response of their American competitors.

568 The importance of including all relevant economic variables as regressors is crucial. In a multivariate regression model, the interpretation of the coefficients alters depending upon the other regressors that are included as independent variables. The coefficient β_k represents the change in the value of the dependent variable given a unit change in x_k holding all other regressors constant. If important variables are omitted from the regression, than they are not being held constant for purposes of understanding β_k. Leaving out a relevant regressor is generally taken as *prima facie* evidence that the estimated equation is not reliable.

569 Unit cost declines for integrated circuits can exceed 30% for each doubling of cumulative volume. See the discussion of learning economies in Appendix B.

Thus, given conditions of production in this industry, it is to be expected that firms in international competition may likely pass on, in terms of price increases, less than 100% of the exchange rate changes and indeed probably much less than 100% of the exchange rate changes. A critical variable will be what competitors in the industry in both countries are doing with respect to prices.

Another behavioral factor to be considered is dumping. U.S. market share losses were significant in 1984 and 1985 when Japanese producers were dumping in the U.S. market. Data collected by the U.S. International Trade Commission showed dramatic declines in the prices of imported Japanese DRAMs and EPROMs. From September 1984 to September 1985, the imported price of Japanese 64K DRAMs fell by 77%. The decline for 256K DRAMs was an even more dramatic 93%. The decline for the 128K EPROM was 82%. These price changes occurred at a time when the real yen/dollar exchange rate had been essentially constant for four years (1982 to 1985).

Exchange rate changes also will not affect trade flows where U.S. firms have been driven from the market by Japanese dumping (as in DRAMs). Once out of the market, it is extremely difficult, technologically, to recapture high volume commodity IC production.[570]

Description of the Models

The models focus on the economic factors that are expected to affect the volume of U.S. imports of integrated circuits from Japan and the volume of U.S. exports of integrated circuits to Japan. The models of trade are conventional in the sense that they include variables found in other studies of imports and exports and are estimated in a familiar functional form.[571] They

---

570   See discussion in Appendix B on Barriers to Entry.

571   The following sources were consulted with respect to model specification: Kenneth Bernauer, "Effectiveness of Exchange-Rate Changes on the Trade Account: The Japanese Case," *Economic Review*, Federal Reserve Bank of San Francisco (Fall 1981), pp. 55-71; Peter B. Clark, Dennis E. Logue and Richard J. Sweeney (eds.), *The Effects of Exchange Rate Adjustments* (The Proceedings of a Conference sponsored by OASIA Research, U.S. Department of the Treasury, April 4-5, 1974); Robert M. Dunn, Jr., "Flexible Exchange Rates and Oligopoly Pricing: A Study of Canadian Markets," *Journal of Political Economy* 78 (January/February 1970): 140-151; Irving B. Kravis and Robert E. Lipsey, "Prices and Market Shares in the International Machinery Trade," *The Review of Economics and Statistics* 64 (February 1982): 110-116; Paul R. Krugman and Richard E. Baldwin, "The Persistence of the U.S. Trade Deficit," *Brookings Papers on Economic Activity* 1 (1987): 1-43; Catherine L. Mann, "Prices, Profit Margins, and Exchange Rates," *Federal Reserve Bulletin* (June 1986): 366-379; John F. Wilson and Wendy I. Takacs,

are less conventional in including specific supply-side variables that are considered important in influencing trade in integrated circuits.

U.S. Imports of Integrated Circuits From Japan

The following reduced form model was used to estimate the volume of U.S. imports of integrated circuits from Japan:

$$\ln \text{RUSIM} = \beta + \beta_1 \ln \text{RUSELE} + \beta_2 \ln \text{USCAPA}$$

$$+ \beta_3 \ln \text{ICPROD} + \beta_4 \ln \text{RUSICP}$$

$$+ \beta_5 \ln \text{JICPX} + \beta_6 \ln \text{REX} + e$$

where:

RUSIM: real volume of U.S. imports of integrated circuits from Japan. Source: U.S. Department of Commerce.

RUSELE: real U.S. shipments of computer equipment. Source: U.S. Department of Commerce.

USCAPA: U.S. capacity utilization rate for wafer fabrication. Source: SIA.

ICPROD: Japanese production of integrated circuits (in units). Source: MITI.

RUSICP: real U.S. domestic price index for integrated circuits (1980 = 100). Source: Bureau of Labor Statistics.

RJICPX: real Japanese export price index for integrated circuits (1980 = 100). Source: The Bank of Japan.

REX: real ¥/$ exchange rate. Source: IMF.

[Note: nominal values were deflated by the wholesale manufacturing price index (1980 = 100) for both the United States and Japan.]

"Differential Responses to Price and Exchange Rate Influences in the Foreign Trade of Selected Countries," *The Review of Economics and Statistics* 61 (February 1979): 267-279.

The equation was estimated using quarterly data for the period 1981Q1 to 1986Q4. Neither of the price variables nor the variable for U.S. demand (RUSELE) were statistically significant and they were dropped from the final equation. The equation was estimated using an ordinary least squares regression technique.[572] The results are provided below:

Independent Variable	Estimated Coefficient	Standard Error	t-Statistic
USCAPA	1.274	0.121	10.499
ICPROD	1.090	0.045	24.363
REX	0.461	0.172	2.684

R^2 = .9716
Adjusted R^2 = .9673
F-Statistic (3, 20) = 227.73
D.W. = 2.499
Standard error = 0.10
Critical values of t are 2.528 (99.0%) and 2.845 (99.5%)

All of the coefficients were of the expected sign. The overall fit of the regression equation was very high as shown in panel one of Figure A.2, where the actual imports and estimated values from the regression equation are plotted. One of the most interesting results of the regression is the importance of supply side forces in both Japan and the United States in determining U.S. imports of integrated circuits from Japan. U.S. imports were positively correlated with the level of capacity utilization in the U.S. industry, indicating that Japanese imports have increased as capacity constraints were confronted in the United States. The relatively more abundant Japanese supply reflects higher capital investment spending over the period as discussed in chapter 3. U.S. imports from Japan were also positively correlated with Japanese production, indicating that the U.S. market was in part an outlet for excess supply in Japan.

The real exchange rate was also statistically significant, but variations in the exchange rate had less of an effect on import volume than the other

---

572 Regressions were also performed using a second degree polynomial distrubuted lag model with the far endpoints constrained to zero. The exchange rate variable was lagged. These models resulted in poorer overall fit and a number of coefficients for the lagged values were not significant.

FIGURE A.2

U.S. IMPORTS OF INTEGRATED
CIRCUITS FROM JAPAN
($ MILLION)

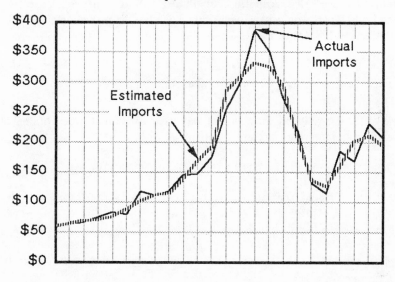

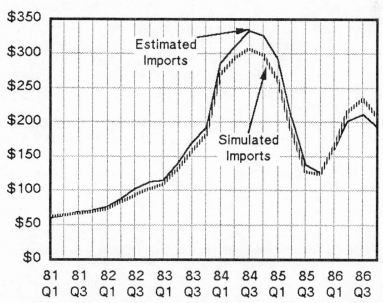

variables in the equation. In order to illustrate the exchange rate effect, U.S. imports of integrated circuits were simulated using the regression equation assuming that the exchange rate remained constant over the period at its 1981 level.[573] The simulated import levels are compared to estimated import levels under actual conditions in panel 2 of Figure A.2. The graph makes clear that while movements in the exchange rate had a small effect on quarterly imports, the trend and relative magnitude of imports were not significantly affected by movements in the ¥/$ rate. Indeed, under the constant exchange rate scenario, cumulative U.S. imports of integrated circuits from Japan would have been only 4.0% less than they actually were over the period 1981Q1 to 1986Q4.

U.S. Exports of Integrated Circuits to Japan

The following reduced form model was used to estimate the volume of U.S. exports of integrated circuits to Japan:

$$\ln \text{RUSX} = \beta + \beta_1 \ln \text{RJELEC} + \beta_2 \ln \text{ICRATIO}$$

$$+ \quad \beta_3 \ln \text{RPJDIC} + \beta_4 \ln \text{RPUSXIC}$$

$$+ \quad \beta_5 \ln \text{REX} + e$$

where:

RUSX: real volume of U.S. exports of integrated circuits to Japan, measured by the real volume of Japanese imports of integrated circuits from the United States converted to dollars at the real exchange rate. Source: Japan Tariff Commission.

RJELEC: real volume of Japanese production of electronics equipment. Source: Japanese Electronics Institute.

ICRATIO:Japanese integrated circuit inventory divided by integrated circuit production (in units). Source: MITI.

---

573 Over the period, the real value of the yen compared to the U.S. dollar weakened from 1981Q1 to 1985Q1 and generally strengthened from 1985Q1 to 1986Q4.

RPJDIC: real domestic price index of Japanese integrated circuits (1980=100). Source: The Bank of Japan.

RPUSXIC:real U.S. export price index for integrated circuits (1980=100). Source: Bureau of Labor Statistics.

REX: real ¥/$ exchange rate. Source: IMF.

[Note: nominal values were deflated by the wholesale manufacturing price index (1980=100) for the United States and Japan.]

The equation was estimated using quarterly data for the period 1981Q1 to 1986Q4. Japanese domestic integrated circuit prices were not statistically significant and were dropped from the final equation. The equation was estimated using an ordinary least squares regression technique.[574] The results are provided below:

Independent Variable	Estimated Coefficient	Standard Error	t-Statistic
RJELEC	0.967	0.130	7.42
ICRATIO	-0.402	0.048	-8.40
RPUSXIC	-0.534	0.246	-2.17
REX	-0.458	0.133	-3.43

R^2 = .9534
Adjusted R^2 = .9436
F-Statistic (4, 19) = 97.12
D.W. = 2.495
Standard error = 0.071
Critical values of t are 2.086 (97.5%) and 2.845 (99.0%)

All of the coefficients were of the expected sign. The overall fit of the regression equation was very high as shown in panel one of Figure A.3, where the actual imports and estimated values from the regression equation are plotted.

---

574 Regressions were also performed using a second degree polynomial distributed lag model with the far endpoints constrained to zero. The price and exchange rate variables were lagged. These models resulted in poorer overall fit and a number of coefficients for the lagged variables were not significant. Additionally the long-run elasticities (the sum of the lagged coefficients) were very close to the coefficients produced by the OLS regression.

FIGURE A.3

U.S. EXPORTS OF INTEGRATED
CIRCUITS TO JAPAN
($ Million)

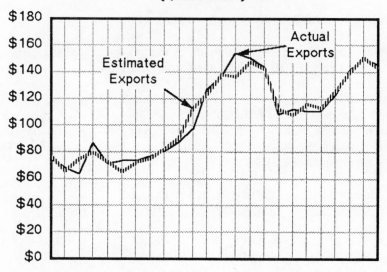

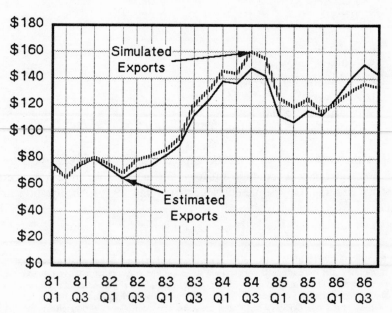

The results show a positive correlation between Japanese demand for integrated circuits and exports of integrated circuits from the United States. The coefficient implies that holding all other factors constant, a 1% increase in Japanese demand results in a 0.967% increase in U.S. exports. At the same time there is a negative correlation between U.S. exports to Japan and the ratio of inventory-to-production. The inventory-to-production ratio was used as a measure of relative Japanese integrated circuit supply. This result implies that as Japanese inventories decrease (increase) purchases of U.S. integrated circuits increase (decrease), suggesting that purchases of U.S. product increases as the scarcity of domestic supply increases. In other words, the fact that U.S. exports of integrated circuits were strongly correlated to Japanese demand in downstream markets and inversely related to inventory buildup in the Japanese semiconductor industry indicates that Japanese users/consumers tend to import semiconductors from abroad only when domestic demand cannot be met by domestic production.[575] While the domestic price of Japanese integrated circuits was not statistically significant in explaining exports of U.S. integrated circuits, the deflated export price index for U.S. integrated circuits, a proxy for U.S. supply, was very significant. This result adds further evidence to the hypothesis that Japanese consumers of integrated circuits appear to give first preference to Japanese suppliers because Japanese consumers are sensitive to the price of the U.S. product, substituting out of U.S. integrated circuits when U.S. prices increase, while not following the same behavior with respect to the domestic product when domestic prices increase.

The real exchange rate was also statistically significant, but variations in the exchange rate had less of an effect on import volume than the other factors in the equation. In order to illustrate the exchange rate effect, U.S. exports of integrated circuits to Japan were simulated using the regression equation assuming that the exchange rate remained constant over the period at its 1981 level. The simulated import levels are compared to estimated import levels under actual conditions in panel 2 of Figure A.3. The graph makes clear that while movements in the exchange rate had a small effect on quarterly imports, the trend and relative magnitude of imports were not significantly affected by movements in the ¥/$ rate. Indeed, under the constant exchange rate scenario, cumulative U.S. exports of integrated circuits to Japan would have been only 3.4% higher than they actually were over the period 1981Q1 to 1986Q4.

---

575 A number of observers of the Japanese semiconductor market have commented that Japanese consumers purchase foreign semiconductors only when a domestic source is not available. *See, e.g., Nihon Keizai* (March 20, 1985); *Far Eastern Economic Review* (August 22, 1985); BA Asia, Ltd., *The Japanese Semiconductor Industry 1981/82* (1982), p. 136.

APPENDIX B

THE ECONOMICS OF SEMICONDUCTOR PRODUCTION AND COMPETITION

It is useful, for purposes of understanding the current dynamics in semiconductor competition, to analyze the economics of production in the semiconductor industry and the competitive implications that derive from these conditions of production. Semiconductor production does not fit within the parameters of the perfect competition paradigm in microeconomics. International commercial rivalry in semiconductors is even further removed from the standard treatment of classical trade theory.[576] It is not possible, therefore, to use the positive or normative conclusions of standard microeconomics and trade theory as a basis for understanding the semiconductor industry or for evaluating public policies for this industry.

---

576 Kenneth Flamm makes this point for technology-intensive industries generally: "The powerful paradigm of efficient, competitive markets producing a socially optimal allocation of resources rests on the assumption of a mature, widely diffused technology used to produce a standardized commodity. This scenario falls wide of the mark when a technology-intensive product like computers is considered. Instead, a realistic model of competition in a high-tech industry must include elements such as continuous investments in creating a superior, closely held technology; advanced, differentiated products over which an innovator holds a monopoly (albeit temporarily); and the significant monopoly rents received by an innovator justifying and financing continued investments in research and development." Kenneth Flamm, *Targeting the Computer* (Washington, D.C.: The Brookings Institution, 1987), p.12.

This appendix describes how integrated circuit production is characterized by significant learning economies and other economies of scale, the structural conditions to which those economies have given rise, the competitive dynamics that derive from the technical conditions of production, and the resulting implications for understanding current economic and policy questions related to international semiconductor production and trade.

THE ECONOMICS OF SEMICONDUCTOR PRODUCTION

Semiconductor production in general, and integrated circuit production in particular, are characterized by significant economies of scale. Economies of scale are those factors that enable a firm or industry to produce large volumes at lower average cost than small volumes.[577] What is of interest is the relationship between *average costs* and *scale of output*.

A useful way to analyze economies of scale is in terms of three categories or types of production organization: (1) product-specific economies, (2) plant-specific economies, and (3) multi-plant economies. Product-specific economies are those associated with the volume of any single product made and sold. Plant-specific economies are those associated with the total output -- possibly encompassing many products -- of an entire plant or plant complex. Multi-plant economies are those associated with a firm's operation of more than one plant.[578]

Essentially there are three different kinds of factors that may bring about scale economies: (1) fixed cost factors; (2) factors pertaining to external economies, and (3) technological factors.

Fixed cost factors pertain to industries where a large minimum outlay constraint is required before production can commence. As the volume of production expands, the less is the fixed cost outlay per unit of output. These fixed cost factors have become increasingly important for integrated circuit production, especially with the advent of VLSI technology.

External economies generally derive from financial factors rather than from physical or technological factors.[579] For example, a firm may be able to purchase large quantities of an input from another firm (in another industry) at a lower price than small quantities of the same input. Here, however, any

577   Kelvin Lancaster, *Introduction to Modern Microelectronics* (Chicago: Rand McNally and Co., 1969), p. 88.

578   These categories have been suggested by Scherer. See F. M. Scherer, *Industrial Market Structure and Economic Performance* (Boston: Houghton Mifflin Company, 1980), p. 81.

579   C.E. Ferguson, *Microeconomic Theory* (Homewood, Illinois: Richard D. Irwin, Inc. 1972), pp. 236-37.

economies of scale accruing to the firm purchasing production inputs are derived entirely from circumstances of the supplying firm or industry.

Technological factors refer primarily to conditions of production that are subject to increasing returns to scale. Under such conditions a firm may be able to increase its output by a greater percentage increase than the increase in inputs.[580] Other things equal, a larger company will be in a better position to overcome indivisibilities -- allowing either fuller use of capacity or the use of more specialized, efficient equipment. The primary source of scale economies in semiconductor manufacturing arise from the technological conditions of production.[581]

Learning Economies or Dynamic Scale Economies

Learning economies, which derive from technological factors associated with the production process, are a form of dynamic scale economies.[582]

---

580 More formally, such scale economies are present when a t-fold proportionate increase in all inputs yields a t'-fold increase in output, where $t' > t > 1$.

581 Economies of scope are scale economies associated with the production of more than one product in a specific plant or plant complex. (Economies of scope would fall within Scherer's category of plant-specific economies.) The economies of interest concern the interaction between individual product volume and the agglomeration of multiple products.

> *In addition to economies deriving from the size or scale of a firm's operations (concepts at least intuitively familiar to most economists), there is also the possibility that cost savings may result from simultaneous production of several different outputs in a single enterprise, as contrasted with their production in isolation, each by its own specialized firm. That is, there may exist economies resulting from the scope of the firm's operations.*

Briefly stated, economies of scope are present when the cost of producing two products together or in combination is less than the total cost of producing each product separately. Such scope economies are also present in integrated circuit wafer fabrication. Formally, $f(A,B) < [f(A,0) + f(0,B)]$. *See, e.g.,* John C. Panzar and Robert D. Willig, "Economies of Scale in Multi-Output Production," *Quarterly Journal of Economics* 91 (August 1977): 481-93. The quotation is from William J. Baumol, John C. Panzar and Robert D. Willig, *Contestable Markets and the Theory of Industry Structure* (New York: Harcourt Brace Jovanovich, Inc. 1982), p. 71.

582 Dynamic economies of scale or learning economies refer to the fact that cost reductions occur as *cumulative* output increases, which means that the cost economies are related to a lengthening period of time. Economies of scale, on the other hand, arise when average costs fall as output for a *given production period* increases.

Integrated circuit production is a classic case of learning economies.[583]

Composite learning is a joint manufacturing effort which involves everyone from the line operator through corporate management. For a particular operation which has a target or standard hours per unit (E), the average unit hours (aveU_x) for the first unit through any given unit(x) is a function of:

(a.) the ability to learn a new technique (k);

(b.) the rate at which the technique is mastered (N); and

(c.) the production experience (X).

Mathematically, this functional relationship is stated as:

$$\text{aveU}_x = kEX^N \tag{1}$$

where aveU_x = the cumulative average hours for
first X units,

k = the ratio of initial unit hours to
standard hours per unit (E),

X = the unit measured (cumulative units),

N = the statistical rate of learning.[584]

Three basic equations can be derived from this relationship:

$$\text{aveU}_x = KX^N \tag{2}$$

$$U_x = (N+1)KX^N \tag{3}$$

$$tU_x = KX^{N+1} \tag{4}$$

---

583 Scherer, *Industrial Market Structure*, p. 82; Richard Baldwin and Paul R. Krugman, "Market Access and International Competition: A Simulation Study of 16K Random Access Memories," *NBER Working Paper No. 1936* (June 1986), pp. 5-6; Douglas W. Webbink, *The Semiconductor Industry: A Survey of Structure, Conduct and Performance* (Federal Trade Commission Staff Report, January 1977), Chapter III.

584 J.G. Abramowitz and G.A. Shotluck, Jr., *The Learning Curve: A Technique for Planning, Measurement and Control* (IBM Report No. 31. 101, 1970), sections II and III.

where (2) represents the cumulative average cost, (3) is the unit cost at any given unit and (4) is the total cost up to and including any given unit. The rate of learning is of such a nature that, given a constant rate of production, a doubling of cumulative production reduces cumulative average cost per unit by a specific percentage. This percent reduction in average cost per unit is constant throughout the learning cycle.

Integrated circuit production is characterized by significant learning economies. For example, production of DRAMs, SRAMs and EPROMs, high volume MOS-memory products, are subject to these learning economies and are generally used as "technology-drivers" for integrated circuit production. That is, given the relationship between cumulative output and learning, semiconductor firms do much of their "learning" on these commodity memory products. This learning is transferable to other, lower-volume MOS products.[585]

The learning economies express themselves in yield improvements, particularly at the wafer fabrication stage. Yield is the measure of manufacturing proficiency in integrated circuit production and is stated as the percentage of devices which begin the production process which ultimately become useable parts. Improvements in yield lower unit costs dramatically.

The sensitivity of the manufacturing process gives rise to a very distinctive form of learning-by-doing. Suppose that a semiconductor chip has been designed and the manufacturing process worked out. Even so, when production begins the yield of usable chips will ordinarily be very low. That is, chips will be produced, but most of them -- often 95 percent --

---

585 For example, DRAMs, SRAMS and EPROMs (memory devices) and microprocessors (logic devices) are produced with much of the same equipment. They will be produced with different processes (i.e., fabrication steps), but some learning experience gained in DRAM, SRAM or EPROM production will be applied to microprocessor production. The importance of technology drivers to achieving learning economies was summarized in a recent report by ICE:

> *One of the ramifications of targeting potentially higher profit product areas is that commodity markets can fall by the wayside. For example, all U.S. merchant manufacturers except TI and Micron have gotten out of the DRAM market citing that it is an unprofitable product area. (Motorola appears to be on the fence.) DRAMs have been a process driver for many of these companies (a process driver is a product which can be made in high volumes on an advanced process technology to gain experience in that technology and drive costs down.) Without DRAMs to fill that role, other products such as SRAMs and EPROMs have to be used.... It should be noted that, with Japanese competition heating up in these areas, large U.S. companies that expect to survive must be able to take a stand in at least one commodity product line.*

Integrated Circuit Engineering Corporation, *Status 1987,* p. 2-26.

will not work, because in some subtle way the conditions for production were not quite right. Thus, the manufacturing process is in large part a matter of experimenting with details over time. As the details are gotten right, the yield rises sharply. Even at the end, however, many chips still fail to work.[586]

The Learning Curve and Integrated Circuit Production

A "learning curve" is a statement of the relationship between costs and cumulative production or experience. "The curve that relates unit cost to accumulated volume is called the learning curve."[587] If the constant cost reduction is 15%, the improvement in cost is said to be on an 85% learning curve. More generally, with a constant reduction of x% the improvement is designated as being on a 100% - x% learning curve. As a planning tool the learning curve is very important. It enables production managers to know what the approximate unit cost will be at any anticipated output level.[588]

The cost economies represented by the learning curve (i.e., the reduction in average cost with increases in cumulative volume) are due to experience and learning, including changes in technology and production techniques. The predominant cost economies found in integrated circuit production are those due to learning economies.

Several characteristics of these learning economies should be noted. First, learning by doing on the part of production workers is only one, relatively unimportant, source of such economies. Most are generated by improvements in the production process.... Second, most learning economies are not an automatic by-product of production, but rather are produced by the deliberate efforts of firms.... Third, learning economies, though identified with cumulative past production by the industry, may also be a function of time in production.... Fourth, although some learning readily becomes general knowledge and thus a public good, much is either uniquely applicable to a particular operation or can be transferred to another facility only with technical assistance from the firm

---

586 Baldwin and Krugman, "Market Access," pp. 5-6.

587 A. Michael Spence, "The Learning Curve and Competition," *The Bell Journal of Economics* 12 (1981): 49.

588 For example, the average cost per unit at the 1000th unit for an 85% learning curve equals approximately 1/0.85 times the average cost per unit at the 2000th unit: $\text{aveU}_{1000} = 1.176\ (\text{aveU}_{2000})$. See Webbink, *Semiconductor Industry*, pp. 49-50, for a discussion of how various companies use the learning curve in their business decision making.

having the know-how. Consequently, a large portion of the benefits produced by learning accrues to firms doing the learning.[589]

Other economies of scale discussed above are also present in integrated circuit production and are included in industry estimates of the learning curve. These include both fixed cost factors (e.g., substantial R&D costs) as well as the increasing capital-intensiveness associated with higher volume production (what Lancaster has grouped under technological factors). There are also external economies of scale (volume discounts) in buying the various materials (chemicals, gases, acids, etc.) used in production of integrated circuits.[590]

Generally, it is industry practice to plot unit cost (or price as a proxy for cost) as a function of cumulative volume using total manufacturing cost. Thus, this learning curve would include not only economies from experience but also scale economies due to those elements of fixed cost and scale of production that are captured by depreciation of plant and equipment and R&D.[591] An illustrative learning curve is plotted in Figure B.1.[592]

Industry Structure: Barriers to Entry, Market Contestability and Economic Concentration

The effect of shrinking the size of the circuits on a chip, moving from MSI through LSI to VLSI, has had significant effects on the market structure of the semiconductor industry. The move to VLSI production has dramatically increased the capital requirements and minimum scale of operation for integrated circuit production. This change has significantly affected barriers to entry in the industry.

By definition, a barrier to entry to a market is a factor which permits a firm or firms to raise price above a competitive level (above "economic cost") without attracting new entry. The traditional literature on entry barriers comes from Joe Bain's seminal work *Barriers to New Competition*.[593] Five

---

589 J. Tilton, *International Diffusion of Technology: The Case of Semiconductors* (Washington, D.C.: The Brookings Institution, 1971), pp. 85-86.

590 Webbink, *Semiconductor Industry*, Section III.A.4.

591 As already indicated above with respect to the "technology-driver" argument, economies of scope also exist in integrated circuit production.

592 Note that what is plotted in the graph is price, not cost, since cost data is not publically available.

593 Joe S. Bain, *Barriers to New Competition* (Cambridge, Mass.: Harvard University Press, 1956).

FIGURE B.1

DRAM LEARNING CURVE 1974-1986
Price Per Bit (Millicents)

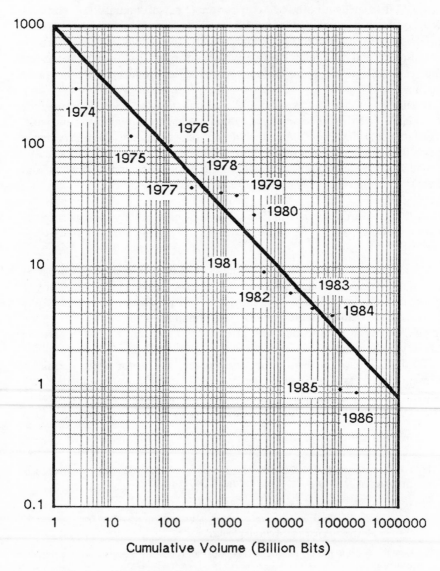

Cumulative Volume (Billion Bits)

SOURCE: Dataquest, October 1986

broad types of barriers to entry can be gleaned from the literature: (1) limited access to key resources, (2) absolute cost barriers, including capital barriers, (3) economies of scale, (4) product differentiation, and (5) predatory action.[594] At least three of these types of entry barriers are important for high volume integrated circuit production -- absolute cost barriers, economies of scale and predatory actions. Indeed if the Japanese actions in MOS memories are successful in driving out most or all of their U.S. competitors from high volume MOS memory production through predatory action, this predatory pricing example will remain as a significant entry barrier to any firm contemplating entry into MOS memory production.

In Bain's terminology the absolute capital requirements for high volume integrated circuit production represent a significant entry barrier. The capital requirements for integrated circuit production have increased rapidly in the past decade as geometries have shrunk drastically and the capital intensity of the production process has increased dramatically. The capital requirements (plant, equipment and R&D) for state of the art production of the latest EPROM product (i.e., for only *one* density) have increased almost five-fold since 1977. At that time the capital requirements for production of the 16K EPROM (the state of the art product at the time) were approximately $35 million. Today, the capital requirements for production of the 1MB EPROM are in excess of $160 million.[595]

Finally there are significant economies of scale in integrated circuit production, primarily related to learning.[596] The presence of these learning economies confers significant advantages on the firm or firms that can gain market share (cumulative volume) at the expense of its rivals. More importantly, in the context of barriers to entry, the existence of learning economies gives firms in the market a significant advantage over potential entrants who must sustain significant losses in the process of gaining market share and volume increases that will bring down unit costs.

By keeping its price low initially, the pioneer can stimulate rapid expansion of demand for its product and therefore progress farther down its learning curve before others begin competing. Also, with an initial cost

---

594 Scherer, *Industrial Market Structure,* ch. 8 and Daniel B. Suits, *Principles of Economics* (New York: Harper & Row, 1970), ch. 19.

595 These capital requirements represent an entry barrier not only in Bain's sense but also in the sense of sunk costs as used in the literature on contestable markets. That is, the EPROM market would not be considered a contestable market. The concept of market contestability makes the distinction between fixed costs, which are recoverable, and sunk costs, which are not recoverable. Baumol, Panzar and Willig, *Contestable Markets,* ch. 10.

596 As Bain emphasized, for any positive value for capital requirements (sunk costs), the barrier to entry will be higher the greater the economies of scale.

advantage, the pioneer may choose to pursue an aggressive low-price policy that higher cost rivals have difficulty emulating. If it can underprice its rivals, it will almost surely maintain a dominant market share, and with a larger market share it will enjoy more of the learning-by-doing economies and hence hold a continuing cost advantage, reinforcing its exclusionary pricing incentive. Only by accepting initial losses can rivals beginning with lower cumulative volume compete their way to a position of approximate equality.[597]

The attempt of entry by Korean manufacturers into high volume DRAM production is instructive on this point. Following the 1982 announcement by the Korean government of a "Semiconductor Industry Promotion Plan" (which included a variety of measures to encourage an indigenous manufacturing capability in semiconductors) three of Korea's largest chaebol (industrial groups) -- Samsung, Lucky-Goldstar, and Hyundai -- made a massive commitment to enter semiconductor manu-facturing (estimated at between $1-$2 billion).[598] The Korean firms entered full-scale production of 64K DRAMs in late 1984 and early 1985. To their surprise and consternation, the Korean firms found that Japanese 64K DRAM prices were less than half the Korean's cost of production and the Korean producers incurred substantial losses.[599] A Seoul journal observed that

Japanese manufacturers [have] come out with a dumping offensive to dominate the world semiconductor market from the beginning. They came out with a dumping offensive that does not even recover production costs in order to overturn their competitors . . . Japan's dumping offensive which is striking a major blow at our country's semiconductor industry has only now acquired systems for mass production of the 64K DRAM and is going on the final stages in development of the 256K DRAM and cannot escape bitter struggle as it is disrupted by Japan's bud-nipping tactics.[600]

As a result, the Korean firms pulled back from concentration on mass memory products (64K and 256K DRAM) into product areas less likely to be subject to "cut-throat pricing" by Japanese producers.[601] However, all three firms are still attempting, with significant government assistance, to try again

---

597   Scherer, *Industrial Market Structure,* pp. 250-51.

598   Korea Exchange Bank, *Monthly Review* (May 1985).

600   *Hanguk Ilbo* (March 31, 1985), p. 4; *Journal of Commerce* (July 3, 1987), p.3A.

601   *Business Korea* (October 1986), p. 70.

with the IMB DRAM based on technology acquired from U.S. companies.[602] Indeed, the Korean Government sees its role as encouraging these firms to continue their attempts to enter the industry by reducing the risks associated with entry. An official of the Korean Ministry of Science and Technology stated that "the government must provide the motive factor for technological innovation by providing the support measures for compensating for risks involved in such technological innovation and for proper recovery of investment costs in technological innovation."[603]

The Korean experience, supports the contention that entry barriers are significant for MOS memory production. The fact that huge conglomerate corporations, with their large financial resources, combined with significant government assistance, have not yet been successful in breaking into high volume MOS memory production after three years, is compelling evidence that entry barriers in this industry are significant.

INTERNATIONAL COMPETITIVE DYNAMICS IN THE SEMICONDUCTOR INDUSTRY

The Semiconductor Industry and International Trade

As the above discussion concerning the technical conditions of production makes clear, to understand the market dynamics of the global microelectronics industry, the analyst must go beyond the parameters of standard trade theory based on concepts of perfect competition and determinable equilibrium outcomes. In recent years there has been a growing body of literature that departs from the assumptions of standard trade theory by focusing on trade under conditions of increasing returns to scale and imperfect competition. These models offer a new and much more useful way of analyzing trade, particularly trade in manufactured products.[604]

The enduring influence of neoclassical economic theory in general, and the theory of international trade in particular, is based on its generality, internal consistency, and determinateness. Price changes can be related all the way back to income distribution in comparing one equilibrium state to another. Its major weakness is that the entire model is based on the assumption that economic systems operate without friction. More concretely, this means that productive factors (physical structures, capital equipment,

---

602 *Maeil Kjongjie Sinmun* (September 5, 1985), p. 6.

603 *Kim Song-ch' ol in Kisul Kwanli,* No. 2 (1985).

604 Elhanan Helpman and Paul R. Krugman, *Market Structure and Foreign Trade: Increasing Returns, Imperfect Competition, and the International Economy* (Cambridge, Massachusetts: The MIT Press, 1985).

workers, etc.) are instantaneously and costlessly shifted from one use to another, from producing a particular article in one location to producing another commodity elsewhere, in response to market price signals. The entire process of adjustment, and the distribution of the costs of the adjustment, are ignored. The dynamic process of economic change is left out of the formal model.

In the international area, this has been slowly changing under constant confrontation from both empirical evidence and from those economists primarily concerned with dynamic change and adjustment costs. Thus, even some of the major practitioners of the neoclassical school have expressed dissatisfaction with the current model. Robert Baldwin has stated that "the present state of trade theory is far from satisfactory" and laments the fact that the most significant factors affecting the nature of international trade are "the ones for which our understanding of the process is the weakest." [605] Gottfried Haberler, in surveying the theoretical and empirical literature concerned with evaluating traditional trade theory states that "the picture which emerges is that of a mosaic of interrelated, overlapping and occasionally conflicting theories and models, each applicable to certain situations." [606]   And Paul Krugman recently asserted that "it is hard to reconcile what we see in manufactures trade with the assumptions of standard trade theory." [607]

The central neoclassical theory explaining the composition and direction of a country's trade is what has been termed the Heckscher-Ohlin (H-O theory) factor abundance theory. This theory, which is quite simplistic but has been developed into a logically elegant model, states that a country will export those products whose production uses intensively the country's relatively abundant resources and imports those products whose production uses intensively the country's relatively scarce resources. This theory was developed and came to be accepted before any formal empirical testing was performed.

Since Leontief's classic 1953 article, which empirically demonstrated that U.S. exports and imports had the opposite factor intensity that the H-O theory would predict, there has been extensive research on the determinants

---

605 Robert E. Baldwin, "Testing Trade Theories: A Comment," in *International Trade and Finance: Frontiers for Research* ed. Peter B. Kenen (Cambridge: Cambridge University Press, 1975), pp. 151, 154.

606 Gottfried Haberler, "Survey of Circumstances Affecting the Location of Production and International Trade as Analyzed in the Theoretical Literature," in *The International Allocation of Economic Activity* eds. Bertil Ohlin, Per-Ove Hesseborn, and Per Magnus Wijkman (New York: Holmes & Meier Publishers, 1977), pp. 1-24.

607 Paul Krugman, "New Theories of Trade Among Industrial Countries," *American Economic Review* 73 (May 1983): 343.

of trade and new theories and explanations presented to explain the empirical results.[608] Recent advances in the literature have been based on economies of scale and product differentiation.[609] These theories are directed at explaining three aspects of world trade that contradict the neoclassical model: (1) much of world trade is between countries with similar factor endowments, (2) a large part of trade consists of a two-way exchange of similar products, and (3) much of the expansion of trade in the post war period has occurred without sizeable resource allocation and income distribution effects.[610] These theories are dynamic and encompass both trade and international direct investment in manufactured goods. The major difference is that these explanations focus on economies of scale internal to the firm, not on differences in technological innovations, as the basis for trade.[611] Krugman summarizes the basic ideas of this theory as follows:

> *We distinguish between two kinds of trade: inter-industry trade based on comparative advantage, and intra-industry trade based on economies of scale. The industrial structure of a country's production will be determined by its factor endowments. Within each industry, however, there is assumed to be a wide range of potential products, each produced*

---

608 The resulting alternative or complementary approaches have been classified into three groups: neo-factor proportions explanations, neo-technology explanations, and intraindustry trade explanations. The neo-factor, neo-technology, and intraindustry labels are used by Whitman and Krugman, among others. Krugman, "New Theories of Trade Among Industrial Countries;" and Marina von Neumann Whitman, *International Trade and International Investment: Two Perspectives* (Princeton: Princeton University Press, July 1981), Essays in International Finance, No. 143. In addition to these articles, this section has relied on a number of surveys of the literature including: Harry P. Bowen, "U.S. Comparative Advantage: A Review of the Theoretical and Empirical Literature" (Washington, D.C.: U.S. Department of Labor, July 1980); W.M. Corden, "The Theory of International Trade", in *Economic Analysis and the Multinational Enterprise* ed. J.H. Dunning (London: George Allen & Unwin, 1974); Gene M. Grossman and J. David Richardson, "Issues and Options for U.S. Trade Policy in the 1980s: Some Research Perspectives," National Bureau of Economic Research, February 1982 (Mimeographed); Haberler, "Survey of Circumstances Affecting the Location of Production;" Robert M. Stern, "Testing Trade Theories," in *International Trade and Finance*, pp. 78-150.

609 Herbert Giersch, ed., *On the Economics of Intra-Industry Trade* (Tubingen: Mohr, Seibeck, 1979).

610 Paul R. Krugman, "Intraindustry Specialization and the Gains from Trade," *Journal of Political Economy* 89 (October 1981): 959-73.

611 Kelvin Lancaster, "Intra-Industry Trade Under Perfect Monopolistic Competition," *Journal of International Economics* 1 (May 1980): 151-75; Paul R. Krugman, "Scale Economies, Product Differentiation and the Pattern of Trade," *American Economic Review* 70 (December 1980): 950-59; Avinash Dixit and Victor Norman, *Theory of International Trade* (Digswell Place, Welwyn: Cambridge University Press, 1980), pp. 281-94.

under conditions of increasing returns. Because of these scale economies,
each country will provide only a limited number of the products in each
industry, with the pattern of intraindustrial specialization -- which country
produces what -- essentially arbitrary.[612]

What is important about these recent theoretical expositions is the explicit
recognition that the pattern of intraindustrial specialization is essentially
arbitrary. The comparative advantage characteristics that explain these trade
patterns are not those of countries, but of firms and products (industries).
The attempts to explain the empirical anomalies of trade as seen from the
perspective of neoclassical trade theory, have pushed trade economists in the
direction of more dynamic considerations used in development and
international investment theories. Trade and investment thus can be seen as
different stages of a firm's efforts to extract the maximum flow of benefits
from its specific competitive advantages as conditions change over time.

International Trade in Semiconductors Under Conditions of Oligopoly and
Increasing Returns

International semiconductor production and trade takes place under
oligopolistic conditions. The industrial structure of the semiconductor
industries in Japan, Western Europe and South Korea exhibits characteristics
of imperfect competition. These industries are dominated by a small number
of firms, and because of their relative size in the market, each individual firm
possesses some control over the market. This is referred to as an
"oligopolistic" market structure.

In an oligopolistic market structure, it is difficult to predict how firms will
behave because the market displays characteristics existing under both
perfect competition and monopoly. Under perfect competition, a large
number of firms, all viewing themselves as price takers, will compete until
output is driven to the point that price is equal to the marginal cost of
production in the market. Under a monopolistic industrial structure, we
expect the single supplier, which views itself as a price maker, to produce up
to the point that its marginal revenue for an increment of output is equal to
its marginal cost. This pricing strategy will usually result in a market price
that is higher than would be derived under perfect competition, and a lower
level of output in the market.

Economic models of oligopoly must describe market dynamics that fall
somewhere in between the perfect competition and monopoly models.

---

612 Krugman, "New Theories of Trade Among Industrial Countries," p. 344.

Although no general theory exists, typical economic models for oligopoly predict that firms will engage in various forms of strategic behavior. Firms may choose to collude and restrict output to raise the market price above the price that would result in the competitive solution; or conversely, they may choose to engage in some form of competition which can evolve into economic warfare to drive other firms out of the market. In the latter scenario, a firm that has the greatest resources to sustain losses is more likely to survive.

Recently, several models of oligopoly have been developed to analyze international trade flows.[613] One such model, developed by J. Brander and P. Krugman, has broad application to the global microelectronics industry. The Brander/Krugman model of international trade (which assumes an oligopolistic market in both the home and foreign countries) characterizes an industry in which firms operate in segmented markets (due to transportation costs or some other type of barrier) so as to prevent resale. Under such conditions, oligopolists can price discriminate in the two markets to maximize their total revenues. The Brander/Krugman model also incorporates a certain type of strategic behavior by the oligopolistic firms -- that they take rival firm's behavior as given and attempt to maximize revenues assuming competing firms will continue to produce at their current levels and not retaliate (nor do they collude in an attempt to monopolize the market). This is referred to as "Cournot" behavior.[614]

Based on these assumptions, the model predicts that the oligopolists will sell in both their home and foreign markets and that oligopolistic competition will result in firms dumping in their respective foreign markets. At first, it may appear counter-intuitive that the market would even support an equilibrium in which firms in different countries producing the same good would incur additional costs (transportation costs) in order to sell in foreign markets. But even with the same production functions and market demands, the Cournot rivalry predicts international trade. This is because each firm has a smaller share in the foreign market relative to its home market share because of the transportation costs. Under these circumstances, the profit maximizing oligopolist perceives that he is facing a higher marginal revenue function in the foreign markets. Therefore, he equates his marginal costs to the marginal revenues in both markets and ends up price discriminating.

---

613 Two such models can be found in the following articles: J. A. Brander, "Intra-industry Trade in Identical Commodities," *Journal of International Economics* 13 (1981): 1-14; J.A. Brander and P. Krugman, "A Reciprocal Dumping Model of International Trade," *Journal of International Economics* 15 (1983): 313-321.

614 This type of strategic behavior was first analyzed by Antoine Augustin Cournot (1801-77), a French economist and mathmetician.

But according to the assumptions in the model, marginal revenue is the same in both markets. Because of the transportation cost, the firm has a smaller profit margin in the foreign market than in the home market and the firm is dumping in the foreign market.[615]

Therefore, in an oligopolistic market structure, economic theory suggests that even when no apparent cost advantages exist, because firms have some degree of market power, they may choose to engage in international trade and dump in the foreign market. Thus, under the conditions in the model, dumping is rational economic behavior.

More insight into the dynamics of the global microelectronics industry can be gained by examining the implications of learning economies which characterize semiconductor production. Traditional trade theory is built on the assumption of constant returns to scale, and so it is not helpful in understanding the global microelectronics industry.

Paul Krugman has developed another model which analyzes international trade in an oligopolistic market structure where economies of scale prevail.[616] Krugman's model also incorporates two assumptions found in the economic model described above: (1) markets can be segmented (to allow for price discrimination by the oligopolist); (2) they engage in strategic rivalry of the "Cournot" type. Based on these assumptions, this model shows that in the presence of scale economies, if a government protects the home market from foreign competition, domestic firms can exploit the scale economies through increased market share in the domestic market. This translates into a lower cost for exports to foreign markets as well. Therefore, domestic protection can be used as a form of export promotion when scale economies are present.

There is a positive feedback from output to marginal cost to output. By protecting one market, the government gives the domestic firm greater

---

615 The following excerpt from Helpman and Krugman provides more insight into the technical economic points of this model: "Each firm is a low cost shipper to its own market, a high cost shipper to the other market. It must have a smaller market share in the foreign market (unless transport costs are zero in which case market shares are equal); this lower market share means a lower perceived elasticity of demand and hence a higher marginal revenue. In equilibrium, this higher marginal revenue exactly offsets transportation costs. This difference in perceived elasticity of demand means that the two firms are in effect price discriminating or dumping." *Market Structure and Foreign Trade*, p. 107.

616 Paul R. Krugman, "Import Protection as Export Promotion: International Competition in the Presence of Oligopoly and Economies of Scale," in *Monopolistic Competition and International Trade* ed. Henry K. Kierzkowski (Oxford:Oxford University Press, 1984), pp. 182-193.

economies of scale, while reducing those of its foreign competitor. Thus decreasing costs are at the heart of the story.[617]

A circularity exists between costs of production and output. The greater the output for a firm, the lower the marginal cost in production, which bestows a price advantage in the market for the producer. This price advantage enables the firm to capture a large market share in both the domestic and foreign markets, which triggers the cost-output cycle again. If production costs continually decline over the entire range of output, it would theoretically enable a firm to monopolize the industry.

The Economic Basis of the Japanese Industry's Competitive Challenge to American Market Leadership

The world semiconductor industry is gradually being taken over by oligopolistic firms. The Japanese conglomerates have been successful at maneuvering themselves into their present position - a position that poses a serious challenge to the technological leadership that has traditionally been held by the U.S. industry.

Cooperative Efforts and Shared Costs by the Japanese Industry and Government

The Japanese government has been instrumental in developing the Japanese semiconductor industry. The government has provided joint funding for large scale R&D projects with Japanese manufacturers. As discussed in Chapter 3, the VLSI project resulted in the Japanese producers achieving technical parity in the MOS memory markets by the early 1980s.[618]

Joint R&D projects gave the Japanese producers a tremendous cost advantage over the American industry. By pooling information and efforts for these very risky and costly projects, they were able to minimize investment expenditures in R&D in key product and process areas. Their American counterparts, on the other hand were investing in R&D projects independently. This led to more duplication of effort for the U.S. industry as a whole, which is clearly less efficient, more wasteful and more risky.

---

617 Ibid., p. 187.

618 "A direct result of the VLSI project was the emergence of the Japanese semiconductor industry as a dominant factor in the U.S. market for high-integration memory products." Kyoko Sato, *Japanese Semiconductor Industry Yearbook* (Tokyo:Press Journal, Co., 1985), p. 26.

Import Protection as a Basis for Export Drives

The Japanese semiconductor industry has always enjoyed some form of protection of its domestic market. Prior to the early 1970s, its market was explicitly protected by trade barriers. After that time, the market was implicitly protected by: 1) informal agreements, among Japanese conglomerates to buy semiconductors from domestic producers, and 2) rigid distribution systems in the domestic market. This is evident in market data for Japanese. Even when the Japanese industry was in its infancy and the U.S. industry was clearly the technological leader, the U.S. industry was never able to capture more than 10 percent of the Japanese market.[619]

The strategic protection provided to the domestic Japanese market, enabled the Japanese producers to exploit learning economies inherent in semiconductor production. As the Japanese industry matured into a viable competitor in the global markets, it had increased economic incentives to capture more market share in foreign countries to further exploit learning and scale economies as discussed in the previous section.

The Economic Logic of Dumping

The Japanese industry's objective was to gain market share for strategic MOS memory products in the United States. This would enable them to exploit learning economies and reduce production costs for these products. Furthermore, they could also apply this learning to the production of other semiconductor devices, such as ASICs, to achieve lower costs of production in those areas as well. Strong economic incentives were present for the Japanese to gain market share even by selling devices in the unprotected U.S. market at prices that were lower than prices in their domestic market and even lower than average and marginal cost. In the economics literature, this is referred to as "dumping" in the foreign market.[620]

Since the early 1980s, the Japanese have targeted strategic semiconductor devices - DRAMs and EPROMs - and "dumped" them in foreign markets. As the Japanese producers have increased their share of the U.S. and other third country markets, the U.S. merchants producer's share has subsequently declined. If the Japanese producers do obtain a global monopoly in this fashion, the economies of the scale and learning economies that such a

---

619 Semiconductor Industry Association, *Japanese Market Barriers in Microelectronics* (Memorandum in Support of a Petition Pursuant to Section 301 of the Trade Act of 1984 as Amended, June 14, 1985).

620 Yamamura and Vandenberg, "Japan's Rapid-Growth Policy on Trial: The Television Case," discuss overinvestment and the logic of dumping by Japanese electronics companies.

position would offer will provide barriers to market entry and help to solidify a long-term monopoly position.

Conglomerate Structure and Cross-Subsidization

The Japanese semiconductor producers have engaged in this dumping campaign since the early 1980s. Because they are large, diversified conglomerates, they are able to forego adequate rates of return and even incur losses on the production of these devices. Also, the Japanese conglomerates typically enjoy close associations with banking institutions (a situation that is restricted in the U.S.). This enables these producers to continue to make the large-scale investments in R&D and capital equipment that are necessary to maintain a technical edge in the market. Also cross-subsidization is made possible by large government contracts for the development of telecommunications equipment. This option is clearly not available to producers in the U.S., where the telecommunication industry is run by the private sector and monitored by the FCC to promote competition in this market.

Advantages to Upstream (SME) and Downstream (Systems) Producers

The development of VLSI technology has shifted competitive advantage from the small entrepreneurial firms, typified by the U.S. merchants, to the large vertically integrated firms, such as the Japanese producers.

VLSI technology has led to a convergence of circuit and systems design. This confers a tremendous advantage to the vertically integrated firm, because it requires that both system and circuit development be coordinated. Given the proprietary nature of these technologies, it is far easier for a large conglomerate to carry out such development than internally independent firms, which may both deal with a variety of firms including each other's competitors. Furthermore, it is becoming evident that the U.S. downstream industry would be in jeopardy without the availability of a domestic semiconductor industry to provide a complete range of devices.

VLSI process technology is more capital-intensive and requires larger scale, greater automation, and more capital equipment. Consequently large expenditures in R&D and equipment are required in the "upstream" industry as well. Large-scale vertically integrated firms can better afford to develop VLSI process technologies as well as provide critical technological inputs for VLSI circuits.

Finally, the upstream industries are dependent on a healthy U.S. semiconductor industry. If the U.S. semiconductor industry declines, sales in the upstream industries likewise decline. The SME and materials producers are less able to maintain the necessary expenditure on R&D and, therefore, will not be able to maintain their technological advantage.

THE NATURE OF COMMERCIAL RIVALRY IN WORLD SEMICONDUCTOR PRODUCTION

International production and trade of semiconductors, as the previous sections have illustrated, is not the type of economic activity where conventional microeconomic and trade theory is a useful guide to either empirical analysis or public policy. Technological innovation is the driving force of this industry. Spending on research and development and investment in plant and equipment are key determinants of current and future market share. Learning economies and other economies of scale drive reductions in production costs, making worldwide market share a key determinant of the average cost of production. The positive feedback loop between increases in market share and reductions in cost make losses in market share, for any given technology, extremely difficult to recapture.[621] While cost and market share dynamics may favor larger firms, the rate of innovation of new technological innovations may be fostered by smaller, start-up firms that don't have an economic interest in monopoly rents associated with current technology. Public policy formation must keep both issues in mind.

Because of the important relationship between market share increases and cost reductions, international market access is crucial for semiconductor producers. U.S. producers must be able to obtain open access to the Japanese market, especially now that the Japanese market is the largest market in the world for semiconductor consumption. Continued restricted access to the Japanese market for U.S. producers will mean a continued competitive edge for Japanese producers in world competition as discussed above.[622]

Relative rates of spending on R&D and plant and equipment will be critical determinants of future cost competitiveness and market shares. Past and current R&D spending will determine technological progress and the pace of innovation. Capital spending increases for fabrication and assembly

---

621 Kenneth Flamm, "Internationalization in the Semiconductor Industry" in Joseph Greenwald and Kenneth Flamm, *The Global Factory* (Washington, D.C.: The Brookings Institution, 1985), pp. 68-94, for a discussion of U.S. losses to Japan in transistors. "The lesson learned was that a competitive advantage, once lost, is exceedingly difficult to regain."

622 See also the results in Baldwin and Krugman, *"Market Access"*, where their simulation suggests that Japanese home market protection was *decisive* in giving Japanese firms the ability to compete in world markets.

facilities lead to increased yields and scale economies, further reducing unit costs. Thus continued trends in relative R&D and capital spending for U.S. and Japanese firms do not augur well for future trends in world market share for U.S. producers.

GLOSSARY OF TERMS AND ACRONYMS

ASIC
: Application Specific Integrated Circuit. An integrated circuit tailored for a specific use. ASICs are often custom devices.

BESSY
: An electron accumulator ring for synchotron radiation constructed jointly by the West German Government and the Land Government of Berlin.

bipolar
: One of two main types of transistors (along with MOS). Bipolar transistors were the dominant semiconductor devices of the 1950s. They operate at higher speeds than MOS devices, making them especially useful for such signal processing as radar and communications.

bit
: A binary digit. A bit is the smallest unit of storage in a digital computer and is used to represent one of the two digits in the binary number system.

BMFT
: West Germany's Ministry of Research and Technology.

CAD
: Computer Aided Design.

captive
: Firms which manufacture semiconductors for use in their own end products.

chaebol
: South Korean industrial group.

chip
: A small piece (typically less than one square centimeter) of a semiconductor wafer. Also used to refer to a packaged integrated circuit.

CIS	Center for Integrated Systems at Stanford University.
CMOS	Complementary Metal Oxide Semiconductor; possesses n-channel (negative-conducting properties) MOS transistors and p-channel MOS transistors on the same chip; known for low power dissipation and density of elements per unit area.
CNET	France's Center for Telecommunications Studies.
CNS	France's Norbert Segard Center, administered by the Center for Telecommunications Studies.
COCOM	Coordinating Committee on Multilateral Export Controls. A multinational body made up of representatives of the NATO powers and Japan to regulate the flow of Western technology.
COSY	The Compact Storage Ring for Synchotron Radiation. A West German research project using superconducting magnets for X-ray lithography.
DARPA	Defense Advanced Research Projects Agency, U.S. Department of Defense.
DESY	A synchotron R&D project in Hamburg, West Germany, concentrating on the use of X-ray lithography to manufacture electronic switching circuits.
DGT	France's Directorate-General of Telecommunications.
DIELI	France's Directorate of Electronics Industries and Data Processing.
diode	A two-terminal electronic device that allows current to flow freely in one direction only.
DOD	Department of Defense.
DRAM	Dynamic random access memory. A type of semiconductor in which the presence or absence of a capacitive charge represents the state of a binary storage element. The charge must be periodically refreshed.
DSB	U.S. Defense Science Board.

dumping
Selling a product in a foreign market at a price below "fair market value," e.g., below what it is sold for in its home market or selling it at a price below its cost of production, including profit.

EAR
U.S. Export Administration Regulations.

ECL RAMs
Emitter coupled logic random access memory. A high speed device used in supercomputers and mainframe cache memories.

EPROM
Erasable Programmable Read Only Memory. The contents of the device may be erased through exposure to ultraviolet light, and new information may be written to the device afterwards.

ES2
European Silicon Structures.

ESPRIT
European Strategic Program for Research and Development in Information Technologies. A program administered by the European Economic Community to promote joint R&D in the information technologies.

ETL
Japan's Electrotechnical Laboratory, administered by the Ministry of International Trade and Industry.

ETRI
Korea's Electronics and Telecommunications Research Institute.

EUREKA
A European multinational R&D effort in artificial intelligence, robotics, supercomputers, advanced microelectronics, new materials, optoelectronics, and high powered lasers.

FHG
West German Association of Institutes of Applied Research.

gallium arsenide (GaAs)
A compound semiconductor material. GaAs semiconductors are much more difficult to manufacture than silicon semiconductors, but permit much higher speeds.

gate   i) The basic digital logic element where the binary value of
                     the output depends on the value of the inputs.   ii)   The
                     primary control terminal of an MOS device.

gate   An IC consisting of a regular arrangement of gates that
arrays   arrays are interconnected to provide custom functions.

gate   The basic unit of measure for digit circuit complexity, based
equivalents   on the number of elementary logic gates that would have to
                     be interconnected to form the same circuit function.

GATT   General Agreement on Tariffs and Trade.

GICI   France's Interministerial Group for Integrated Circuits.

ICs   Integrated circuits. An array of transistors and diodes on a
                     single piece of silicon crystal that is interconnected in such a
                     way as to allow it to perform the function of a complete
                     electronic circuit. ICs are the largest and most important
                     family of devices in the semiconductor industry.

ICE   Integrated Circuit Engineering Corporation.

indium   A compound material used for optoelectronics.
phosphide

ITAR   U.S. International Traffic in Arms Regulation.

ITCs   U.S. Investment Tax Credits.

JDB   Japan Development Bank.

JECC   Japan Electronics Computer Company.

JFTC   Japan Fair Trade Commission.

JTECH   U.S. Japanese Technology Evaluation Program.

KAIST   Korean Advanced Institute of Science and Technology.

KDB   Korean Development Bank.

keiretsu   Group of affiliated companies in Japan, usually   centered
                     on a major bank.

Japan Key Technology Center	A Japanese Government/industry institution established in 1985 to channel government funds into high risk, high technology R&D.
KIET	South Korean Institute of Electronics Technology.
KIETUS	KIET office located in California.
Kijoho	Special Japanese legislation in effect from 1978 to 1985 which provided exemptions from Japan's Antimonopoly Law, preferential loans, and tax benefits to specific information and machinery industries.
LETI	France's Electronics and data Processing Technology Laboratory.
lithography	The transfer of a pattern or image from one medium to another, as from a mask to a wafer. The transfer can be effectuated through the use of light, x-rays, or beams of ions or electrons.
LSI	Large Scale Integration. LSI devices contain 100 to 5,000 gate equivalents or 1,000 to 16,000 bits of memory.
mask	A patterned screen, usually of glass, used to allow exposure of selected areas of a photoresist-coated wafer by a light source.
MCC	Microelectronics and Computer Technology Corporation, U.S.
MCNC	Microelectronics Center of North Carolina.
merchant	A firm whose primary business is the manufacture of semiconductors for sale to other firms.
microprocesor	A single IC chip that performs all the central processing-unit functions of a computer.
MITI	Japan's Ministry of International Trade and Industry.
MOF	Japan's Ministry of Finance.

MOS	Metal oxide semiconductor. One of two main types of transistors (along with bipolar); consists of semiconductor body (silicon) with silicon-dioxide gate dielectric and metal gate.
MPT	Japan's Ministry of Post and Telecommunications.
MSI	Medium Scale Integration. ICs containing 10 or more gate equivalents but less than 100.
MTI	South Korean Ministry of Trade and Industry.
NACA	U.S. National Advisory Committee for Aeronautics, the forerunner of NASA.
NICs	Newly Industrializing Countries.
NIF	South Korean National Investment Fund.
NTT	Nippon Telephone and Telegraph.
OEM	Original Equipment Manufacturer. A company which manufactures end-products which incorporate semiconductors. The term embraces captive producers as well as electronics firms which consume but do not produce semiconductors.
OIEC	Optoelectronic Integrated Circuit. An integrated circuit that converts light signals into electronic signals.
ONR	U.S. Navy's Office of Naval Research.
OTA	U.S. Office of Technology Assessment.
PTTs	An acronym used to refer to the European Post and Telecommunications authorities.
RAM	Random Access Memory, which stores digital information temporarily and can be changed as required. It constitutes the basic storage element in most computers.
RBOCs	Regional Bell Operating Companies. Formerly part of the AT&T system, the RBOCs became independent companies pursuant to the judicial consent decree breaking up the AT&T system.

ROM   Read Only Memory. Permanently stores information used repeatedly -- such as microcode or characters for electronic display. Unlike RAM, ROM cannot be altered.

SEMATECH   Semiconductor Manufacturing Technology. A U.S. semiconductor industry consortium formed to conduct R&D in advanced semiconductor manufacturing technologies.

SIA   Semiconductor Industry Association.

silicon   The basic material used in the manufacture of semiconductors.

SJRD   Korean Semiconductor Joint Research Center (Seoul).

SME   Semiconductor Manufacturing Equipment.

SORTEC   A Japanese industry-government project to develop semiconductor manufacturing technology.

SRAMS   Static RAMs. A type of RAM which does not require periodic refresh cycles, as does dynamic RAM.

SRC   Semiconductor Research Corporation (North Carolina, U.S.).

synchotron   A particle accelerator which emits intense light. Synchotron radiation is being widely explored as a potential source of lithography for manufacturing semiconductors with submicron circuit widths.

technology driver   IC products (usually DRAMs, SRAMs and EPROMs) that are manufactured in high volumes. Manufacturing them permits learning of the manufacturing process which in turn results in reductions in production costs. This knowledge is often transferable to products that are produced in lower volumes.

technopolis   Regions within Japan designated by MITI to grow into technology-oriented cities consisting of approximately 200,000 residents, research parks, universities, corporate R&D facilities, and venture businesses. Each region is eligible for low-interest government loans, R&D subsidies, tax breaks, and other preferential government programs.

VHSIC   Very High Speed Integrated Circuit.   Also, the R&D
                         project established by that name by the Department of
                         Defense.

VLSI   Very Large Scale Integration.   VLSI devices are ICs that
                         contain 5,000 or more gate equivalents or more than 16,000
                         bits of memory. (Some sources designate devices with 1,000
                         or more gate equivalents as "VLSI")

wafer   Semiconductor material, usually silicon, on which individual
                         chips or slices can be fabricated and cut into prescribed
                         pieces for individual integrated circuits.

WSTS   World Semiconductor Trade Statistics.

x-ray   The use of x-rays to transfer a pattern or image from   one
lithography   medium to another. X-ray lithography is being explored as
                         a possible technology for manufacturing semiconductors
                         with sub-micron circuit widths.

Bibliography

Abramowitz, J.G. and Shotluck, G.A. Jr. *The Learning Curve: A Technique for Planning, Measurement and Control.* IBM Report No. 31.101, 1970.

Anchordoguy, Marie. *The State and the Market: Industrial Policy Towards Japan's Computer Industry.* Boston: Harvard Business School, January 27, 1987.

Bain, Joe S. *Barriers to New Competition.* Cambridge, Massachusetts: Harvard University Press, 1956.

Baldwin, Richard and Krugman, Paul R. *"Market Access and International Competition: A Simulation Study of 16K Random Access Memories."* NBER Working Paper No. 1936. (June 1986).

Benz, Stephen, and Richards, Timothy. *Government Procurement of Semiconductors.* Semiconductor Industry Association, 1986.

Bernauer, Kenneth. "Effectiveness of Exchange-Rate Changes on the Trade Account: The Japanese Case." *Economic Review.* Federal Reserve Bank of San Francisco, Fall 1981.

Borrus, Michael. *Reversing Attrition: A Strategic Response to the Erosion of U.S. Leadership in Microelectronics.* University of California, Berkeley: BRIE Working Paper No. 13, March, 1985.

Bowen, Harry P. *U.S. Comparative Advantage: A Review of the Theoretical and Empirical Literature.* Washington, D.C.: U.S. Department of Labor, July 1980.

Brander, J.A., and Krugman, P. "A Reciprocal Dumping Model of International Trade." *Journal of International Economics* 15 (1983): 313-21.

Braun, E., and Macdonald, S. *Revolution in Miniature.* Cambridge: U.K.: Cambridge University Press, 1978.

Brueckner, Leslie, and Borrus, Michael. *Assessing the Commercial Impact of the VHSIC (Very High Speed Integrated Circuit) Program.* University of California, Berkeley: BRIE Working Paper No. 5, December 1984.

Clark, Peter B., Logue, Dennis E., and Sweeney, Richard J., eds. *The Effects of Exchange Rate Adjustments.* The proceedings of a conference sponsored by OASIA Research, U.S. Department of the Treasury, April 4-5, 1974.

Commission of the European Communities. Communication of the Commission to the Council. *Draft Council Decision* (adopting 1986 ESPRIT Workprogramme) COM(85) 602 Final (November 12, 1985).

————. Communication of the Commission to the Council. *Toward a European Technology Community.* COM(85) 350 Final (June 25, 1985).

————. Communication of the Commission to the Council. *Towards a European Technological Community.* COM(85) 530 Final (September 30, 1985).

————. Communication from the Commission to the Council. *The Second Phase of ESPRIT.* COM(86) 269 Final (May 21, 1986).

————. Communication from the Commission to the Council. *EUREKA and the European Technology Community.* COM(86) 664 Final (November 20, 1986).

————. First Report by the Commission to the Council. *Community Projects in the Field of Microelectronics at July 15, 1983.* COM(83) 564 Final (October 7, 1983).

————. Third Report by the Commission to the Council and the European Parliament. *Community Actions in the Field of Microelectronic Technology.* COM(85) 776 Final (December 23, 1985).

Committee on the Role of the Manufacturing Technology Program in the Defense Industrial Base. Manufacturing Studies Board Commission on Engineering and Technical Systems. *Manufacturing Technology: Cornerstone of a Renewed Defense Industrial Base.* Washington, D.C.: National Academy Press, 1987.

Corden, W.M. "The Theory of International Trade." In *Economic Analysis and the Multinational Enterprise.* Edited by J.H. Dunning. London: George Allen & Unwin, 1974.

Dataquest. *Building a Japanese Techno-State: MITI's Technopolis Program Underway.* San Jose, California: Dataquest Incorporated, 1987.

Defense Science Board. *Task Force on Semiconductor Dependency.* November 30, 1986.

Dixit, Avinash and Norman, Victor. *Theory of International Trade.* Digswell Place, Welwyn; Cambridge University Press, 1980.

Dunn, Robert M., Jr. "Flexible Exchange Rates and Oligopoly Pricing: A Study of Canadian Markets." *Journal of Political Economy* 78 (January/February 1970): 140-51.

Elektrotechnische Studievereniging Delft. *Electrotechniek in Het Licht van de Rijzende Zon.* (April 1982).

Federal Coordinating Council on Science, Engineering and Technology (FCCSET), Committee on High Performance Computing. *Annual Report.* January 1987.

Ferguson, Charles H. *American Microelectronics in Decline,* MIT Draft, December 1985.

Ferguson, C.E. *Microeconomic Theory.* Homewood, Illinois: Richard D. Irwin, Inc. 1972.

Finan, William F., and LaMond, Annette M. "Sustaining U.S. Competitiveness in Microelectronics: The Challenge to U.S. Policy." In *U.S. Competitiveness and the World Economy.* Edited by Bruce R. Scott and George C. Lodge. Boston: Harvard Business School Press, 1985: 144-175.

Flaherty, M. Therese, and Itami, Hiroyuki. "Finance." In *Competitive Edge: The Semiconductor Industry in the U.S. and Japan.* Edited by Daniel I. Okimoto, Takuo Sugano, and Franklin B. Weinstein. Stanford: Stanford University Press, 1984.

Flamm, Kenneth. *Targeting the Computer.* Washington, D.C.: The Brookings Institution, 1987.

Foster, M. *Telecommunications Equipment Standards and Certification Procedures for Japan.* Tokyo: Foster Associates International, October 1984.

Gadbaw, Michael, and Richards, Timothy. *The Protection of Intellectual Property Rights in Developing Nations.* Boulder, Colorado: Westview Press, forthcoming.

General Accounting Office. *Observations on the U.S.-Japan Semiconductor Arrangement.* April 1987.

Giersch, Herbert, ed. *On the Economics of Intra-Industry Trade.* Tubingen: Mohr, Seibecyk, 1979.

Greenwald, Joseph, and Flamm, Kenneth. *The Global Factory.* Washington, D.C.: The Brookings Institution, 1985.

Grossman, Gene M., and Richardson, J. David. *"Issues and Options for U.S. Trade Policy in the 1980s: Some Research Perspectives."* National Bureau of Economic Research. February 1982 (Mimeographed).

Haberler, Gottfried. "Survey of Circumstances Affecting the Location of Production and International Trade as Analyzed in the Theoretical Literature." In *The International Allocation of Economic Activity.* Edited by Bertil Ohlin, Per-Ove Hesseborn, and Per Magnus Wijkman. New York: Holmes & Meier Publishers, 1977.

Haklisch, C.S. *Technical Alliances in the Semiconductor Industry.* NYU Center for Science and Technology Policy, February 1986.

Helpman, Elhanan, and Krugman, Paul R. *Market Structure and Foreign
    Trade: Increasing Returns, Imperfect Competition, and the
    International Economy.* Cambridge, Massachusetts: The MIT Press,
    1985.
Hiromatsu, Hitoshi. *Denwa no Muko wa Konna Kao: Denden Kosha KDD
    no Uchimaku.* Tokyo: 1980.
Hiroshi, I. "Antitrust and Industrial Policy in Japan." *In Law and Trade
    Issues of the Japanese Economy.*
Hofstadter, R. *The American Political Tradition.* New York: Vintage Books,
    1974.
House Ways and Means Committee Subcommittee on Trade. *High
    Technology and Japanese Industrial Policy: A Strategy for U.S.
    Policymakers.* October 1, 1980.
Howell, Thomas; Benz, Stephen; and Wolff, Alan. "International
    Competition in the Information Technologies." *Stanford Journal of
    International Law* 22 (1986): 215-262.
Integrated Circuit Engineering Corporation. *Status 1987: A Report on the
    Integrated Circuit Industry.* Scotsdale, Arizona: ICE, 1987.
Janow, M.E. "Whither the Future of Japanese Industrial Development
    Policies." In VI *Michigan Yearbook of International Legal Studies 11*
    (1984): 111-131.
Johnson, C. *MITI, MPT and the Telecom Wars: How Japan Makes Policy for
    High Technology.* University of California, Berkeley: BRIE
    Working Paper No. 21, September 11, 1986.
Karatsu, Hajima. *A Friendly Talk on a Serious Topic.* June 13, 1986
    (Mimeographed).
Kravis, Irving B., and Lipsey, Robert E. *"Prices and Market Shares in the
    International Machinery Trade."* The Review of Economics and
    Statistics 64 (February 1982).
Krugman, Paul. "New Theories of Trade Among Industrial Countries."
    American Economic Review 73 (May 1983): 343-47.
_____. "Import Protection as Export Promotion: International
    Competition in the Presence of Oligopoly and Economies of Scale."
    In *Monopolistic Competition and International Trade.* Edited by
    Henry K. Kierzkowski. Oxford: Oxford University Press, 1984.
_____. "Intra-Industry Specialization and the Gains from Trade." *Journal
    of Political Economy* 89 (October 1981): 959-73.
_____. and Baldwin, Richard E. "The Persistence of the U.S. Trade
    Deficit." *Brookings Papers on Economic Activity 1* (1987): 1-43.
_____. "Scale Economies, Product Differentiation and the Pattern of
    Trade." *American Economic Review* 70 (December 1980): 950-59.
Lancaster, Kelvin. *Introduction to Modern Microelectronics.* Chicago: Rand
    McNally and Co., 1969.

_____. "Intra-Industry Trade Under Perfect Monopolistic Competition." *Journal of International Economics* 1 (May 1980): 151-75.

Levin, Richard C. "The Semiconductor Industry." In *Government and Technical Progress*. Edited by Richard R. Nelson. New York: Pergamon Press, 1982: 9-100.

Malbera, F. *The Semiconductor Business*. Madison: University of Wisconsin Press, 1985.

Mann, Catherine L. "Prices, Profit Margins, and Exchange Rates." *Federal Reserve Bulletin* (June 1986): 366-79.

Manufacturing Studies Board and National Materials Advisory Board, Commission on Engineering and Technical Systems, National Research Council. *The Semiconductor Industry and the National Laboratories: Part of a National Strategy*. Washington, D.C.: National Academy Press, 1987.

Millstein, J.E. "Decline in an Expanding Industry; Japanese Competition in Color Television." In *American Industry in International Competition*. Edited by Laura Tyson and John Zysman. Ithaca, New York: Cornell University Press, 1983.

National Academy of Sciences. *Balancing the National Interest*. Washington, D.C.: National Academy Press, 1987.

National Materials Advisory Board. *An Assessment of the Impact of the Department of Defense Very High Speed Integrated Circuit Program*. Washington, D.C.: National Academy Press, 1982.

National Science Foundation, Division of Electrical, Communications, and Systems Engineering, and Consultants. *Effects of a Substantial Loss in Capability of the U.S. Semiconductor Industry on "Upstream" and "Downstream" Industries*. September 5, 1986, draft.

Office of Technology Assessment. *Microelectronics Research and Development*. Washington, D.C.: U.S. Government Printing Office, March 1986.

_____. *Information Technology R&D*. Washington, D.C.: U.S. Government Printing Office, 1985.

_____. *International Competitiveness in Electronics*. Washington, D.C.: U.S. Government Printing Office, 1983.

_____. *Technology, Innovation and Regional Economic Development*. Washington, D.C.: U.S. Government Printing Office, July 1984.

Office of U.S. Trade Representative. *Annual Report of the President of the United States on the Trade Agreements Program (1985)*. Washington, D.C.: Government Printing Office, July 1984.

Okimoto, D.I., Sugano, T. and Weinstein, F.B., eds. *Competitive Edge: The Semiconductor Industry in the U.S. and Japan*. Stanford, California: Stanford University Press, 1984.

Panzar, John C. and Willig, Robert D. *"Economies of Scale in Multi-Output Production."* Quarterly Journal of Economics 91 (August 1977): 481-93.

President's Commission on Industrial Competitiveness. *Global Competition: The New Reality.* Washington, D.C.: U.S. Government Printing Office, January 1985.

Sato, Kyoko. *Japanese Semiconductor Industry Yearbook 1985.* Tokyo: Press Journal, Inc., 1985.

Scherer, F.M. *Industrial Market Structure and Economic Performance.* Boston: Houghton Mifflin Company, 1980.

Semiconductor Industry Association. *Japanese Market Barriers in Microelectronics (June 14, 1985).*

_____. *The Effect of Government Targeting on World Semiconductor Competition.* Washington, D.C.: SIA, 1983.

Stern, J.P. "Japan's R&D Tax Credit System." *Journal of the American Chamber of Commerce of Japan* (April 1987).

Stern, Robert M. "Testing Trade Theories." In *International Trade and Finance Frontiers for Research.* Edited by Peter B. Kenen. New York: Cambridge University Press, 1975: 78-150.

Stowsky, Jay. *Beating Our Plowshares Into Double-Edged Swords.* University of California, Berkeley: BRIE Working Paper No. 17, April 1986.

Tatsuno, Sheridan. *MITI's Take Lead Strategy Shifts into High Gear.* San Jose, California: Dataquest Incorporated, 1984.

_____. *Japan's Technopolis Strategy.* New York: Prentice Hall Press, 1986.

Tilton, J. *International Diffusion of Technology: The Case of Semiconductors.* Washington, D.C.: The Brookings Institution, 1971.

United National Centre on Transnational Corporations. *Transnational Corporations in the International Semiconductor Industry.* New York: United Nations, 1986.

U.S. Department of Commerce, International Trade Administration. *An Assessment of U.S. Competitiveness in High Technology Industries.* February 1983.

_____. *A Competitive Assessment of the U.S. Semiconductor Manufacturing Equipment Industry.* Washington, D.C.: U.S. Government Printing Office, March, 1985.

U.S. Government Accounting Office. *United States -Japan Trade: Issues and Problems.* September 21, 1979.

U.S. International Trade Commission. *64K Dynamic Random Access Memory Components from Japan.* U.S.I.T.C. Publication No. 1862, Final, June 1986.

_____. *Changes in the U.S. Telecommunications Industry and the Impact on U.S. Telecommunications Trade.* U.S.I.T.C. Pub. No. 1642, June 1984.

_____. *Eraseable Programmable Read Only Memories from Japan.* U.S.I.T.C. Pub. No. 1927, Final, December 1986.

Van Wolferen, K.G. "The Japan Problem." *Foreign Affairs* (January 1987).

Webbink, Douglas W. *The Semiconductor Industry: A Survey of Structure, Conduct and Performance.* Federal Trade Commission Staff Report, January 1977.

Wilson, John F., and Takacs, Wendy I. "Differential Responses to Price and Exchange Rate Influence in the Foreign Trade of Selected Countries." The *Review of Economics and Statistics* 61 (February 1979).

Yamamura, Kozo. "Joint Research and Antitrust: Japanese vs. American Strategies." In *Japan's High Technology Industries.* Edited by H. Patrick and L. Meissner. Seattle: University of Washington Press, 1986.

Yamamura, Kozo, and Vandenburg, Jon. "Japan's Rapid Growth Policy on Trial." In *Law and Trade Issues of the Japanese Economy.* Edited by G.R. Saxonhouse and Kozo Yamamura. Seattle and London: University of Washington Press, 1986: 238-83.

Index